Contents

THE
100 BEST
EXCHANGE-TRADED FUNDS
YOU CAN BUY
2012

- Tips to Assess Your Risk Tolerance
- Advice on Investing in Commodity-Based Funds
- Portfolio Strategies Using ETFs

PETER SANDER AND SCOTT BOBO

Adams media

AVON, MASSACHUSETTS

Published by
Adams Media, a division of F+W Media, Inc.
57 Littlefield Street, Avon, MA 02322. U.S.A.
www.adamsmedia.com

ISBN 10: 1-4405-3281-8
ISBN 13: 978-1-4405-3281-8
eISBN 10: 1-4405-3284-2
eISBN 13: 978-1-4405-3284-9

Printed in the United States of America.

10   9   8   7   6   5   4   3   2   1

Library of Congress Cataloging-in-Publication Data
is available from the publisher.

This publication is designed to provide accurate and authoritative information with
regard to the subject matter covered. It is sold with the understanding that the publisher
is not engaged in rendering legal, accounting, or other professional advice. If legal advice
or other expert assistance is required, the services of a competent professional person
should be sought.
—From a *Declaration of Principles* jointly adopted by a Committee of the American Bar
Association and a Committee of Publishers and Associations

Many of the designations used by manufacturers and sellers to distinguish their product
are claimed as trademarks. Where those designations appear in this book and Adams
Media was aware of a trademark claim, the designations have been printed with initial
capital letters.

This book is available at quantity discounts for bulk purchases.
For information, please call 1-800-289-0963.

PART I

THE ART AND SCIENCE OF INVESTING IN EXCHANGE-TRADED FUNDS

You may have read about it in *The Wall Street Journal* back in March 2011. Or you may have heard about it elsewhere.

In a public announcement at an asset management conference, investment powerhouse Charles Schwab made public its design for a new type of retirement plan: specifically, a new type of 401(k) plan managed on behalf of its clients. This plan would consist of nothing but exchange-traded funds—ETFs for short. Further, Schwab would let its investors trade—that is, buy and sell—those ETFs at no charge.

We've come a long way, baby.

Way back when—up until the 1970s, anyway—stock investing was basically for the rich—famous or not. It was a closed and very private alliance between an exclusive set of individuals and their stockbrokers. Those individuals bought individual stocks, largely at their brokers' recommendation. They typically paid hundreds of dollars in commissions to buy and sell, so they held onto their stocks for years. Business didn't change as much or as fast in those days, so that was probably okay.

Mutual funds, which were started to provide a managed alternative to individual and some institutional investors, have been around since the 1920s in one form or another. The post–World War II prosperity led to a boom in saving and investing, combined with tax and compliance clarifications in the Securities Act of 1933 and the Investment Company Act of 1940. Now the average investor didn't have to join the broker club. He or she could buy a mutual fund and expect it to pay for retirement—or if the investor also had one of the common legacy pensions, it could finance the American Dream.

The mutual fund in its traditional form first appeared as a fund called the Massachusetts Investors Trust. Now you didn't need a broker—you just traded with the investment company, usually with a phone call and by mailing checks back and forth. That fund took care of your money and invested it in individual stocks, and a few times a year, you would receive a printed report of what the fund had invested in. It didn't require much time or much expertise.

Trouble is, you didn't know what you were investing in until the report came, which was long after you had invested in the fund (or divested yourself of it). The fund would charge you up-front fees—sales charges—to get in, and sometimes to get out. It would even levy a nefarious "12b-1" fee as a marketing charge to—guess what—market the fund to someone else. Sometimes these fees, or "load," were buried in the fund's performance. You could invest in a "no-load" fund, but somewhere or another you'd still pay anywhere from 1 percent to 2.5 percent or more of the fund's value every year for the services of the fund manager.

Still, the commission structure, ambiguities, and time requirements of investing in individual stocks, coupled with an increasing public demand for investments, made mutual funds a real success story. By 1970, some 360 funds were available with combined assets of about $48 billion.

It was the wave of self-directed retirement savings, spearheaded by IRAs and the 401(k), creations of Congress in the early 1980s, that really caused mutual funds to take off.

But some investors were still not happy with the costs and opacities of traditional mutual funds. Some just wanted an inexpensive and easy-to-follow way to invest in a stock index or a selection of stocks, to get the diversification and growth without the time, energy, effort, and cost of buying individual stocks. That cry was first heard by John Bogle of Vanguard Funds in the late 1970s. Vanguard pioneered very low cost index-based mutual funds, which still exist today.

That fund and its brethren spearheaded another leg of the mutual fund boom, which has led to more than 7,000 mutual funds today holding more than $11 trillion in assets.

But investors wanted to reduce costs further and speed and simplify the process of buying and selling funds. They wanted to sell Fund A and buy Fund B at a current market price during the trading day, they wanted to know what that price would be, and they wanted to pay little to no commission. They wanted to use the order placement tools of the day, allowing limit orders, stop loss orders, and so forth.

Indeed, they wanted to buy and sell funds—*bundles* of stocks or other securities—just the way they bought and sold stocks. Online, real time, at the push of a button.

Responding to this demand, State Street Global Advisors (SSGA) came up with an idea. They would create a fund and list it on an exchange. They would buy and sell shares of that fund to and from the general public. The fund would be tied to a popular index—the Standard & Poor's 500 index, and would hold an assortment of stocks as close as possible to the contents and weighting of that index. The investor would know exactly what those stocks were, and how much of each was held. As those stocks rose and fell, the asset value (the net asset value or NAV) of the fund would rise and fall throughout the trading day. Although influenced by other market forces, the price of the fund would move accordingly.

Enter the exchange-traded fund, or ETF.

In this case, it was called the SPDR S&P 500 Trust. This first SPDR came to market in 1993. "SPDR" stands for S&P Depositary Receipts, a now-arcane phrase that has largely disappeared from the vernacular, although the term SPDR hasn't. In fact, it has become the flagship brand for the 100-plus funds offered by SSGA. It is traded under the ticker symbol SPY and is listed later in this book.

Today, ETFs are the hottest, fastest-growing thing out there. They have grown from humble beginnings in the 1990s to about 1,300 funds managing $1 trillion in assets. Although still smaller in total assets managed, they are giving traditional mutual funds a run for their money.

For many investors, they are also giving individual stocks a run for their money.

As we've made clear in other books in the *100 Best* series, we advocate—and provide tools for—individual investors to buy and sell individual stocks. We like individual stock investing and think that too many people are afraid of it; it isn't as hard as it looks.

But we also recognize that people don't want to spend all of their time looking at all of their money. They want ways to invest in things like international stocks or emerging country infrastructure or alternative energy without spending the time and overcoming the ambiguities of investing in those rather unfamiliar and—well—foreign corners of the investing space.

We think ETFs have a significant role to play for all investors, even for the most sophisticated individual stock investors. ETFs can play a substantial role in any stock portfolio and in any portfolio strategy. And now we have the first all-ETF 401(k) plan on the doorstep.

As with other forms of investment, it's important to understand what you're doing, and seek value—the greatest value—where there is value to be had among a number of complex choices.

It is in that spirit that we bring you the first of a new series: *The 100 Best ETFs You Can Buy 2012.*

In the Spirit of . . . *100 Best Stocks*

Our *100 Best Stocks* series is based on the premise that you can do this investing thing yourself. You can be your own investment manager. You can make your own informed investing decisions, and manage your investments, time permitting. At the very least, you can become more knowledgeable about what to ask your hired professional investment manager or financial advisor, if you so prefer. Either way, you become a better investor.

In book form we can't possibly give you everything you need to know about 100 companies so that you can simply log on and start buying. We can't give you fish. There's too much to know, and we can't possibly keep it "fresh" in publishing cycle-dependent book form.

We can't give you fish, but we can *teach you how* to fish. We can share enough knowledge about common-sense, value-driven investing in either stocks or ETFs to help you make informed decisions. And we can share our set of *100 Best* choices, which gives you an informed place to start—a good fishing hole, if you will.

We've now applied this formula to three different investing spaces. First is our flagship book, *The 100 Best Stocks You Can Buy*, a favorite for fifteen years and most recently revamped this year. More recently, we've added *The 100 Best Aggressive Stocks You Can Buy*, and *The 100 Best Technology Stocks You Can Buy*. Each title is available in a 2012 edition. Each title employs the same approach—find value, invest strategically, learn how to fish, and find 100 good places to do it.

In this book, *The 100 Best Exchange-Traded Funds You Can Buy 2012*, we set out to do exactly the same. Except that now, instead of fishing for companies, we are fishing for ETFs. Is it the same? Is it different? Short answer: yes. It is the same, *and* it is different.

It is the same because in *The 100 Best Exchange-Traded Funds You Can Buy 2012*, like the other series titles, we look for value. Good results for the risk and cost involved. We look for funds you can understand, just like in the *Stocks* books, where we look for companies you can understand. We give you the facts you need, plus a short narrative interpretation of the story and the pros and cons of a particular fund. There are lots of places to get the facts. There are few places to get the interpretation and the pros and cons, especially applied consistently across a selection of funds.

So how is our ETF book different? First, we aren't analyzing a company, so the discussion and interpretation of a story is different. We don't have products, brands, marketplace excellence, supply chain excellence, innovation results, or deep layers of management and employees to examine. What we have with funds is more factual and less intangible. We have a list—a list of stocks, bonds, or commodities that comprise the fund. And we have some statistics reflecting how that composite of securities has performed over time. We have some mostly factual knowledge about how the index the fund is constructed around works. But there really isn't a story about most funds. It's like analyzing how a group of people work together, rather than understanding the personality, skills, and history of a single individual.

Now you know a little about how we position this book with the *100 Best Stocks* series and how it resembles and differs from those books. You're probably thinking it's time to get on with the story, and you're right. First, a little roadmap.

In the rest of Part I, we will explain the basics of ETFs—what they are, how they work, who offers them, and what kinds are out there. We won't go into depth on the mechanics of ETFs but rather will focus on what you need to know to make intelligent selections. It's not just about picking ETFs but also how to use them in your portfolio, so we'll offer some advice about where and how to use ETFs in your own personal portfolio strategy—which will look similar to the framework presented in the *100 Best Stocks* books, if you've followed us there. Then we'll give a short overview of how we picked our 100 Best ETFs. Finally, we will turn you loose with our short, two-plus page writeups on each of the 100 chosen ETFs.

Let's start at the beginning.

What Are ETFs?

ETF stands for "exchange-traded fund." But what does that mean?

When defining a phrase, we like to take it apart, word by word, to capture the meaning and start to understand it better. Suppose we start with the last word in the phrase—*fund*.

Fund, in the investing world, is a company that invests in other securities —stocks, bonds, futures contracts, cash instruments, you name it. That fund, in turn, sells its own securities—shares—allowing you to own and participate in your share of that fund when you buy it. So now we have this fund, owning a collection of securities issued by individual companies or entities, and that fund has issued shares that you can buy.

That's where the *exchange traded* part comes in. Exchange traded (we'll do both words at once) means that you can buy and sell the fund's shares on an exchange. Typically, today that exchange is the so-called "Arca" exchange, an electronic exchange now merged with the old New York Stock Exchange. The details aren't important; for most of us investors, an exchange is an exchange— they're all fast enough and cheap enough and easy enough that it doesn't matter.

Since the fund trades on an exchange, it can be traded throughout the day, based on supply and demand, just like a stock. There are quotes just like a stock, including a "bid" and an "ask" quote, if you're familiar with those concepts. (If you're not familiar, that's not really important either, if you're investing rather than trading.) And just like a stock, the price can change throughout the day based on supply and demand for the shares of the fund.

The Exchange-Traded Advantage

Why do people invest in exchange-traded funds? What's so great about them, anyway?

There are many reasons to invest in funds as opposed to individual stocks—diversification, participation in obscure markets, analysis time, etc. We'll examine ETF investing as part of your overall investing strategy shortly. For now, it makes sense to discuss the advantage of ETFs over other kinds of funds.

When boiled down, there are two core advantages of ETFs. There are others, but the two you need to know right off the bat are:

1. *Transparency.* When you buy a fund, you would like to know what's in that fund. What's under the hood, pure and simple, right? Not that you have to know everything about every security in the fund, but you'd like to see, at least in a general sense, what the fund owns and how much of it. ETFs offer that transparency. You can see the fund holdings every night, not just on a printed quarterly statement. An adjunct to this notion of transparency: Most ETFs (all but thirty-four "actively managed" funds, in fact) are constructed around an established index. The fund buys and sells stocks according to predetermined rules and guidelines about following the index, not always one for one (we'll get into that) but pretty close to the index. So you don't have a fund manager making decisions you don't know about or may not approve of.

2. *Cost.* Cost is the 800-pound gorilla that really got the whole thing started. Because ETFs follow indexes and trade like stocks (simpler) and because the investing public got tired of paying big bucks for investment managers who couldn't even match the performance of major stock market indexes like the S&P 500 Index, ETFs came into existence as a low-cost model. Fees for equity ETFs average about 0.6 percent, in contrast to something north of 1 percent for traditional mutual funds (it used to be further north of 1 percent than it is now—thanks, of course, to competition from ETFs). That doesn't sound like much, but if you have $100,000 invested, it might be a difference of $1,000 per year *every year* you own the fund. That adds up. Further, it is much easier to buy and sell ETFs. Yes, you'll have to pay a brokerage commission, which might be $10 or less at an online broker, but it is much easier to get in, to get out, and to change your fund preferences.

An "F" or an "N" or a "P"

Those who are familiar with ETFs—or those who have read ahead—know that there are different forms of exchange-traded funds. Some of these are conventional while others are organized and set up differently.

The standard ETF is technically an investment company designed to sell shares to the public and use the proceeds to invest in securities, as previously described. ETFs own the securities, and all of an ETF's investors own a share of that basket. Each share has a net asset value (NAV) equal to the total fund holdings divided by the total number of shares the ETF has issued. Each shareowner owns exactly that NAV.

As ETFs tried to put more and different types of securities, such as commodity futures contracts, into their baskets, a funny thing happened. The mechanism for buying and selling futures contracts created small losses every time the contract was rolled over into the next month's contract. This effect, called *contango*, caused an almost automatic, built-in loss for these funds and will be described later. It is also difficult and sometimes expensive to own physical commodities, like precious metals.

Because of the difficulties inherent in actual ownership, several fund providers brought to market a new form of "fund" called an exchange-traded note (ETN). They aren't really funds at all because they don't own a basket of securities. Rather, each ETN is an unsecured debt instrument issued by a financial institution, the value of which varies according to the index or commodity price it is set up to follow.

Before the 2008 collapse of key financial institutions like Bear Stearns and Lehman Brothers, ETNs gained a lot of popularity as a way to invest in specialized markets. Today, there are about 165 ETNs in existence.

Since an ETN technically isn't an ETF, there must be another important acronym out there that covers both of these things, right? Indeed, there is: the all-inclusive ETPs—simply, *exchange-traded products*. There are 1,293 ETPs.

Indexes, Plus

Most ETFs have been tied to indexes. That is, their holdings replicate or attempt to replicate the performance of a popular or not-so-popular stock or bond index. Those indexes might be created by a large, "blue-chip" financial institution like S&P or Deutsche Bank, or they might be created by a smaller "boutique" index provider like Russell (as in Russell 2000) or MSCI Inc.—a ". . . provider of investment decision support tools to investment institutions"—or by any one of dozens of other firms in the business.

An ETF will decide to utilize such an index and, of course, pay its provider a fee for that use. Not surprisingly, many indexes have been custom-created during the ETF boom to serve niche needs. An example is the NASDAQ OMX Clean Edge Global Wind Energy Index, which supports our PowerShares Global Wind Energy Portfolio (PWND) *100 Best ETF* pick.

Indexes can track the largest and most well-known stock and bond market indices—the S&P 500, NASDAQ 100 Index, or the Barclays Capital U.S. Aggregate Bond Index. Many indexes fall between these major market indexes and the boutique indexes such as the NASDAQ OMX Clean Edge Global Wind Energy Index—they track narrower market segments by market capitalization (such as the S&P Small Cap 600 Index) or style (growth or value) or international markets or specific sectors (like financials or technology) or specific industries, like infrastructure or computer networking.

Index-based ETFs attempt to "track" their chosen indexes by holding a basket of securities representing those indexes. They buy and sell every security in the basket—or a statistical sampling of that basket, as investors buy or redeem ETF shares. They do this in batch mode instead of selling 1.3 shares—or whatever—of Apple when you sell your 100 shares of the SPDR S&P 500 Trust ETF. But at least for U.S-based funds trading in large-cap stocks, these buys and sells happen fairly quickly—and the recent advent of so-called *high-frequency trading* and some of its tools has made it faster. Faster is better, because the true contents of your ETF will more closely match the index.

GETTING OFF TRACK

When you buy an ETF, you aren't buying an index directly, because there's nothing to buy. An index is simply a measurement of a market or market segment. Instead, you're buying a basket, or a collection, of actual shares or securities that ideally match the index.

But a particular fund or ETF may be slow to update the portfolio for a variety of reasons. If an index contains 500 stocks, the logistics of making all those buys and sells is difficult. If the ETF specializes in international stocks, many of those markets aren't even open when you are buying or selling your ETF shares. Therefore, a fund's actual contents may vary from the securities in the index and their weighting.

As a result, ETFs calculate, which is a statistical evaluation of the differences in content and timing between the contents of an ETF and the index it is set up to track. ETFs that have a high tracking error may not deliver the results you expect in a particular market segment. We'll discuss tracking error among other ETF performance metrics under "ETFs—Just the Facts" later in this section.

Weight, Weight, Don't Tell Me

Indexes actually do two things to shape the contents of a fund that tracks them. First and most obvious, an index provides the list of securities that an ETF needs to own, either exactly or as a representative statistical sample, if that is in the stated operational mode of the fund.

Second, it provides the *weighting* of the securities in that fund. Apple, Inc., and Microsoft may be part of the S&P 500 and thus will be included in the SPDR S&P 500 Trust ETF. But *how much* Apple? *How much* Microsoft? That's a critical question, and the index involved must have a weighting scheme. That weighting could be by *market capitalization* (biggest cap stock gets the top spot) or it could be *equal weighted*, where every security is held in the same proportion, or it could be on some more exotic or esoteric criterion, like dividends (dividend weighted) or earnings (earnings weighted) or some other scheme.

We will return to the subject of weighting later. It is important, for every weighting method has its advantages and disadvantages.

ETFS: UP AND TO THE RIGHT

And just how many ETFs are there? You now know that ETFs are a relatively new phenomenon in the investing space. We started with one in 1993. Since then, the idea has caught on, as we can see from these numbers from one of the leading providers in the industry:

YEAR	NUMBER OF ETFS
1993	1
1997	19
2001	102
2005	204
2009	819
2010	1,099
2011	1,293 (August)

(*Source: State Street Global Advisors*)

The 1,293 number may include some funds that have been discontinued or that don't trade in the United States. We've seen numbers from other sources as high as 1,310. But you get the idea. We expect the existing ETF numbers to rise, and the number retired to rise as well, particularly with Merrill Lynch's August 2011 decision to shut down its "HOLDRs," a unique and somewhat outdated form of ETF.

Actively Managed ETFs

Recently, actively managed ETFs have been introduced. These permit the fund manager to buy and sell individual securities according to the strategy stated in the fund's prospectus. Here, the line between an index-based ETF and a fully managed mutual fund starts to blur. These funds offer the benefits of active management and diversification, all at a lower cost.

There are only thirty-four such funds in the 1,293-fund universe at present, and only eleven of those are equity funds. That said, we expect this niche within a niche to grow rapidly in the next few years as people get used to using the ETF format to invest.

How Big Are These Funds?

Like most businesses—or households for that matter—a handful achieve huge size and scale, while the rest of the pack, perfectly good businesses or households in their own right, well, they run with the pack.

In the ETF space, there are some really gigantic funds. Of the approximately $1.1 trillion invested in exchange-traded products today, the top three funds make up almost $200 billion, or just under 20 percent of that.

Here's a bit more about how they break down, size-wise. The *median* equity-based ETF has assets of about $68 million (that's with an "m," not with a "b"). Of the approximately 1,293 funds out there, 157 of them have assets of more than $1 billion, and 290 of them have assets under $10 million. The rest fall in between, although you can see from the median that a significant number are closer to $10 million than $1 billion.

The largest fund? It's the SPDR S&P 500 Trust (SPY), the one that kicked it all off in 1993, with assets of $93 billion. The second largest is the SPDR Gold Trust (GLD), which tracks the price of gold, with assets of $63 billion. The third largest is a bit of a surprise—the Vanguard Emerging Markets Index Fund (VWO)—at about $50 billion. That in itself should show how ETFs can be used (and are used) to pick up exposure to more challenging segments of the market, in this case, emerging markets. Incidentally, we included two of these three funds—the SPY and VWO funds—in our *100 Best ETFs* list.

A Few More ETF Tidbits

The 100 Best Exchange-Traded Funds You Can Buy 2012 is not really intended to make you an ETF expert. Rather, we want to give you a good start toward understanding how to *use* ETFs to accomplish your investing objectives. That said, it's worth sharing, or reinforcing, a few more facts and truths about just what ETFs are and how they work.

1. ETFs are traded on a stock exchange. Like stocks and unlike mutual funds, that means ETFs:

   - Trade like a stock during market hours
   - Trade with standard order types such as market orders, limit orders, and stop-loss orders to set and/or execute at certain price points
   - Are fully quoted, with a real time bid and ask price as well as most recent price traded
   - Are usually subject to normal brokerage trading commissions, but there are no other "loads" or sales charges. Some financial service companies may offer free commissions for certain ETFs traded online.

   These features do a lot to increase price transparency, reduce cost, and to make trading easier than ordinary mutual funds.

2. Like mutual funds, ETFs have ongoing management, operating, and marketing expenses. These expenses are expressed as an annualized percentage of the ETF's net assets and are deducted from the fund's net asset value. The percentage is known as the "expense ratio" and ranges from 0.05 percent for the simplest index funds to 2.25 percent for some complex leveraged funds. The median is 0.60 percent for equity ETFs, although we prefer a lower figure. More to come under "Selecting the 100 Best ETFs."

3. ETFs may or may not trade at the value of their underlying assets. Depending on market conditions, the price paid may be at a premium or discount to the ETF's NAV. Ordinarily these premiums or discounts are very small, usually less than a tenth of a percent, but if the ETF is small and illiquid (that is, not a lot of trading activity), the "premium/discount" is worth watching.

4. Unlike many mutual funds, ETFs have no minimum investment. You can buy just one share if you want, although you'll still pay a full commission.

5. ETFs tend to be tax efficient. Most ETFs are some form of an index fund, and as most indexes are relatively stable, there isn't a lot of buying and selling of securities within the fund. Therefore, capital gains and losses are usually minimal. When redemptions occur, ETFs can usually handle them without creating a taxable transaction within the fund. So, unlike mutual funds, where you will pay capital gains taxes on holdings sold even if you don't sell your shares, ETFs generally do not create a taxable event until you sell the fund itself. There

are exceptions, particularly with commodity funds, where each fund must "mark to market" its asset value each year, and you will have to pay taxes on any gains realized. Research your tax concerns on the fund's website and with a qualified tax advisor.

Who Are We to Write about ETFs?

Time for an aside. The text was starting to get a bit heavy here, a bit too deep into the subject at hand. It's time to step back and tell you a little bit about us.

First, you may (or may not) know us as the authors of the *100 Best Stocks* series of books (which we've freely taken the opportunity to mention a couple of times). That qualifies us, right?

Yes, it does help. Just as we were able to extend our tested *100 Best Stocks* approach into *The 100 Best Aggressive Stocks* and the *100 Best Technology Stocks*, we think we can offer something useful about ETFs for the same group of individual investors. We understand the idea of culling down 1,300 funds into a useful *100 Best* list mainly aligned to the idea of investing for value.

We are value finders, regardless of how it's delivered. The value may be anchored to safety and current cash returns, or it may come in the form of growth and growth potential. The *100 Best Exchange-Traded Funds* were all chosen with this in mind.

We function as a team. But a team is made up of individuals, so here is a brief summary of who we are, where we came from, and how our experiences relate to bringing you the *100 Best Exchange-Traded Funds You Can Buy 2012*. If you've read any of the sister *100 Best Stocks* books, these biographical sketches will look familiar.

Peter Sander

Peter is an independent professional researcher, writer, and journalist specializing in personal finance, investing, and location reference, as well as other general business topics. He has written twenty-seven books on these topics, done numerous financial columns, and conducted independent privately contracted research and studies. He came from a background in the corporate world, having experienced a twenty-one-year career with a major West Coast technology firm.

He is most definitely an individual investor, and has been since the age of twelve, when his curiosity at the family breakfast table got the better of him. He started reading the stock pages with his parents. He had an opportunity during a one-week "project week" in the seventh grade to read and learn about the stock market. He read Louis Engel's *How to Buy Stocks*, then the pre-eminent—and one of the only—books about investing available at the time (it first appeared in 1953; he thinks he read a 1962 paperback edition). He read Engel, picked stocks, and made graphs of their performance by hand with colored pens on real graph paper. He put his hard-earned savings into buying five shares of three different companies. He watched those stocks like a hawk and salted away the meager dividends to reinvest. He's been investing ever since, and in combination with twenty-eight years of home ownership and a rigorous savings regimen, he has done quite well in the net worth department, pretty much on his own.

Yes, he has an MBA from a top-rated university (Indiana University, Bloomington), but it isn't an MBA in finance. He also took the coursework and certification exam to become a certified financial planner (CFP). But by design and choice, he has never worked in the financial profession. His goal has always been to share his knowledge and experience in an educational way, a way helpful for the individual as an investor and personal financier to make his or her own decisions.

He has never made money giving investment advice or managing money for others, nor does he intend to.

Outside of an occasional warm Friday evening at the harness race track or a nickel-dime-quarter poker game with former work buddies, Peter just doesn't gamble. Not that he thinks it's unethical; he just doesn't like to lose hard-earned money on games of chance. But when it comes to investing, Peter can be fairly aggressive. Not with all of his investments, but with a portion. He is a classic Buffettonian value investor in most ways, investing for value in businesses he understands. He occasionally will make a big bet on something that appears to be an obvious winner.

By nature, Peter has traditionally not been an active fund investor, choosing most of his stocks on his own and preferring not to leave his driving to anyone else. But he applauds these vehicles as a way to diversify his portfolio into some of the far corners and critical sectors of the investing world.

Scott Bobo

Scott is relatively new to the professional writing game, but has been an investor since age fourteen, when he made the switch from analyzing baseball box scores to looking at the numbers and charts in the business section. Cautious from the start, his first stock purchase was an electric utility with a spicy dash of dividend reinvestment. Unfortunately, the investing career was cut short by a lack of investment capital, and eight years later his brokerage firm was nice enough to send him a letter asking him if he was still alive and would he mind terribly taking his business elsewhere. As it turned out, that early 1980s episode was the real start of his investing career, since he now had an income and lived five minutes from a brokerage with half a dozen open Quotron machines.

In his twenty-plus years in engineering and technology management, he's learned that a unique product value proposition is important to the success of any company. He's also learned (the hard way) that proper financial fundamentals are just as critical. From a development manager's perspective, comprehending a new product's risk/reward proposition is one of the keys to a company's success. From an investor's perspective, it's also one of the keys to successful value investing in a dynamic, innovation-driven market.

Like Peter, Scott has always been a value investor. Choosing a company to buy based on momentum or popularity won't always result in a bad pick, just usually so. And while there are plenty of companies out there that can point to a history of increasing stock prices, there are far fewer that can point to a future of the same. Looking hard at the numbers, picking through the pretenders, and finding the contenders is where Scott adds his own value.

Scott likes to use ETFs when there's an identifiable trend in the market with no single clear leader, or there are several players that are all attractive for different reasons. Some may have greater growth potential, some may offer better stability . . . with the right ETF, you can have a little (or a lot) of the best of both worlds. Scott also thinks ETFs are a great way to gain entry into a sector that you may eventually wish to focus on with just a few individual share selections. You can buy the ETF, and if you like its performance, pick those component stocks that most closely align with the performance of the fund.

Scott plays poker too and finds the atmosphere around a poker table to be a bit like the stock market. Everyone knows there's money to be made, but not everyone is willing to do the math. Rather than figure out if they've got a reasonable chance of achieving financial gain with the cards (or stocks) they see in front of them, some simply bet on a combination of hope and the theory that "if you don't bet, you can't win." While that's true, it's also true that if you don't bet, you can't lose. You only have so much money to play with—make the most of it by understanding what you're betting on, where the opportunities are, and what you're up against. This is where this book can help.

Why ETFs?

So the big question many of you are probably asking is, "Why?" Why ETFs? Why ETFs instead of individual stocks, which we've been researching and bringing your way for years?

We consider ETFs to be an excellent way to build a complete portfolio. What do we mean by that?

The truth is that while we like individual stocks because we think, as investors, you should invest in good businesses and manage those investments as if you own the business, that simply isn't practical across an entire investment portfolio. That is, unless you really like doing it and have the time and resources to pull it off.

We think the diversification, the transparency and simplicity, and the access to more obscure market segments, such as emerging country infrastructure, for example, make ETFs a compelling story.

Does that mean you should invest in nothing but ETFs, as Charles Schwab seems to imply by creating the all-ETF 401(k) plan? Maybe, maybe not. Because of the diverse offerings in the current ETF universe, we believe you could put together a pretty good nothing-but-ETF portfolio, although paying the average 0.60 percent expense ratio across your entire portfolio should be a consideration. We actually like the idea of blending ETFs and individual stocks to build a strategic and tiered portfolio.

What is a tiered portfolio?

Read on . . .

ETFs and Portfolio Strategy

For faithful readers of our *100 Best Stocks* series, what follows will again look familiar. But we typically covered it as sort of a "dessert" for the meal, as a way to think strategically about how to place your individual stocks in your portfolio.

Now we cover it as a main course.

What do we mean by "it"? "It" is the segmentation of your portfolio into *tiers*—three tiers to be exact, the foundation, rotational, and opportunistic portfolio—to achieve different purposes and thus to be filled with different kinds of securities. The idea is to center your investing efforts and choices on these tiers and to manage risk. The reason that it's a "main course" in this book is that ETFs can play an important role in building out the portfolio, especially its foundation and rotational segments.

Building a Tiered Portfolio

Just like owning an automobile goes far beyond buying it, investing in stocks or funds goes well beyond just buying and selling them. There should be some underlying strategy shaping your fund or stock picks, and that strategy should lead to a greater whole of maximum returns, short and long term, with minimal risk and cost.

We find that many investors lose the forest in the trees, spending all of their energy trying to find individual stocks or funds without putting enough consideration into their overall investing framework. If they look at the big picture at all, they tend to look at the formulaic covenants of asset allocation, a favorite subject of the financial planning and advisory community, as though the difference between 50 percent equities and 60 percent equities makes all the difference in the world. Sure, it might in the world of pension funds and other institutional investments, where a 10 percent adjustment could move millions into or out of a particular asset class and more or less toward safety, but what about a $100,000 portfolio? Does $10,000 more or less in stocks, bonds, or cash make that much difference?

Perhaps not. And of course, there's more to that story—doesn't it matter more which equities or funds you invest in than just the fact that you're 60 percent in equities? While asset allocation models make for nice pie charts, we prefer to approach big-picture portfolio constructs differently.

Moreover, in connecting *100 Best Exchange-Traded Funds* with our individual stock books, *100 Best Stocks, 100 Best Aggressive Stocks,* and *100 Best Technology Stocks*, the question becomes what percentage of your portfolio should be allocated to each, as well as other assets such as fixed income, real estate, gold, etc.? Further, how can ETFs be used to get exposure to certain sectors, like fixed income, real estate, gold, or even areas of technology that don't lend themselves to individual stock investing? It makes sense to put some thought into your overall portfolio and the *components* of that portfolio and figure out how they all fit together.

Start with a Portfolio in Mind

First, we'll make an assumption: You are not a professional investor. You have other things to do with your time, and time is of the essence. You cannot spend forty, fifty, or sixty hours a week glued to a computer screen analyzing your investments.

To that assumption, we'll add another: As an individual investor, you're looking to beat the market. Not by a ton—20 percent sustained returns simply aren't possible *for all of your portfolio* without taking outlandish risks. But perhaps, if the market is up 4 percent in a year, you'd like to achieve 6, perhaps 7 or 8 percent without taking excessive risks. Or if the market is down 20 percent, perhaps you cut your losses at 5 or 10 percent. You're looking to do *somewhat better* than the market.

Because of time constraints, and owing to your objective to do slightly better than average and because you have *The 100 Best Exchange-Traded Funds* and perhaps our other books already at your fingertips, we suggest taking a tiered approach to your portfolio. The tiers aren't based on the type of assets; they're based on the amount of activity and attention you want to pay to different parts of your portfolio. It's a strategic portfolio approach you would probably take if you were managing a small business—put most of your focus on the products and customers who might bring the greatest new return to your business. Let the rest of your slow, steady customer base function as it has for the long term.

To do this, we suggest breaking up your portfolio into three tiers, or segments. This can be done by setting up specific accounts, or less formally by simply applying the model as a thought process.

Active Portfolio Segmentation

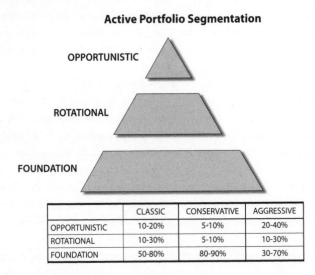

	CLASSIC	CONSERVATIVE	AGGRESSIVE
OPPORTUNISTIC	10-20%	5-10%	20-40%
ROTATIONAL	10-30%	5-10%	10-30%
FOUNDATION	50-80%	80-90%	30-70%

We can't go much further without defining the three segments:

The Foundation Portfolio

In this construct, each investor defines and manages a cornerstone foundation portfolio, which is long term in nature and requires relatively less active management. Frequently, the foundation portfolio consists of retirement accounts (the paradigmatic long-term investment) and may include your personal residence or other long-lived personal or family assets, such as trusts, collectibles, and so forth.

The typical foundation portfolio is invested to achieve at least average market returns through index funds, quality mutual funds, and income-producing assets such as dividend-paying stocks or bonds held to maturity.

A foundation portfolio may contain some long-term plays in commodities or real estate to defend against inflation, particularly in such commodities as energy, precious metals, and real estate trusts. The foundation portfolio is largely left alone, although as with all investments it is important to check at least once in a while to make sure performance—and managers if they're involved—keeps up with expectations.

Most of the ETF selections in this book are well suited to the foundation portfolio. The index funds, international, dividend, fixed income, and many of the specialized funds provide the kind of returns, income, and diversification you're looking for. More specialized ETFs can give you long-term exposure to the key industries described above for the long term, like energy, real estate, precious metals, general commodities, or technology. You can build a diverse foundation portfolio with just a handful of ETFs; in fact, ETFs could logically make up your entire foundation portfolio if you so choose.

The Rotational Portfolio

The second segment, the rotational portfolio, is managed fairly actively to keep up with changes in business cycles and conditions. It is likely in a set of stocks or funds that might be rotated or remixed occasionally to reflect business conditions or to get a little more offensive or defensive.

More than the other portfolios, this portfolio follows the rotation of market preference among different kinds of businesses and business assets. The portfolio is managed to redeploy assets among market or business sectors, between aggressive and defensive business assets, from "large cap" to "small cap" companies, from companies with international exposure to those with little of the same, from companies in favor versus out of favor, from stocks to bonds to commodities, and so forth. Sector-specific exchange-traded funds are a favorite component of these portfolios, as are cyclical and commodity-based stocks like gold mining stocks.

Is this about "market timing"? Let's call it "intelligent" or "educated" market timing. For years, studies have been telling us that it is impossible to effectively time market moves. It is impossible to catch highs and lows in particular investments, market sectors, or even the market as a whole. Nobody can find exact tops or bottoms. But by watching economic indicators and the pulse of business and the marketplace, long-term market performance can be boosted by well-rationalized and timely sector rotation. The key word is "timely." The agile, active investor has enough of a finger on the pulse to see the signs and invest accordingly.

While the idea isn't new, low-cost, well-targeted, easily traded ETFs make practical plays for individual investors. With ETFs, you don't have to liquidate or acquire a whole basket full of investments on your own to follow a sector. There are dozens of ETFs on our *100 Best* list that can be used for rotation.

FINDING THE RIGHT SEGMENT

Want *our* recommendations for how to use a particular ETF? As a handy reference to help you decide how to use a fund strategically in your portfolio, we've made a recommendation in each ETF write-up, labeled "100 Best Strategy." You can find this in the header at the top of each write-up.

If you don't want our recommendation, feel free to ignore this part. Our feelings won't be hurt. Promise.

The Opportunistic Portfolio

The opportunistic portfolio is the most actively traded portion of an active, self-directed investor's total portfolio. The opportunistic portfolio looks for stocks or other investments that seem to be notably under- or overvalued at a particular time or for more aggressive plays to boost the returns of the overall portfolio.

The opportunistic portfolio may be used to generate short-term income or cash, through short-term trading, or "swing" trading, or through short-term equity option strategies. Both topics are beyond the scope of this introduction. This part of the portfolio—or if you prefer to look at it as two separate "twin peaks" on your investing "mountain"—can also be used to layer in some aggressive plays. Perhaps you allocate 20 percent of your portfolio to aggressive stock plays to be held for a year to a few years, and another 10 percent to short-term swing trades to be held for a few days or a few weeks. It depends on what investing styles you're comfortable with and how much time you have to manage your investments.

Generally, ETFs are not opportunistic investments. Because they represent groups of stocks or entire markets, they don't move in sharp "swing" patterns as much. We have identified a few, such as the PowerShares Global Nuclear Energy Portfolio (PKN), as opportunistic in a bet on recovery from the March 2011 Japan disaster and for the nuclear energy industry as a whole, but this is an exception, not the rule.

ARE RETIREMENT ACCOUNTS ALWAYS PART OF THE FOUNDATION?

The long-term objectives and nature of retirement accounts suggest normal inclusion as part of the foundation portfolio. In fact, you can deploy retirement assets as either part of the rotational or opportunistic portfolio. Indeed, it might make a lot of sense. Why? Because returns generated are tax free, at least until withdrawn. Tax-free returns can compound much faster. Because of the importance of these assets, you should only commit a small portion to an actively managed opportunistic portfolio, but it can be a good way to "juice" the growth of this important asset base.

Do As They Do

As individual stock investors, we have used ETF information, specifically the funds' portfolio selections, as a way to identify individual stocks for further research as individual investments. Want to research networking stocks? Just look at the portfolio holdings of the PowerShares Dynamic Networking Portfolio (PXQ). You'll get some good ideas. Or how about stocks that company insiders are buying? Try the Guggenheim Insider Sentiment ETF (NFO).

You get the idea. Both ETFs, by the way, made our *100 Best ETFs 2012* list.

Why *NOT* ETFs?

This section has offered some reasons why ETFs make sense, and some applications of ETFs to your investing enterprise. But are ETFs perfect? Are they the panacea you've long sought to cure all of your investing ills?

For every argument, there's a counterargument, and by way of education if nothing else, it's worth addressing the shortcomings of ETF investing. Here are three:

1. *Overdiversification.* ETFs, by their nature, buy baskets of securities. Such diversification can be a good thing, because it insulates you from the problems an individual company might get unlucky enough to fall into. Oil giant BP and its 2010 Gulf of Mexico disaster is a great example. The energy industry may have a great long-term future, but here's a company that lost as much as half its value because of one incident. Buying an energy ETF with many large multinational producers would insulate you from this threat. But if that ETF has every single producer in its portfolio, you know you're getting the bad ones with the good ones. The success stories will be negated by the failures, and we like to buy success stories.

You know at the outset that you won't—can't—beat the returns of that sector, because you own the whole sector, and you're getting hit with expenses during that ownership. So unless we intend to track a complete index like the S&P 500, we tend to shy away from funds that have too many—say, over 100—stocks.

2. *Now you have a middleman.* So there is cost, and that cost is deducted from your investment continuously. And there is the "tracking error" that arises when the middleman can't adjust the portfolio composition to precisely reflect the index. So you might not get quite the returns you had in mind.

3. *Indexes can be complex.* ETFs, and their indexes, are financial "products." We all know that the past decade has been one of so-called "financial engineering," and some of those engineered products have been—well—overengineered. Some indexes can have very complex and hard-to-understand selection and weighting schemes, which you should take the time to understand before committing lots of cash. (Incidentally, you can usually get to a pretty good description of an underlying index just by entering the name into a search engine.)

So, obviously, these aren't showstoppers; if they were, we wouldn't have produced this book. But these "counterarguments" are worth taking a moment to understand.

The ETF Universe

Now that we've described ETFs in general and laid out some thoughts on how they can be used, it's time to drill down a bit into the world of ETFs and some of the facts and figures about them. Ordinarily we might have put this information earlier, but we thought it made sense to do it after covering the application and strengths of ETFs as investment vehicles. Now you have a better idea of what you're looking *for*, as well as what you're looking *at*.

Basic Stuff

In Table 1, we break down the ETF universe across self-determined lines, that is, what the fund provider tells us. Note that these figures don't add up to the 1,293 figure representing the entire universe, because some funds don't report every stat or may not fit perfectly into a category or may be too new to have a determination.

There are five statistics in this table:

- *Market Cap* tells us the fund's *investment objective* in terms of the size of the companies held in the fund. Large-cap companies generally exceed $5 billion in market cap, while small-cap companies are generally below $1 billion. Note that this is an investment *objective*, but many indexes contain a minority of issues that may fall outside the objective. Furthermore, most funds are set up to comply largely—say 80 or 90 percent—with an index but are given some latitude to deviate. As you can see, most ETFs are classified as large cap, as large-cap issues tend to dominate their makeup unless specifically excluded.
- *Style*. Funds can be classified by the "styles" made popular in the mutual fund space—"growth" for companies with significant earnings or stock-price growth or some combination, "value" for companies with strong basic financial fundamentals. While we've always argued that growth is a component of value, this designation shows which way the index is oriented, if indeed it is oriented one way or another—most ETFs are classified as blends.
- *Leverage*. Funds that are *leveraged* are specially constructed to magnify the movement of an index, either up or down. These leveraged funds are "financially engineered" to provide 2X (twice) or 3X (three times) an index performance. They are usually riskier—and more expensive—than ordinary "1X" funds, and are usually used for short-term rotations. We have one such fund on our *100 Best ETF* list, and as you can see, most funds are *not* leveraged.

Market Cap	No. of ETFs
Small cap	155
Mid cap	381
Large cap	750
Style	No. of ETFs
Growth	320
Value	377
Blend	589
Leverage	No. of ETFs
Unleveraged	1,134
2X	120
3X	56

Expense Ratio	No. of ETFs
<0.25%	258
0.25–0.50%	337
0.50–0.75%	437
>1.0%	20
Vintage (time since inception)	**No. of ETFs**
<1 year	281
1–5 years	722
5–10 years	203
>10 years	104

Table 1: Basic ETF Statistics

- *Expense Ratio.* Here we show a breakdown of ETFs by expense ratio, the annual expense rate taken against assets and deducted from NAV. As you can see, there are plenty of ETFs with expenses below half a percent. Complex funds, or funds with a large international content, are typically more expensive.
- *Vintage.* An ETFs vintage refers to its time since inception. As you can see, a vast majority of funds are relatively new to the universe. New funds have new ideas—or are cheaper than older funds—but, like companies, you should be a bit more careful about using a fund that doesn't have an established track record.

Sectors

Table 2 shows how funds break down by market sector—Energy, Industrial, Material, etc. Not every fund focuses in a sector; in fact, most don't, so the total number of sector-oriented funds is 370. In many screeners, these can be broken down further into specific industries, which helps if you're trying to isolate funds with exposure to water or computer software—but if you want computer networking or water infrastructure, you'll have to dig deeper. Note that search engines can sometimes fill the void—enter "water infrastructure ETF" or "networking ETF" and you'll often get a decent result; it's just hard to pair that criterion with others to do a screen search.

ETFs by Sector	No. of ETFs
Business Services	0
Consumer Services	30
Energy	45
Environmental	11
Financial	72
Health and Biotech	28
Industrial	34
Material	54
Software and Hardware	21
Technology	40
Telecom	15
Utilities	20
TOTAL	370

Table 2: ETFs by Sector

Geography

Some ETFs, but not all, are aligned to particular geographies and report themselves accordingly. Tables 3 and 4 are fairly self-explanatory. Again, a fund does not have to invest 100 percent in a country or region; 80 to 90 percent is usually enough. Further, whether or not a fund is for "Mexico" is determined by whether the fund trades on the local stock exchange, not whether the company is actually located or headquartered there, so you may see some holdings that appear not to fit. *EAFE*, by the way, is "Europe Australasia Far East."

ETFs by Region	No. of ETFs
Americas	423
Asia	72
Australasia	3
BRIC	5
EAFE	10
Europe	84
Global Ex-U.S.	9

ETFs by Region	No. of ETFs
Global Multi-Region	99
Latin America	15
Middle East/Africa	9
Pacific Ex-Japan	8
TOTAL	737

Table 3: ETFs by Region

ETFs by Country	No. of ETFs
USA	348
China	18
Japan	13
Canada	7
Brazil	6
India	6
Mexico	3
Russia	3
United Kingdom	3
Australia	2
Poland	2
South Korea	2
Taiwan	2
Austria	1
Belgium	1
Chile	1
Colombia	1
France	1
Germany	1
Hong Kong	1
Indonesia	1
Ireland	1
Israel	1
Italy	1
Malaysia	1

ETFs by Country	No. of ETFs
Netherlands	1
Peru	1
Singapore	1
South Africa	1
Spain	1
Sweden	1
Switzerland	1
Thailand	1
Turkey	1
Vietnam	1
TOTAL	437

Table 4: ETFs by Country

ETF Sponsors—Who Makes These Things, Anyway?

We feel strongly that it helps to understand the major players in the ETF space in order to understand the space itself. Knowing who the players are helps to comprehend and evaluate their offerings, just as you would know something about a particular Toyota or Ford car model just from being familiar with the brand at a higher level.

With that in mind, we offer this section, which identifies and summarizes the thirty-six largest and most important ETF and ETN providers, or *sponsors*. These thirty-six sponsors account for some 1,258 of the 1,293 fund products we believe are out there. Not surprisingly, different providers specialize in different things across the ETP product landscape, from equity and index funds to more specialized sector, strategy, commodity, inverse, and leveraged funds.

The biggest in the group, BlackRock (which offers the iShares brand), SSGA (SPDRs), and Invesco (PowerShares), account for more than 80 percent of the assets invested (as of the end of 2009) and a little more than a third of the total fund names offered.

There are thirty-six identifiable ETF sponsors. With twenty-one of thirty-six sponsors having funds on our list, our *100 Best ETFs* list is well diversified across the spectrum of sponsors. Table 5 summarizes the thirty-six sponsors. Following that is a little more description and detail of these major and not-so-major players.

Sponsor	No. of Funds	No. 100 Best ETFs	Brand, Comments
AdvisorShares Investments LLC	10		specialized active and enhanced ETFs
ALPS Advisors Inc.	3		mostly a fund marketer
Barclays Capital Inc.	81	2	iPath, mostly commodity ETNs
BlackRock Fund Advisors	226	17	iShares, largest family of funds
Charles Schwab Investment Management, Inc.	14	2	broad market equity funds
Claymore Advisors LLC	5		specialty, strategy
Credit Suisse Asset Management LLC	4		complex hedge-fund–like funds
DB Commodity Services LLC	10	2	commodity funds through PowerShares
Deutsche Bank Ag (London)	1		commodity funds through PowerShares
Direxion Funds	51		all but 3 are leveraged
ELEMENTS	14	4	mostly commodity ETNs
ETF Securities USA LLC	7	1	physical commodity backed
FaithShares Advisors LLC	5		Christian faith-oriented
Fidelity Mgmt. & Research Co.	1		one fund so far
First Trust Advisors LP	61	4	strategy, Morningstar, Value Line
FocusShares	15	1	new, lowest-cost sector/strategy funds
Global X Mgmt. Co. LLC	35	2	countries, specific industries
Goldman Sachs & Co.	2		two complex funds
GreenHaven Commodity Services LLC	1	1	one industry standard commodity fund
Guggenheim Funds Distributors LLC	43	3	specialty, strategy
IndexIQ Advisors LLC	14		global, international
Invesco PowerShares Capital Mgmt. LLC	156	17	broad and complete offering
Javelin Investment Mgmt. LLC	1		one-trick contrarian pony
JP Morgan Funds	3		small player so far
Merrill Lynch Holdrs	17		going off the market
PIMCO	14	1	mostly bond funds
ProShares	122	3	mostly leveraged

Sponsor	No. of Funds	No. 100 Best ETFs	Brand, Comments
RevenueShares LLC	6		complex index funds
Russell Investments, Inc.	17	1	specialty funds
Rydex Investments	36	3	specialty and leveraged approaches
SSGA/State Street	101	13	SPDRs—oldest, one of biggest brands
UBS Global Asset Mgmt.	24	2	variety, including commodity ETNs
United States Commodity Funds LLC	9		large commodity futures funds
Van Eck Associates Corp.	40	4	Market Vectors, specialty sectors
Vanguard Group, Inc.	64	11	low-cost, broad-based funds
WisdomTree Asset Mgmt., Inc.	46	6	innovative specialty funds

Table 5: ETF/ETN Fund Sponsors

AdvisorShares Investments LLC

AdvisorShares entered the ETF industry as a relative latecomer in September 2009. AdvisorShares partnered with financial author Harry Dent Jr. to launch the Dent Tactical ETF (DENT), an actively managed fund. Its funds are specialized and relatively "high-touch"; its largest fund is the Cambria Global Tactical ETF (GTAA). No AdvisorShares funds made this year's *100 Best ETF* list.

U.S. Listed ETFs: 10
Expense Ratio Range: 0.95%–1.85%
Avg. Expense Ratio: 1.35%

ALPS Advisors Inc.

ALPS was one of the first firms to actively market ETFs and ETF strategies to the financial advisor community but remains small with three total and specialized funds. Its biggest role is one of marketer/distributor of other funds to the financial planning community, but it has its own funds as well. Its largest fund is the specialized Alerian MLP (Master Limited Partnership) ETF. No ALPS funds made this year's *100 Best ETF* list.

U.S. Listed ETFs: 3
Expense Ratio Range: 0.54%–0.85%
Avg. Expense Ratio: 0.65%

Barclays Capital Inc.

Barclays was one of the pioneers in the ETF space, but has sold off its largest ETF business, iShares. It remains as the purveyor of the "iPath" brand of funds, mostly ETNs following the commodity markets. In 2009, Barclays agreed to sell its Barclays Global Investors unit, which includes iShares, to BlackRock for approximately $13.5 billion. BlackRock is one of the world's largest publicly traded investment management firms, and the combined entity has more than $2.7 trillion in assets under management. The iPath Dow Jones—AIG Commodity Index Total Return Medium-Term Notes Series A ETN is its largest fund. There are two iPath ETNs on the *100 Best ETF* list (JJS and GSP).

U.S. Listed ETFs: 81
Expense Ratio Range: 0.35%–0.95%
Avg. Expense Ratio: 0.73%

BlackRock Fund Advisors (iShares)

As a pioneering, large ETF family (along with Invesco (PowerShares) and State Street Global Advisors (SPDRs)), iShares was started by Barclays Global Investors and Morgan Stanley in 1993. In 2009, Barclays sold its Barclays Global Investors unit, including iShares, to BlackRock in a large deal. At that time, there were 180 iShares funds. Today there are about 228, covering a wide range of investment styles and needs, mostly in the equity space. The largest fund is the iShares MSCI EAFE Index Fund (EFA), which is not on our *100 Best ETF* list, but seventeen of its other funds are on the list, giving iShares the nod as our single largest provider.

U.S. Listed ETFs: 226
Expense Ratio Range: 0.09%–0.95%
Avg. Expense Ratio: 0.42%

Charles Schwab Investment Management Inc.

Charles Schwab is one of the country's largest asset managers. In November 2009, Schwab launched a line of ETFs that trades commission-free for clients in Schwab accounts. The Schwab funds tend to give very broad coverage of major market segments, like small-cap stocks, and do so at a very low expense ratio. We have two Schwab funds on the *100 Best ETF* list, SCHA and SCHB.

U.S. Listed ETFs: 14
Expense Ratio Range: 0.06%–0.35%
Avg. Expense Ratio: 0.14%

Claymore Advisors LLC
See *Guggenheim Funds Distributors, LLC.*

Credit Suisse Asset Management LLC
In February 2010, Credit Suisse launched the Credit Suisse Long/Short Liquid Index (Net) ETN (CSLS), which is designed to offer exposure to hedge-fund–like returns by tracking the performance of non–hedge fund, transparent market measures. The Credit Suisse funds are highly specialized; none made the *100 Best ETF* 2012 list.

U.S. Listed ETFs: 4
Expense Ratio Range: 0.45%–0.85%
Avg. Expense Ratio: 0.6%

DB Commodity Services LLC
DB (Deutsche Bank) structures ten commodity funds based on its own indexes and offers them under the PowerShares (Investco) brand. There are two PowerShares DB commodity funds on our list: the PowerShares DB Energy Fund ETF (DBE) and the PowerShares DB Oil Fund ETF (DBO). See *Invesco/PowerShares.*

Deutsche Bank Ag (London)
This is similar to DB Commodity Services LLC, listed above, with funds packaged and distributed through Invesco PowerShares. There is one fund, the PowerShares DB Agriculture Fund ETF, listed in this group for U.S. trading; it is not on our *100 Best ETFs* list.

Direxion Funds
Founded in 1997, Direxion Shares runs a series of leveraged funds, which, in its words, "apply the power of X" to a broad range of index and specialized equity fund selections. In 2008, it became the first to provide 3X leveraged ETF products, designed to track daily investment results of 300 percent of the performance of its benchmarks. Its largest fund is the Direxion Financial Bull 3X Shares ETF. There are currently no Direxion funds on the *100 Best ETF* list, but these funds are prime for consideration in rotational portfolios to capture short-term market movements or to amplify returns in key market segments.

U.S. Listed ETFs: 51
Expense Ratio Range: 0.55%–0.95%
Avg. Expense Ratio: 0.94%

ELEMENTS

ELEMENTS is a brand name of exchange-traded notes (ETNs) originally issued by Bank of America subsidiary Merrill Lynch and sometimes sponsored by other organizations, like HSBC and the Swedish Export Credit Corporation. ELEMENTS ETNs track specialized markets and strategies, including commodities like gold, agriculture, and biofuels; currencies and a few equity strategies such as small-cap and large-cap value. The largest fund, Elements Rogers International Commodity Index ETN (RJI), is on the *100 Best ETF* list, as are three others.

U.S. Listed ETFs: 14

Expense Ratio Range: 0.75%–0.75%

Avg. Expense Ratio: 0.75%

ETF Securities USA LLC

Headquartered in London, ETF Securities specializes in physical commodity funds, specifically oriented toward precious metals. ETFS started in 2003 with the world's first physical gold fund, ETFS Gold Trust (SGOL), which is still its largest fund. Its first U.S. fund started in August 2009, and one fund, the ETFS Physical Precious Metal Basket Shares ETF (GLTR), is on our *100 Best ETF* list for 2012.

U.S. Listed ETFs: 7

Expense Ratio Range: 0.3%–0.6%

Avg. Expense Ratio: 0.5%

FaithShares Advisors LLC

FaithShares occupies a unique niche in the ETF landscape, offering five ETFs utilizing indexes aligned with Christian values. In December 2009, FaithShares launched its first three ETFs, including funds focusing on Christian, Catholic, and Baptist values. The largest is the FaithShares Christian Values Fund (FOC), but there are no funds on the *100 Best ETF 2012* list.

U.S. Listed ETFs: 5

Expense Ratio Range: 0.87%–0.87%

Avg. Expense Ratio: 0.87%

Fidelity Management & Research Company

So far, investment giant Fidelity is a "one-trick pony" when it comes to ETF offerings, although we expect this to change. Its subsidiary Fidelity Management & Research LLC (FMR) offers the Fidelity NASDAQ Composite Index Tracking Stock (ONEQ), which is currently not on our *100 Best ETFs* list.

U.S. Listed ETFs: 1
Expense Ratio Range: 0.3%–0.3%
Avg. Expense Ratio: 0.3%

First Trust Advisors LP

Founded in 1991, First Trust Advisors is a fairly major player in the ETR space. It manages more than $32 billion in assets, and offers an array of size/style funds, sector funds, specialty funds, and global funds, many of which are based on more "active" indexing strategies designed to beat the market. Of our four First Trust ETF selections, two follow value-oriented Value Line indexes, one a value-oriented Morningstar index, to achieve a stronger value orientation.

U.S. Listed ETFs: 61
Expense Ratio Range: 0.45%–0.95%
Avg. Expense Ratio: 0.68%

FocusShares

FocusShares is a unit of discount broker Scottrade, and in March 2011, launched a suite of U.S. equity ETFs, including sector-specific funds and broad-based products. Its largest fund is the Focus Morningstar US Market Index (FMU) and we have the Focus Morningstar Health Care Index ETF (FHC) on our *100 Best ETF* list. FocusShares funds tend to be well designed and less expensive than most, but also new and untested; we expect to include more of them on future *100 Best ETF* lists.

U.S. Listed ETFs: 15
Expense Ratio Range: 0.05%–0.19%
Avg. Expense Ratio: 0.16%

Global X Management Company LLC

Global X Funds is a New York–based provider of exchange-traded funds specializing in ETFs to cover global markets and specific segments of those markets. Our two Global X picks, the Global X China Materials Fund (CHIM) and the Global X China Consumer Fund (CHIQ), are good examples of this up-and-coming fund provider's offering. The Global X Silver Miners ETF (SIL) is their largest fund.

U.S. Listed ETFs: 35
Expense Ratio Range: 0.49%–0.78%
Avg. Expense Ratio: 0.66%

Goldman Sachs & Co.

Goldman isn't so much mentioned because of what it's done in the ETF space, as it has only two funds, GS Connect S&P GSCI Enhanced Commodity ETN (GSC), and another taken over from Claymore, the Claymore CEF Index Linked GS Connect ETN (GCE). Do these funds sound complex and sophisticated? In a word—yes. With GS, it's more about what it *could* do as a creator of complex and specialized (and expensive) funds. No Goldman funds are on our *100 Best ETF* list.

U.S. Listed ETFs: 2
Expense Ratio Range: 0.95%–1.25%
Avg. Expense Ratio: 1.1%

GreenHaven Commodity Services LLC

GreenHaven Continuous Commodity Services was founded in 2006 as a privately owned investment advisor for trading commodity futures contracts. The firm has created one exchange-traded fund, the GreenHaven Continuous Commodity Index Fund (GCC), which tracks the performance of an index it developed in 1957. It is a well-regarded fund in this space, and is on our *100 Best ETF* list.

U.S. Listed ETFs: 1
Expense Ratio: 0.85%

Guggenheim Funds Distributors, LLC

Guggenheim Funds acquired Claymore Securities in 2009, and officially changed the name of the company's ETF products in September 2010. Guggenheim's ETF offerings consist of many innovative products, including several based on insightful strategies like insider trading (Guggenheim Insider Sentiment Fund—NFO—on our list), enhanced indexes, and specialty sectors. There are three Guggenheim funds on our *100 Best ETF* list.

U.S. Listed ETFs: 43
Expense Ratio Range: 0.12%–0.75%
Avg. Expense Ratio: 0.5%

IndexIQ Advisors LLC

IndexIQ lists a series of fifteen funds that are, at this writing anyway, a bit rich and sophisticated for their blood. In IndexIQ's own words, it offers "hedge fund replication ETFs that cover the top hedge fund investment styles, the first ETFs of their kind. IndexIQ prides itself on what it refers to as 'Rules-Based Alpha Investment,' a strategy which seeks to combine the benefits of traditional passive index-based investing with the alpha potential sought by the best actively managed funds." Its largest fund currently is the IQ Hedge Multi-Strategy Tracker (QAI). Okay, not now, but maybe someday.

U.S. Listed ETFs: 14
Expense Ratio Range: 0.48%—0.79%
Avg. Expense Ratio: 0.72%

Invesco PowerShares Capital Management LLC

With its PowerShares brand, Invesco has become one of the "Big 3" powerhouses in the ETF space (the others are BlackRock's iShares and State Street Global Advisors (SSGA)'s SPDRs). Founded in 2003, the company claims to "[lead] the intelligent ETF revolution." It offers approximately 156 funds (a frequently changing number) owned in more than 130 countries and listed on multiple exchanges around the world. Its largest and most famous entry is the PowerShares QQQ Trust, Series 1 (QQQ), but there are seventeen others on our list in various places, mostly in general equity and strategy/sector funds.

U.S. Listed ETFs: 156
Expense Ratio Range: 0.2%–0.95%
Avg. Expense Ratio: 0.59%

Javelin Investment Management LLC

Javelin, a one-trick pony founded in 2008, offers the JETS Contrarian Opportunities Index Fund (JCO), an obviously contrarian strategy-focused ETF. We did not pick this one for our list.

U.S. Listed ETFs: 1
Expense Ratio : 0.58%

JP Morgan Funds

You might expect a powerhouse like JP Morgan Chase & Company to be a bigger player in the ETF/ETN industry, but not so to date. In the ETF world, JP Morgan is best known for its Alerian Master Limited Partnerships Index ETFs (AMJ and BSR), which tracks energy pipeline and storage-based partnerships that trade on the U.S. exchanges. None found their way onto our *100 Best ETF 2012* list.

U.S. Listed ETFs: 3
Expense Ratio Range: 0.85%–0.85%
Avg. Expense Ratio: 0.85%

Merrill Lynch Holdrs

Merrill Lynch offers a series of specialized ETFs under the "HOLDRs" brand. HOLDRs are trust-issued receipts that represent beneficial ownership in a group of stocks. The details are beyond scope, but this ownership form did not allow the flexibility offered by other ETF forms, and as of late August 2011, this brand, once one of the largest in the ETF space, announced its discontinuance. Accordingly, there are no entries on our *100 Best ETFs* list.

U.S. Listed ETFs: 17

Expense Ratio Range: NM

Avg. Expense Ratio: NM

PIMCO

Founded in 1971, Pacific Investment Management Co. is the world's largest bond fund manager. In 2008, PIMCO entered the ETF market with a series of bond ETFs. The largest of its fourteen current offerings is the PIMCO Enhanced Short Maturity Strategy Fund (MINT); we have the actively managed PIMCO Build America Bond Strategy Fund (BABZ) on our *100 Best ETF* list.

U.S. Listed ETFs: 14

Expense Ratio Range: 0.09%–0.55%

Avg. Expense Ratio: 0.25%

ProShares

Launched in 2006, ProShares is the world's largest manager of short and leveraged funds. Short ProShares were the first ETFs designed to go up when the benchmarks go down and vice versa. Ultra ProShares were the first ETFs to double the daily performance of their tracking indices or benchmarks. ProShares' largest fund is the ProShares UltraShort 20 Year Treasury (TBT). We have three relatively conservative ProShares short funds on our list covering the S&P 500, NASDAQ 100, and S&P Small Cap 600 indexes.

U.S. Listed ETFs: 122

Expense Ratio Range: 0.85%–0.95%

Avg. Expense Ratio: 0.95%

RevenueShares LLC

RevenueShares offers six ETFs using a revenue-weighted model to track broad stock indexes. Its largest fund is the RevenueShares Large Cap Fund (RWL). There are currently no RevenueShares funds on the *100 Best ETF* list.

U.S. Listed ETFs: 6
Expense Ratio Range: 0.49%–0.6%
Avg. Expense Ratio: 0.53%

Russell Investments, Inc.

Through the years, Russell Investments has been mainly a provider of indexes for other ETFs to use. A number of providers, including State Street Global Advisors (SSGA) and BlackRock/iShares have created funds around these indexes, some of which are on our *100 Best ETF* list. In 2011, Russell introduced its first ETFs to the U.S. market. We have its Russell Equity ETF, an ETF "fund of funds" that holds other ETFs, on our *100 Best ETFs 2012* list.

U.S. Listed ETFs: 17
Expense Ratio Range: 0.37%–0.69%
Avg. Expense Ratio: 0.51%

Rydex Investments

Rydex Investments offers thirty-six ETF products, covering mostly specialty approaches to broader markets, typically at attractive expense ratios. It offers equal-weighted funds for the S&P and S&P sectors and some leveraged and inverse funds covering the broader markets. One leveraged fund, the Rydex 2X S&P 500 ETF, is on our *100 Best ETF* list.

U.S. Listed ETFs: 36
Expense Ratio Range: 0.2%–0.7%
Avg. Expense Ratio: 0.44%

State Street Global Advisors (SSGA)

As much as anyone, SSGA can be credited with the creation of the ETF industry. In 1993, it offered the original "SPDR" (S&P Depositary Receipt, for you trivia buffs) to track the general S&P 500 index, and it is still one of the largest and most popular funds today (SPY). Today it has expanded that offering to approximately 101 funds covering a broad assortment of equity and bond funds, many tracking specially created S&P indexes. Thirteen of the *100 Best ETFs* for 2012 are SSGA "SPDR" funds.

U.S. Listed ETFs: 101
Expense Ratio Range: 0.09%–0.65%
Avg. Expense Ratio: 0.36%

UBS Global Asset Management

UBS, or Union Bank of Switzerland, offers several ETN products under the E-TRACS brand, which are designed to track the performance of various commodities and sectors. Its largest fund is the UBS E-TRACS Alerian MLP Infrastructure Index (UPLI). We selected two commodity-based ETFs for our list: the UBS E-Tracs DJ UBS Commodity Total Return ETN (DJCI) and the UBS E-Tracs UBS Bloomberg CMCI Food Trust ETN (FUD).

U.S. Listed ETFs: 24

Expense Ratio Range: 0.3%–0.85%

Avg. Expense Ratio: 0.71%

United States Commodity Funds LLC

United States Commodity Funds LLC manages several exchange-traded funds that track the prices of different commodity futures contracts sold on the New York Mercantile Exchange (NYMEX). Its offerings enable investors to invest in the price of oil, natural gas, gasoline, and heating oil. As direct investors in futures contracts, these funds have had problems over the years with "contango" effects (rolling over and paying a premium to do so each month). They have also dominated some of their commodity sectors to the point that regulators threatened position limits, which in turn caused prices to go out of synch with net asset values—in short, these funds have not tracked their core commodity price as well as one would expect. Its largest fund is the United States Natural Gas Fund (UNG), but there are none on our *100 Best ETFs* list, as other funds and sectors have done better.

U.S. Listed ETFs: 9

Expense Ratio Range: 0.45%–0.95%

Avg. Expense Ratio: 0.66%

Van Eck Associates Corporation

Van Eck Associates Corporation has been a player in the mutual fund space in 1955 and offers a set of funds under the brand name Market Vectors. These ETFs offer exposure across an array of markets, including hard assets (commodities), commodity producers, international, specialty, and bond markets. Some Market Vectors ETNs offer leveraged or inverse exposure to currencies. Its largest fund is the Market Vectors Gold Miners ETF (GDX), which, along with the Junior Gold Miners ETF (GDXJ), is on our *100 Best ETFs* list. We also have the clever Market Vectors Agribusiness Fund (MOO) and the Market Vectors Global Alternative Energy Fund (GEX).

U.S. Listed ETFs: 40   Expense Ratio Range: 0.16%–1.43%

Avg. Expense Ratio: 0.59%

Vanguard Group, Inc.

Founded by pioneer investor and fund manager John C. Bogle in 1975, the Vanguard Group is renowned for its low-cost index fund offerings in both the mutual fund and ETF spaces. Vanguard ETFs cover a range from international markets to broad domestic indexes to highly targeted sectors like real estate. Its expense ratios are notably lower than most of the alternatives. Vanguard's largest ETF is the Vanguard MSCI Emerging Markets ETF (VWO), which, along with ten other funds, is on our *100 Best ETFs* list.

U.S. Listed ETFs: 64
Expense Ratio Range: 0.06%–0.35%
Avg. Expense Ratio: 0.18%

WisdomTree Asset Management, Inc.

As the name might imply, WisdomTree is an innovative developer of both ETFs and indexes on which its own and other ETFs are based. These proprietary indexes commonly employ unique and innovative approaches toward selection and weighting schemes, such as dividend and earnings-based weightings, which many feel address the structural flaws built into market cap and equal-weighted indexes that most ETFs track. WisdomTree offers an assortment of earnings and dividend-oriented international and sector equity funds, as well as a few plays in the currency space. There are currently six WisdomTree ETFs on the *100 Best ETFs* list.

U.S. Listed ETFs: 47
Expense Ratio Range: 0.28%–0.95%
Avg. Expense Ratio: 0.51%

The ETF "Department Store"

Now it's time to shift gears a bit to the characteristics and thought process behind our *100 Best Exchange-Traded Funds 2012* selections.

First on the list is to connect what you might be shopping for in your portfolio to what's out there. We think of it as sort of a department store—you're looking for a certain type of ETF (or ETN). Like a shopping trip, you decide what you need, then find the department or the aisle in the store containing the selections to choose from.

If you've researched ETFs, you've probably discovered that there are seven ways to Sunday to categorize them. Market cap, style objective, sector, geography, asset class, investment philosophy, sector exposure, and industry exposure are among the many. We thought this list was a bit confusing and hard to work with, so we simply sat down and came up with eleven of our own categories cutting across the ETF universe.

When we started, we wanted to create a diverse, "complete" department store, with an appropriate number of funds "on the shelf" in each. We set goals for the number of funds in each category and kept pretty close—but not exactly—to that goal as we got further into the research. Here are the departments in our "store," with the number of ETFs qualified for the *100 Best ETFs 2012* list in parenthesis:

- *General Equity/Index* (15). These are larger funds designed to cover large and broadly based segments of the U.S. equity (stock) space—S&P 500, NASDAQ, Russell 2000, and broad mid-cap and small-cap selections. The SPDR S&P 500 Trust (SPY) and the NASDAQ QQQ Series I Trust (QQQ) both live here.
- *International Equity/Index* (7). These larger funds cover broad equity segments outside, or "ex" the United States, mostly Pacific or a combination of Pacific and European markets. The SPDR Global 100 (IOO) and Vanguard Emerging Markets Index Fund (IWO) can be found here.
- *Dividend* (7). This group specializes in achieving high returns through dividends and dividend growth; some are broad market, some are narrower and pay higher yields like the SPDR S&P International Telecom ETF (IST).
- *Fixed Income* (6). For investors preferring the relative safety of bonds to stocks, this group has relatively high yields and a few choices among long and intermediate maturities, as well as some specialized "Build America Bonds" funds.
- *Commodity—General* (5). This group is for investors who want a diverse basket of commodities. Most of these investments, like the iPath S&P GSCI (Goldman Sachs Commodity Index) Total Return ETN (GSP) are ETNs, not ETFs.
- *Commodity—Specific* (8). Here we get into specific commodity or commodity groups, like energy, metals, precious metals, and agricultural commodities.
- *Strategy/Sector* (30). The thirty equity funds in this "department" buy companies to target either a specific sector or industry, like gold miners or energy producers or alternative energy or infrastructure, or they deploy specific strategies that we align to, like the PowerShares Buyback Achievers Portfolio (PKW), which specializes in companies that buy back their own shares.
- *Country/Region* (10). Here we find the funds targeted to specific regions or countries. Generally, we like the long-term prospects for Japan and

most of Asia and Latin America. We like China too but in a guarded way, so we picked two funds that specialize in specific sectors within China we feel are safer—the Global X China Materials Fund (CHIM) and the Global X China Consumer Fund (CHIQ).

- *Real Estate* (4). We think real estate will see better days for patient investors, and current yields are attractive. These funds mostly buy Real Estate Investment Trusts (REITs).
- *Actively Managed* (4). Although it's a new and largely untested idea, we wanted to stick a toe into the "actively managed" space, where the passive index ETF base is replaced with an active fund manager. One of the four funds in this "department" is the Russell Equity ETF (ONEF), which is actually an ETF owning a portfolio of ten ETFs. A fund of funds, if you will.
- *Inverse/Leveraged* (4). Finally, we get to another group we wanted to stick a toe into. This group is for more sophisticated investors looking to achieve a simple, largely short-term rotational investing objective, for example, to short the market in anticipation of a near-term decline. We offer three generalized "short" funds and one 2X leveraged fund in this group.

What Makes a Best ETF Best?

Now we're going to dig deeper into our thought processes behind our *100 Best Exchange-Traded Funds 2012* selections. We'll take you on a tour of some of the higher-level criteria, or characteristics, we look for in an ETF. At this point, we would like to point out that despite the wide array of data tracked and presented by most ETF portals for each ETF, this is still an inexact science. Even though we are buying a fund, and even though there are a lot of facts and statistics available for a fund, for us it's kind of like buying a business. In buying a business, it's more about how the pieces fit together and what your gut tells you about the result than it is about the pieces themselves.

Applicability

We start off with a "touchy-feely" criterion: Does a fund apply to what we feel to be today's typical "retail" individual investor? Does the fund capture a market segment that makes sense to own?

In this light, we tend to reject very complex, leveraged, hedge-fund–like funds that probably don't suit the average do-it-yourself/can't-watch-daily investor. We've also eliminated funds that, for instance, are specific to Europe or a European country. Although we put a few ETNs on the list to give some commodity exposure, we shied away from those because of credit-risk issues and understandability. We also avoided certain sponsors like IndexIQ because we thought those funds were a little too specialized for this space. Finally, we made only baby steps into the leveraged and inverse arena, for these vehicles have more merit for professional, full-time investors.

Understandability

If we had a hard time understanding a fund, its purpose, or its underlying index, we tended to avoid it. Some of the fund and index descriptions are so full of jargon and buzzwords that we worried about the underlying straightforwardness of the ETF. If there appeared to be too much "financial engineering" involved, we walked on those too. (As an aside, we wish some of these funds would hire consumer-friendly professional writers like us, to make some of their statements, even their "Stated Purpose" statements, more user-friendly and clear!)

Size

Size matters, although it isn't a show starter or stopper. Up to a point, the bigger a fund, in terms of total assets, the better. The fund gets "economies of scale" efficiencies and may be able to (should be able to) lower its expenses. More importantly, the fact that a fund has grown large is an indication of acceptance in the marketplace—that is, other investors, and probably some pretty big ones, have taken the bait. Size usually means liquidity—which follows as our next criterion.

That said, we didn't always select based on size. While we like to see more than, say, $50 million in total assets, we selected a few newer funds or sharply focused funds with assets under $10 million. Sometimes, we think size gets in the way; when a fund controls too much of a market, like the SPDR Gold Trust (GLD), it can draw regulatory scrutiny for controlling too much of the gold market, as did the U.S. Oil Fund (USO) with the oil futures market years ago. A fund that's too big, especially in the commodity sector, may drive prices up simply because of its size and thus not be able to buy the underlying securities cost effectively.

Liquidity

Liquidity refers to the ability to buy or sell ETF shares at a reasonable price, which is in turn a function of an ETF's daily trading volume. If the fund is small, and there is insufficient volume, the fund may be subject to large price swings. If you try to sell your shares and there are no buyers that particular day, you may get less than what you want. Finally, such shares are vulnerable to market disruptions, like the famous "Flash Crash" of May 2010. They may be also subject to a larger bid-ask spread, meaning if the wholesale, "bid," or buy price from you is substantially less than the retail "ask" price, you could take a small haircut on the shares someday.

Most ETFs should be bought and held for the longer term, minimizing liquidity risks. We didn't eliminate an ETF because of poor liquidity, but if there were two identical funds and one was more liquid, that was taken into consideration. Generally, investors buying a fund that trades less than 5,000 or so shares per day should be wary of liquidity issues.

Experience

Like a business—or a prospective employee—an ETF with more experience (that is, that has been in existence longer) is generally more desirable. It's easier to see how the fund has performed, and if there are major flaws in the design of the underlying index, they will have already become apparent. And of course, there will be a performance track record to look at. The ETF space as a whole is quite new, and there are more than 200 funds to come to market in the last year alone. Again, we didn't reject any fund simply because of inexperience, but it was a factor.

Expenses

One of the compelling arguments for ETFs in the first place is cost. Since these funds track indexes in a fairly automatic way, why should they cost a lot to run? The average equity expense ratio is 0.60 percent, and we typically sought funds with ratios below this figure, unless they were smaller and more specialized. One thing that turned us off was relatively simple funds with a large asset base and a high expense ratio. The 0.60 percent figure may make sense, but on a $10 billion fund, the fund manager is collecting some $60 million a year—quite a paycheck for buying an index, trading with it in the markets, and sending out reports.

By way of example, the iShares MSCI Emerging Markets Index (EEM) has total assets of $38.9 billion and an expense ratio of 0.69 percent. Should they be paid $265 million a year to run this fund? We don't think so, and picked the Vanguard MSCI Emerging Markets Fund (VWO), which uses the same index, has $49.9 billion in assets, and an expense ratio of 0.22 percent instead.

THE POWER OF YIELD

As some of you have already read in our *100 Best Stocks You Can Buy* series, we like dividends. Dividends provide current income, and give us some return while we wait for something better to happen with the value of a business and the price of a stock. Generally, we preferred funds with relatively higher yields for their segments, and picked seven ETFs based on their dividends alone. Those thinking about investing in a commodity ETN or an inverse fund should realize no dividends will be paid.

Diversification/Focus

Although financial engineers can measure and calculate diversification benefits to several decimal places, this factor remains one of our "touchy-feely" criteria. True, the benefits of investing in a fund in the first place center on diversification, particularly on an index-based (not actively managed) portfolio. But, as we pointed out earlier, it is possible to overdiversify. An ETF with too many holdings is more likely to track the market, not beat it, and it holds the bad and ugly in a segment along with the good. But if you want to invest in small-cap stocks and want a lot of diversification so you can lock it away and not worry about the fate of Acme Buggywhips, Inc., more is better.

Diversification can be a plus or a minus, as can *focus*, the opposite of diversification, depending on the context. Our selections include both highly diversified and fairly highly targeted funds. If an ETF has a specific objective, like alternative energy, we prefer maybe thirty to fifty holdings; if a broader index or an assortment of countries, maybe 100–200 holdings. But we picked some funds with up to 1,700-plus holdings.

Portfolio

Here's where the rubber really meets the road for us.

By nature, and by experience as authors of the *100 Best Stocks You Can Buy* series, we are stock pickers. We like good businesses; good businesses make good stocks. And if we like the looks of an ETF portfolio, and would want to own it ourselves, that's a major plus. We think you can tell by looking at "what's under the hood," and we spent a lot of time—more than most analysts—doing this. Put another way, it's the best way to test an index: If the index produces a list of stocks you'd want to own and weights them the way you would in the portfolio, that's a major passing grade, particularly if you're like us and want to invest in what's best going forward, rather than looking in the rear view mirror, as most performance statistics do.

It's not that we don't consider past performance; it's that we put more weight in future performance. In the same way that a company's intangible factors like brand, market presence, supply chain, and channel excellence are leading indicators of future performance, we believe the contents of a portfolio is one of the best indicators of a fund's future performance.

Performance

But we don't—and can't—ignore past performance, can we? Heck no. And just for the record, we don't.

For most ETFs, we looked at the past year's and the past three year's performance against the S&P 500 index. If you can't beat the S&P 500 index, you might as well invest in that index (through the SPDR S&P 500 Trust ETF, for instance) and head for the golf course.

Of course, with some sectors like alternative energy or even "regular" energy, which suffered a downturn at the beginning of our three-year horizon, we didn't really expect to beat the index. Also, if a fund tracked something safer than the index, or safer than stocks in general, like the Guggenheim Defensive Equity ETF (DEF), we didn't expect performance to measure up to the general stock market as represented by the S&P. But we did expect, in these cases, for the fund to perform better during a downturn.

IT'S NOT JUST ABOUT WHERE YOU FINISH

Performance measures can be very sensitive to timing. What you see reported will depend on when the measure started. As an example, we're continually amused at financial professionals who tell us that "the stock market gained nothing, actually lost ground over the last ten years." Why? Because ten years ago was the year 2000 and early 2001, when the markets as measured by most indexes reached all-time highs. So if your starting point is at an all-time high, even with pretty solid performance since then, you'll still show a flat or negative result. Same goes with funds—when measuring fifty-two-week or three-year performance, it helps to know where that time line starts (for us, July 2010 and July 2008, respectively).

As it turns out, we used another metric pretty extensively—the value of $10,000 invested at fund inception. That got us away from the tricky starting point issues and from trying to interpret percentages. Simply, if you invested $10,000 when the fund started, where would you be today? How far would you have dropped during the 2008–2009 crisis? How would you have recovered? These end-of-year figures over a series of up to five years can tell a lot (and if you go to an ETF portal like Fidelity, you can see more history than we show). And, for all of us investors, at day's end it's about how our money grows, right?

The caveat, of course, is that not all funds start at the same time, so a fund in existence for ten years will probably show higher figures than a fund existing for only one or two. Thus, the figures are more meaningful to compare internally, that is, looking at change over time *within* the fund, and comparing the *change* to other funds. Ten thousand invested in the iShares Latin America 40 Index Fund (ILF) in 2001 would be worth more than $70,000 today; does this compare well with another fund in existence for only two years and worth $15,000 today? Not based on just these figures alone.

ETFs—Just the Facts

As we move closer to presenting our *100 Best ETFs 2012* list, we feel it's important to lay out a simple glossary and make a few comments about the items contained in the ETF narratives, particularly for those of you familiar with our *100 Best Stocks* format and less familiar with funds.

A TRIP TO THE OL' DATA FISHIN' HOLE

Before venturing into that, this is as good a place as any to recognize Fidelity Investments and their "ETF Research" portal as our primary information source. While much of this information comes *through* the portal *from* the fund sponsor itself, we found Fidelity's organization (and the site's response time) to be efficient and effective. We also discovered that being Fidelity account holders gave us access to a little more information, but think that most investors can get what they need without an account. We did look at some other portals, too. We like Morningstar (*www.morningstar.com*), but felt that the Yahoo!Finance ETF portal (*www.finance.yahoo.com*) left something to be desired. Another ETF-specific portal called "ETFdb" (*www.etfdb.com*) has some interesting data selections but stopped far short of being the complete resource we were looking for.

Remember that we are teaching you to fish here, not giving fish—so you'll have to unpack your rod and reel and do some further research in one of these portal ponds before proceeding. You can also go to the ETF family's own website. These are pretty good too, once you narrow down to a fund family.

In each ETF entry in this book, here's what you'll find:

Portfolio Application

Here we suggest how to use the fund in a tiered portfolio. Most funds make sense for a foundation portfolio, but some, like commodity funds, can be used for rotational portfolios as well. We only had a handful of opportunistic picks, as generally individual stocks and options are more suited for opportunistic, cash-generating plays.

Fund Name

With ETFs, there tends to be a lot in a name. It starts with the fund's brand, like SPDRs, iShares, or PowerShares. Then you'll often see a basic reference to the index, like MSCI or GSCI or S&P followed by a descriptor of the index, which also tends to be a pretty good descriptor of the fund itself. Finally, most names include the fund type, ETF or ETN, or just "Fund," which usually indicates ETF.

Ticker Symbol

This is, of course, the symbol you'll need to do further research or get quotes. A four-letter ticker symbol can indicate a more specialized and newer fund—but not always.

Issuer/Sponsor

The sponsor, or issuer, or provider, or whatever term you choose, creates, markets, and operationally sets up and manages the fund, although other players are usually involved in the mechanics of creating, trading, and financing it. See the section "ETF Sponsors—Who Makes These Things, Anyway?" for more about sponsors.

Description

Here is where we attempted to put our own phrases together to describe the fund: what it has and what it does.

Geography

Most funds are either U.S.; "ex-U.S.," meaning everything except the United States; or "Global," meaning they consider all securities from all countries. Some of our country funds, naturally, have more specific countries or groups of countries as a geographic objective. Note again that geography isn't 100-percent predictive, as most funds have some latitude to venture beyond their index, and most funds base country on where a stock is traded, not its headquarters country.

Morningstar Rating

Just as we don't think we can measure other funds strictly on a quantitative or statistical basis, we don't think others can, either. That said, we wanted to include a couple of the more popular ratings. We'll quote directly from the glossary on the Fidelity website: The Morningstar rating is "a rating based on a Morningstar Risk-Adjusted Return measure that accounts for variation in a mutual fund's monthly performance, and includes the effects of sales charges, loads, and redemption fees, placing more emphasis on downward variations and rewards consistent performance. Funds must have a three-year history to receive a Morningstar Rating." From there, ETFs in the top 10 percent of their group got a five star rating, etc.

We found the Morningstar ratings to be more indicative of recent past performance than the next rating system, the Marco Polo XTF rating. The three-year criterion means that close to half of today's ETPs aren't rated. As a quantitative, rearward-looking measure, we didn't put much weight in the rating but thought you'd like to see it in the narrative.

Marco Polo XTF Rating

The Marco Polo XTF rating attempts to holistically rate ETFs across a variety of criteria, both for performance and operational efficiency. They rate across nine criteria in two categories: "Structural Integrity" and "Investment Analysis." A more complete description can be found through the Fidelity Help/Glossary section of the ETF research portal. We found these ratings to be more indicative of operational efficiency—low expense ratios, solid tracking, and so forth, and comprehensively more useful than the Morningstar rating. Again, this wasn't a selection criterion and is presented FYI only.

Expense Ratio

The expense ratio is appropriately highlighted at the top of the narrative, along with the appropriate "median" benchmark for comparison.

Yield

Yield is the most recent fifty-two weeks' dividends annualized and divided by a fund's current price. Of course, it's an indicator of future dividend performance, but not a commitment. In one case, the PowerShares S&P 500 Buy/Write Portfolio (PBP), we included a nondividend distribution in calculating the yield, since it was distributed as a fairly regular capital gain from covered call option writing, not a pass through of dividends from stocks contained in the fund.

Stated Purpose

Here we took the fund's "Stated Purpose" statement verbatim. As you'll see, some of these are well written and informative; others are jungles of jargon. In almost all cases, they state the exact name of the index a fund tracks, which, of course, is useful for doing further searches to understand the index.

Our Take

This is our "free-form" description and appraisal of the fund, its purpose, its makeup, and its results—our assessment, not theirs.

Why Should I Care?

Here we attempted to drill a bit more into how you might use the fund in your portfolio, and what factors to be cautious of.

Upside

From our "proven" model in *100 Best Stocks*, here we give three reasons why an ETP is attractive . . .

Downside

. . . and three reasons to be cautious about a particular fund.

Inception Date

Pretty simple—the date a fund was launched.

Total Assets

This is the total dollar holdings in a fund, including cash in reserve for investing or distribution.

Total Holdings

Here, we list the number of securities held by a fund, an indicator of focus or diversification.

Percent North America Holdings

To give a snapshot of a fund's geography, we show what percentage is held in United States and Canada-traded firms. Where geography was more important or interesting, we gave more geographic makeup information in the "Our Take" section.

Top 10 Holdings Percentage

Here we attempted to show the concentration, and focus, of a fund. If the top ten holdings make up 60 percent of a fund, that of course makes the fund much more driven by the performance of those holdings. Note that a high "Top 10" can mean focus—or it can reflect the effects of cap weighting. A cap-weighted fund loaded with Apple and Google and other recent winners will have a higher percentage in the Top 10 Holdings Percentage, which can be as much a leading indicator of future risk as one of "focus."

Portfolio Turnover

Portfolio turnover shows the percentage of total holdings, expressed in dollars, that are traded over the past fifty-two weeks as a percentage of total assets. A more active index, like an equal-weighted index, is "rebalanced" more frequently, and will generate more turnover. Bond funds will also have natural turnover as bonds mature. Turnover isn't necessarily bad, especially if you accept the idea proffered by equal-weighted indexes that winners should be sold and reinvested, not ridden for the long term. High turnover with no apparent reason probably means that you should learn more about the index, or that fund managers have too much latitude to make moves away from the index.

Beta Coefficient

Beta is a statistical measure that measures a fund's price performance against a benchmark measuring the performance of the entire market. A beta of greater than 1 means the fund typically amplifies market moves; that is, for every dollar the market moves up, the fund might move up $1.10, if the beta is 1.10. If the beta is less than 1, the fund moves less than the market, and is more defensive than the market, at least historically. If the beta is negative or close to zero, as we see with some of our gold and precious metal picks, it can mean the fund moves in an opposite direction to the market.

R-Squared

R-squared is another statistical measure of fund price movement relative to the broader market, or specifically, a fund's benchmark. If it moves "one-for-one" with the benchmark, the R-squared will be 100.

One-Year Return

Shows how the fund performed over the past fifty-two weeks, net of expenses. We also show the return of the appropriate benchmark over the same period, for equity funds, typically the S&P 500 Index.

Three-Year Return

Shows how the fund performed over the past three years, net of expenses. We also show the return of the appropriate benchmark over the same period, for equity funds, typically the S&P 500 Index. This metric is currently of interest, because it reflects how the fund performed not only in the "up" market cycle of late 2009–mid-2011, but also the down cycle of the 2008–2009 crisis. A fund that did well here might be more defensive.

Tracking Error 1 Year

Tracking error shows how, as a percentage, the fund tracks against its underlying index. A fund with high tracking error and no apparent reason (like international markets being closed during the U.S. trading day) may not trade its underlying securities efficiently as fund shares are bought or sold, or, in using sampling to mimic a larger index, may not be sampling effectively. Tracking error is not a red flag but is a cause for concern if the fund isn't performing well.

Average Daily Volume (Ninety Day)

This is the daily trading volume averaged over a ninety-day period, which gives an idea of the liquidity and trading activity and interest in the fund.

$10,000 Invested at Inception—2006 Through 2011 YTD

This series of figures, described briefly above, refers to the end-of-year values from 2006 through 2010, plus July 2011 year to date, for $10,000 invested in the fund at its inception date. From these figures, you can see the actual ups and downs of these funds as they would have behaved in your portfolio. We caution again, however, that different funds have different inception dates, so a nominal dollar value comparison between Fund A and Fund B, say for the year 2007, doesn't work. It's the relative ups and downs of the series of figures that counts.

What's Under the Hood

Here we show the Top 20 holdings of a fund and their concentration in the fund. We consider this a pretty good indicator of how the fund and its underlying index work. Naturally, we look for concentrations of stocks on our *100 Best* lists for equity funds. If you have a Fidelity account, it is easy to see the entire portfolio for the fund; you can also do this on the fund's website.

Contact Info

Straightforward—the name, address, phone number (for individual investors if they have one), and website for the sponsor firm.

Important "Unlisted" Facts

In the interest of brevity and simplicity, there are at least four factors we examined but didn't include explicitly in each narrative:

Underlying Index

Most of the "Stated Purpose" statements highlight the underlying index used to construct an ETP, so we didn't repeat it in our table. As an investor, it is worth examining the philosophy and the mechanics behind an underlying index. How is it constructed? How does it weight the investments? How often does it rebalance? Some of the sponsor sites provide this information, but most don't give enough detail. The better explanations are usually found on the websites for the actual index providers—MSCI, S&P, Russell, and so forth. The best way to find these? Enter the index name in a search engine.

Index Weighting

Most ETFs use a capitalization weighting or an equal weighting scheme. In a "cap-weighted" index, the amount of a security, in dollars, is held in proportion to its weight in the fund as measured by its market cap. If Apple Inc. is 15 percent of a fund's market cap, then it's held in exactly that proportion. What does that mean? As Apple rises, its market cap rises more or less in proportion to the price increase (assuming the number of shares remains constant) so the weighting of Apple in the fund grows. So there wouldn't be much change at rebalancing time. What does that mean? It means the fund rides its winners longer, but is more vulnerable to downturns, as the fund will tend to hold more of the "high flying" stocks. This happened to the S&P 500 and NASDAQ Composite indexes back in the dot.com boom—as the price of these securities rose, they became a bigger and bigger part of each index, which made them more vulnerable to the debacle that followed.

With this in mind, enter the equal-weighted weighting system, which became popular with investors wary of the risks of market-cap weighting. Now, the rule is, when Apple rises, you sell some to continue to hold it in equal portion to the rest of the issues in the portfolio. That keeps the Apples and Googles of the world from dominating your destiny. Typically, this rebalancing is done only once or a few times a year, so you will ride the winners for a while. But it also might pull you out of these winners before their time, increase transaction costs, and—by definition—weight your portfolio down with more losers (or more opportunities, if you prefer to look at it that way).

We didn't list the weighting scheme in the narrative tables, but you can usually tell by looking at the weights of the holdings ("What's Under the Hood"), or by reading about the index.

Recognizing the downfalls of these two popular systems, others have emerged, including earnings based, dividend based, and a few other more esoteric approaches. We probably have a fairly equal split between market cap and equal weighted funds, with a few dividend and earnings-weighted selections thrown in for good measure.

Premium/Discount, One Year

Because ETFs trade on markets, and because markets set prices based on supply and demand, rather than a direct transfer of NAV, funds may sell at a slight premium or discount to their actual NAV. Since these premiums and discounts typically average under .03 percent, we didn't feel the need to show them. But if you're buying a more exotic, smaller, international, or specialized fund, it's better to pay a discounted price than a premium one, and it's worth looking at the current premium/discount, available on most portals.

Chart Comparison

Finally, most portals allow you to chart the price of a security against a market or against another (or two or three) securities. If you have time, this is a fun game to play—simply chart the ETF you're researching against the S&P 500 (or the SPY ETF) and perhaps against other funds you're trying to compare. You can see how it rises and dips over time compared to other funds, that is, whether it is more aggressive or safer, and whether it is constructed with more timely or market-favored securities.

Selecting the 100 Best ETFs

We've explained ETFs, and we've explained the data analyzed and presented for each ETF. Now comes the question: How did we select the *100 Best ETFs* in the first place?

As we said earlier, and as readers of our *100 Best Stocks* series know, it's about art and science, it's about where a fund has been *and* where it is going, it is about hard facts and about intangibles.

If it were possible to develop a wholly quantitative model to evaluate ETFs, it could be done on a computer, and you wouldn't need this book or any other tools. Problem is, everyone else would have the same computer model, and probably the same fund. If everyone were investing in the same funds, those funds would have more to invest, and would invest in the same portfolio—thus driving those stocks higher—and thus, driving the funds higher. It would be a self-fulfilling prophecy, that is, until everyone bought in, and there wouldn't be enough shares of the individual holdings to go around, and the whole thing would collapse under its own weight.

A vicious circle, and a pretty far-fetched, really, an impossible outcome. The reality is that every investor, individual and institutional, has different needs and different preferences, hence the assortment of different funds.

The reality is that picking a fund is really a matter of determining the fit, determining the underlying quality (expenses, tracking, size, diversification, and performance, etc.). All of those things can be measured, but as we've just explained, they aren't all that makes up a fund. The underlying portfolio, the applicability, the nature of the underlying index, the fund manager, the risk/reward profile—all of these largely intangible factors come into play.

Setting Screens

We started by defining the categories—general equity, international equity, dividend, etc. Then we deployed ETF screens, again with tools supplied by Fidelity Investments in its ETF research portal (*www.fidelity .com*). The screens typically identified the category of fund we were looking for. From there we screened and sorted on a variety of other factors to get best-in-class lists for expense ratio, one-year performance, three-year performance, tracking error, and an assortment of other factors. We made lists of candidates based on these screens.

Making the Final Call

From those lists, we examined each fund—key statistics, portfolio composition, performance measures, distributions—to narrow it down. Some became candidates for further analysis, some were thrown out. Typically, we looked at the sponsor websites and the underlying index methodology through the index provider's website. We did some comparative charting, and we examined *100 Best Stocks* lists.

What we ended up with is what we feel to be the best-in-class set of ETFs for each identified category. Some funds were better at one thing than another, some might appeal more to you because they are cap-weighted or they are not. No matter what, we only claim to have started the research process to have narrowed down your choices to further your research.

At day's end, we feel that these *100 Best Exchange-Traded Funds for 2012* are your best places to start in your quest to add ETFs to your investing portfolio.

PART II

THE 100 BEST EXCHANGE-TRADED FUNDS YOU CAN BUY

Category (No. of funds)	Fund (ETF or ETP)	Symbol	Sponsor	Assets	Yield	Expense ratio %	1-yr performance	Inception Date	$10K at inception through July 2011	Description/Reason chosen
General Equity/ Index (15)	SPDR S&P 500 Trust	SPY	SSGA	$80.2B	1.8%	0.09%	25.7%	1/22/93	$12,314	de facto standard, low exp
	Powershares QQQ Trust, Series I	QQQ	Invesco	$24.3B	0.7%	0.20%	29.9%	5/10/99	$10,365	standard, lots of big tech
	iShares Russell 2000 Growth Index Fund	IWO	BlackRock	$4.2B	0.5%	0.25%	43.4%	7/24/00	$13,514	best of Russell 2000, higher growth
	iShares S&P Midcap 400 Growth Index Fund	IJK	BlackRock	$3.3B	0.6%	0.25%	45.2%	7/24/00	$18,879	strong performer and recovery, narrower than some
	Vanguard Midcap ETF	VO	Vanguard	$3.8B	1.1%	0.12%	38.7%	1/28/04	$17,896	solid portfolio, tracks well
	Vanguard Midcap Growth Index ETF	VOT	Vanguard	$1.3B	0.5%	0.12%	45.7%	8/28/06	$13,484	solid companies, solid industries, solid record
	Rydex S&P 500 Pure Growth ETF	RPG	Rydex	$283.0M	0.4%	0.35%	49.1%	3/1/06	$14,138	best of S&P 500, many 100 Best Stocks
	Rydex S&P Midcap 400 Pure Growth ETF	RFG	Rydex	$678.2M	0.1%	0.35%	56.4%	3/1/06	$16,987	mid-cap plus growth, many 100 Best Aggressive
	Schwab U.S. Broad Market ETF	SCHB	Schwab	$771.5M	1.6%	0.06%	32.4%	11/3/09	$12,819	very broad, very low cost
	Schwab Small Cap ETF	SCHA	Schwab	$519.1M	1.1%	0.13%	39.9%	11/3/09	$14,911	very broad, very low cost
	iShares S&P Small Cap 600 Growth Index Fund	IJT	BlackRock	$2.0B	0.8%	0.25%	42.4%	7/24/00	$21,524	solid returns, mature fund
	iShares S&P Small Cap 600 Value Index Fund	IJS	BlackRock	$1.8B	1.2%	0.25%	31.4%	7/24/00	$22,017	solid long-term performer

Fund	Symbol	Company	Assets	Yield	Expense	Return	Inception	Value	Comments
Vanguard Small Cap Index ETF	VB	Vanguard	$4.4B	1.1%	0.17%	39.5%	1/26/04	$17,449	very broad based, low cost
Vanguard Small Cap Growth Index ETF	VBK	Vanguard	$2.2B	0.4%	0.12%	46.6%	1/26/04	$18,149	broad based, low cost, strong record
iShares S&P Small Cap 600 Index Fund	IJR	BlackRock	$7.5B	1.0%	0.20%	36.8%	5/22/00	$22,189	strong performer, narrower than some
International Equity/Index (7)									
iShares S&P Global 100 Index Fund	IOO	BlackRock	$1.0B	2.6%	0.40%	30.2%	12/5/00	$11,493	market returns, plus some international exposure
iShares MSCI ACWI Ex-U.S. Index Fund	ACWX	BlackRock	$983.2M	2.6%	0.35%	28.8%	3/26/08	$9,521	decent yield, modest expenses
iShares MSCI EAFE Small Cap Index Fund	SCZ	BlackRock	$1.6B	3.5%	0.40%	36.2%	12/10/07	$9,696	decent yield, Japan/Aust strong, small caps
iShares MSCI EAFE Value Index Fund	EFV	BlackRock	$1.4B	3.9%	0.40%	29.1%	8/1/03	$12,190	decent yield, value approach
Vanguard Pacific Stock Index Fund	VPL	Vanguard	$1.6B	4.0%	0.14%	22.9%	3/4/05	$13,372	strong yield, low expenses, Pacific focus
Vanguard Emerging Markets Index Fund	VWO	Vanguard	$49.3M	1.7%	0.22%	23.8%	3/4/05	$23,366	solid country mix, low expenses
Vanguard Europe Pacific ETF	VEA	Vanguard	$7.1B	2.5%	0.12%	32.1%	7/20/07	$8,795	low expenses, Europe/Asia focus
Dividend (7)									
SPDR S&P Dividend ETF	SDY	SSGA	$5.9B	3.3%	0.35%	22.2%	11/8/05	$12,623	like the portfolio, low exp
WisdomTree Equity Income Fund	DHS	WisdomTree	$200.4M	3.5%	0.38%	32.5%	6/15/06	$10,202	growth plus income
First Trust Morningside Dividend Leaders Index Fund	FDL	First Trust	$171.7M	3.6%	0.45%	31.1%	3/9/06	$10,423	lots of 100 Best Stocks

Category (No. of funds)	Fund (ETF or ETP)	Symbol	Sponsor	Assets	Yield	Expense ratio %	1-yr performance	Inception Date	$10K at inception through July 2011	Description/Reason chosen
	iShares Dow Jones Select Dividend Index Fund	DVY	BlackRock	$6.4B	3.6%	0.40%	26.2%	11/3/03	$13,309	growth plus income
	iShares MSCI ACWI Ex-U.S. Health Care Sector Index Fund	AXHE	BlackRock	$3.0M	3.9%	0.48%	23.2%	7/13/10	$12,393	strong sector plus yield
	iShares MSCI ACWI Ex-U.S. Utilities Sector Index Fund	AXUT	BlackRock	$2.6M	7.1%	0.48%	8.7%	7/13/10	$10,639	strong yield, broad foreign exposure
	SPDR S&P International Telecom Sector ETF	IST	SSGA	$9.0M	5.3%	0.50%	32.7%	7/16/08	$11,277	telecom sector strength
Fixed Income (6)	Vanguard Long Term Corporate Bond ETF	VCLT	Vanguard	$164.1M	5.5%	0.15%	5.7%	11/10/09	$11,221	right sized, long term, basic bond portfolio
	SPDR Barclays Capital Long Term Corporate Bond ETF	LWC	SSGA	$35.6M	7.9%	0.15%	5.2%	3/10/09	$13,821	a little more risk, a little more return
	Guggenheim Enhanced Core Bond ETF	GIY	Guggenheim	$5.3M	6.0%	0.32%	2.9%	2/12/08	$11,682	actively managed shorter maturity
	Vanguard Intermediate Term Corporate Bond ETF	VCIT	Vanguard	$561.8M	4.5%	0.15%	7.4%	11/19/09	$11,325	makes the most of shorter maturities
	PowerShares Build America Bond Portfolio	BAB	Invesco	$658.6M	5.5%	0.29%	6.6%	11/17/09	$11,399	corporate returns, muni safety
	PIMCO Build America Bond Strategy Fund	BABZ	PIMCO	$37.5M	5.9%	0.45%	NA	4/20/10	$10,179	actively managed Build America bonds

Category	Name	Ticker	Provider		Expense	Return	Date	Value	Notes
Commodity— General (5)	iPath S&P GSCI Total Return Index ETN	GSP	Barclays	$117.8M	NA	0.75%	26.4%	6/6/06	$6,977	older, more energy weighted
	Elements Rogers Intl Commodity Index Total Return ETN	RJI	Swedish ECC	$941.5M	NA	0.75%	41.6%	10/17/07	$9,501	broad, large, and liquid
	GreenHaven Continuous Commodity Index Fund	GCC	GreenHaven	$733.8M	NA	0.85%	34.8%	1/24/08	$10,612	large, tracks well, performs well
	Elements S&P Commodity Trends Indicator Total Return ETN	LSC	HSBC	$42.7M	NA	0.75%	7.5%	10/10/08	$8,780	innovative weighting, safer?
	UBS ETRACS DJ UBS Commodity Index Total Return ETN	DJCI	UBS	$24.8M	NA	0.80%	25.4%	10/29/08	$11,926	broad basket, less energy, good performance
Commodity— Specialized (8)	UBS ETRACS UBS Bloomberg CMCI Food Trust ETN	FUD	UBS	$43.8M	NA	0.65%	49.5%	4/1/08	$10,981	a whole meal—softs plus livestock
	PowerShares DB Energy Fund ETF	DBE	Invesco	$200.0M	NA	0.75%	28.5%	1/5/07	$12,525	diversified energy, good performing ETF
	PowerShares DB Oil Fund ETF	DBO	Invesco	$595.3M	NA	0.75%	20.9%	1/5/07	$12,323	pure oil play, tracks well, safer during downturn
	iShares Comex Gold Trust ETF	IAU	BlackRock	$7.0B	NA	0.25%	20.6%	1/21/05	$18,879	low expenses, better than larger competitor GLD
	ETFS Physical Precious Metal Basket Shares ETF	GLTR	ETF Securities	$232.1M	NA	0.60%	NA	10/22/10	$12,243	good mix, owns physical assets
	MCLX Biofuels ETN	FUE	Swedish ECC	$9.9M	NA	0.60%	59.5%	2/5/08	$9,835	energy w/o oil & gas, strong recovery

Category (No. of funds)	Fund (ETF or ETP)	Symbol	Sponsor	Assets	Yield	Expense ratio %	1-yr performance	Inception Date	$10K at inception through July 2011	Description/Reason chosen
	Elements Rogers Intl Commodity Index Metals Total Return ETN	RJZ	Swedish ECC	$81.2M	NA	0.75%	36.3%	10/17/07	$12,286	broader than precious metals, defensive
	iPath Dow Jones UBS Softs Subindex Total Return ETN	JJS	Barclays	$58.2M	NA	0.75%	75.8%	6/24/08	$16,041	strongest sector lately
Strategy/Sector (30)	Market Vectors Agribusiness ETF	MOO	Van Eck	$5.3B	0.6%	0.50%	47.8%	8/31/07	$13,437	last year's performance, ag + ag tech portfolio
	iShares MSCI Global Energy Sector Index Fund	IXC	BlackRock	$1.3B	1.9%	0.48%	45.3%	11/12/01	$31,649	solid tracking, low turnover for int'l fund
	PowerShares S&P 500 High Quality Portfolio	PIV	Invesco	$120.4M	1.4%	0.50%	32.9%	12/6/05	$9,619	"cream" of S&P500, many stocks from 100 Best
	PowerShares Morningstar Stock Investor Core Portfolio	PYH	Invesco	$16.9M	1.4%	0.52%	21.3%	12/1/06	$8,349	Morningstar 4-star and moat leaders
	PowerShares S&P 500 Buy/Write Portfolio	PBP	Invesco	$113.1M	7.73%	0.75%	18.5%	12/20/07	$9,373	strategy turns growth into income
	First Trust Value Line 100 ETF	FVL	First Trust	$76.2M	0.1%	0.70%	38.0%	6/12/03	$15,232	Value Line "timeliness" = "1"
	First Trust Value Line Equity Allocation ETF	FVI	First Trust	$7.2M	1.1%	0.70%	24.2%	12/5/06	$11,099	"best" of Value Line 1700 universe
	PowerShares Buyback Achievers	PKW	Invesco	$43.0M	0.6%	0.70%	36.5%	12/20/06	$10,894	compelling strategy, strong long-term results

Fund	Ticker	Provider	Assets	Yield	Expense	Return	Inception		Comments
PowerShares Preferred Portfolio	PGX	Invesco	$1.4B	6.7%	0.50%	13.3%	1/31/08	$9,323	solid yield, some price appreciation
Guggenheim Insider Sentiment ETF	NFO	Guggenheim	$176.7M	0.6%	0.60%	43.1%	9/21/06	$15,241	compelling strategy, strong long-term results
Guggenheim Defensive Equity ETF	DEF	Guggenheim	$26.5M	1.5%	0.60%	30.0%	12/15/06	$10,531	defensive play with some offense
PowerShares Emerging Markets Infrastructure Portfolio	PXR	Invesco	$234.6M	1.1%	0.75%	37.7%	10/16/08	$26,697	infrastructure play, builders not operators
SPDR FTSE/Macquarie Global 100 Infrastructure ETF	GII	SSGA	$42.7M	3.9%	0.59%	21.9%	1/25/07	$9,840	infrastructure, more operators, so higher yield
Market Vectors Gold Miners ETF	GDX	Van Eck	$6.8B	0.7%	0.55%	5.8%	5/16/06	$14,525	gold, w/o commodity fund downsides
Market Vectors Junior Gold Miners ETF	GDXJ	Van Eck	$2.0B	1.4%	0.54%	33.4%	11/10/09	$13,345	gold, with a small cap and international flavor
PowerShares Dynamic Networking Portfolio	PXQ	Invesco	$157.0M	0.0%	0.63%	55.4%	6/23/05	$19,370	important niche, solid performance
Vanguard Information Technology Index Fund	VGT	Vanguard	$1.8B	0.6%	0.24%	28.8%	1/26/04	$13,514	good niche, low cost
WisdomTree Global Natural Resources Fund	GNAT	WisdomTree	$45.5M	2.9%	0.58%	46.5%	10/13/06	$12,861	good blend, dividend weighting
SPDR S&P Global Natural Resources ETF	GNR	SSGA	$169.5M	1.0%	0.40%	NA	9/13/10	$11,827	good ag exposure, low expenses
WisdomTree Large Cap Value Fund	EZY	WisdomTree	$25.7M	1.3%	0.38%	36.6%	2/23/07	$9,641	based on value measures, good strategy, low cost

Category (No. of funds)	Fund (ETF or ETP)	Symbol	Sponsor	Assets	Yield	Expense ratio %	1-yr performance	Inception Date	$10K at inception through July 2011	Description/Reason chosen
	PowerShares Global Wind Energy Portfolio	PWND	Invesco	$24.0M	0.0%	0.75%	-1.2%	7/1/08	$4,239	someday, wind may blow the right way
	Market Vectors Global Alternative Energy Fund	GEX	Van Eck	$133.7M	1.0%	0.60%	2.1%	5/3/07	$4,622	well diversified portfolio, day in sun to come?
	First Trust NASDAQ Clean Edge Smartgrid Infrastructure Core Index Fund	GRID	First Trust	$26.4M	0.9%	0.70%	21.4%	11/16/09	$11,206	infrastructure, smartgrid "plumbing" compelling
	Focus Morningstar Health Care Index ETF	FHC	FocusShares	$5.4M	0.6%	0.19%	NA	3/29/11	$10,718	new fund, low cost, compelling sector
	PowerShares S&P Small Cap Health Care Portfolio	PSCH	Invesco	$158.7M	0.0%	0.29%	45.2%	4/7/10	$13,256	health care sector with small cap pop
	SPDR S&P Biotech ETF	XBI	SSGA	$642.6M	0.0%	0.35%	40.9%	1/31/06	$14,965	good way to play sector
	SPDR Energy Select Sector Fund	XLE	SSGA	$9.0B	1.3%	0.20%	54.0%	12/18/98	$26,715	low cost, established, tracks oil prices well
	PowerShares S&P Small Cap Energy Portfolio	PSCE	Invesco	$104.5M	NA	0.29%	80.1%	4/7/10	$15,121	energy sector strength with small cap pop
	PowerShares Water Resources Portfolio	PHO	Invesco	$1.2B	0.9%	0.64%	29.3%	12/6/05	$13,200	key sector, infrastructure not just utilities
	PowerShares Global Nuclear Energy Portfolio	PKN	Invesco	$25.4M	3.7%	0.75%	18.2%	4/3/08	$7,807	attractive yield, plus long-term nuclear recovery?

Country/Region (10)								
SPDR S&P BRIC 40 ETF	BIK	SSGA	$531.7M	1.9%	0.50%	23.5%	6/19/07	$12,539	best of a vibrant region, good yield
SPDR S&P Emerging Asia Pacific Fund	GMF	SSGA	$714.2M	1.5%	0.59%	23.6%	3/19/07	$14,874	"tigers" and tech oriented
WisdomTree Australia Dividend Fund	AUSE	WisdomTree	$55.1M	5.9%	0.58%	37.2%	6/16/06	$16,637	good yield plus currency tailwind
iShares MSCI Pacific Ex-Japan Index Fund	EPP	BlackRock	$4.0B	3.7%	0.50%	34.9%	10/25/01	$39,182	solid performer, good yield, Australia centered
Global X China Materials Fund	CHIM	Global X	$3.8M	1.2%	0.65%	18.5%	1/14/10	$10,678	right sector play in vibrant but risky country
Global X China Consumer Fund	CHIQ	Global X	$206.6M	1.0%	0.65%	11.7%	12/1/09	$11,073	China trying to strengthen consumer spending
SPDR Russell/Nomura Prime Japan ETF	JPP	SSGA	$15.7M	2.4%	0.50%	11.9%	11/9/06	$8,079	good yield, solid companies, will recover someday
SPDR Russell/Nomura Small Cap Japan ETF	JSC	SSGA	123.7M	1.5%	0.55%	13.9%	11/9/06	$9,239	broad, good industry mix
iShares Latin America 40 Index Fund	ILF	BlackRock	$2.3B	2.2%	0.50%	26.9%	10/25/01	$76,868	stellar long-term performer, good industry mix
SPDR S&P Emerging Latin America ETF	GML	SSGA	$198.8M	1.8%	0.59%	26.1%	3/10/07	$15,888	good industry mix
Real Estate (4)								
Vanguard REIT ETF	VNQ	Vanguard	$9.8B	3.6%	0.12%	37.6%	4/23/04	$16,701	large-cap REITs—all categories
iShares FTSE NAREIT Residential Plus Capped Index Fund	REZ	BlackRock	$159.6M	3.1%	0.48%	41.0%	5/1/07	$10,139	REITs—residential, health care, self storage

Category (No. of funds)	Fund (ETF or ETP)	Symbol	Sponsor	Assets	Yield	Expense ratio %	1-yr performance	Inception Date	$10K at inception through July 2011	Description/Reason chosen
	WisdomTree Global Ex-U.S. Real Estate Fund	DRW	WisdomTree	$132M	12.2%	0.58%	35.4%	6/5/07	$7,744	real estate interests outside U.S., mainly Asia
	PowerShares KBW Premium Yield Equity REIT Portfolio	KBWY	Invesco	$7.7M	4.2%	0.35%	NA	12/2/10	$10,331	mid-cap, small REITs
Actively Managed (4)	Russell Equity ETF	ONEF	Russell	$12.9M	1.5%	0.51%	33.6%	5/11/10	$12,434	fund of funds—contains portfolio of ETFs
	PowerShares Active Real Estate Fund	PSR	Invesco	$23.4M	1.6%	0.80%	24.9%	11/20/08	$20,639	actively managed real estate fund
	PowerShares Active AlphaQ Fund	PQY	Invesco	$10.2M	0.6%	0.75%	39.1%	4/11/08	$11,271	Quantitative and Qualitative Investing Formula
	WisdomTree Dreyfus Commodity Currency Fund	CCX	WisdomTree	$65.1M	0.0%	0.55%	NA	9/24/10	$11,249	strong currencies in commodity-producing ctry's
Inverse/Leveraged (4)	ProShares Short S&P 500	SH	ProShares	$1.8B	NA	0.92%	-18.6%	6/19/06	$7,570	good way to short broad market
	ProShares Short QQQ	PSQ	ProShares	$245.6M	NA	0.95%	-24.4%	6/19/06	$5,242	to short more specific market segment, lots of AAPL
	ProShares Short Small Cap 600	SBB	ProShares	$60.7M	NA	0.95%	-23.0%	1/23/07	$6,410	to short more volatile market segment
	Rydex 2X S&P 500 ETF	RSU	Rydex	$86.8M	1.2%	0.70%	39.3%	11/5/07	$6,244	to magnify results—2X S&P 500

General Equity/Index

The fifteen funds in the General Equity/Index category are designed to give you broad-based exposure to the markets as a whole or to substantial segments of the market. These ETFs would help you diversify and to participate in the markets for the long term. They move more or less with the markets. More specialized mid-cap and small-cap funds and "growth" funds combine somewhat stronger growth potential with somewhat greater risk. The SPDR S&P 500 Trust is the oldest ETF and the traditional favorite for "buying the market." These funds are U.S.-centered and have low expense ratios, in the 0.09 to 0.25 percent range.

100 BEST STRATEGY: **FOUNDATION**

100 BEST CATEGORY: **GENERAL EQUITY/INDEX**

SPDR S&P 500 Trust

Ticker Symbol: SPY ▫ Issuer: State Street Global Advisors (SSGA) ▫ Description: Market Index
Large Cap Blend ▫ Geography: U.S. ▫ Morningstar Rating: 3 stars ▫ Marco Polo XTF Rating: 9.7 ▫
Yield: 1.82% ▫ Expense Ratio: 0.09% (Benchmark: 0.60%)

Stated Purpose

The investment seeks to replicate, net of expenses, the S&P 500 index. The index is composed of 500 selected stocks, and spans over twenty-four separate industry groups. It is heavily weighted toward stocks with large market capitalizations and represents approximately two-thirds of the total market value of all domestic common stocks. The fund holds all of the S&P 500 index stocks. It is comprised of undivided ownership interests called SPDRs. It issues and redeems SPDRs only in multiples of 50,000 SPDRs in exchange for S&P 500 index stocks and cash.

Our Take

The SPDR S&P 500 Trust, often referred to by market professionals as just plain "SPDRs" or occasionally by its ticker symbol SPY, is the original ETF. Conceived in 1993 to give investors a handy and inexpensive way to "buy the market," this fund continues to be one of the quintessential ways to do just that.

The fund is large and highly liquid, and—no surprise—tracks the market very closely with a beta coefficient of 1.00 and an R-squared measure of 100 percent. The fund is market-cap weighted, meaning that the portfolio is weighted toward the stocks with the largest market cap. Shares of companies that do well, such as Apple, get heavier weightings. But with 501 stocks, the fund is well diversified. That said, it is *too* diversified for investors looking to beat the market. The 1.82 percent yield isn't bad and beats most other short-term returns today.

Why Should I Care?

If you want to simply keep up with market performance, typically over the long haul but also as individual stocks start to look scary, this is the place to be. It is a cornerstone holding for a large number of investors, and sets the standard for the ETF industry.

Upside

- Tracks markets closely
- Very low expenses
- Very liquid and easy to trade

Downside

- Can't beat the market
- Cap weighting means you pay more for winners
- Not much small- or mid-cap exposure

Just the Facts

INCEPTION DATE: **January 22, 1993**

TOTAL ASSETS: **$80.2 billion**

AVERAGE DAILY VOLUME: **173 million**

TOTAL HOLDINGS: **501**

PERCENT NORTH AMERICA HOLDINGS: **99.5%**

TOP 10 HOLDINGS PERCENTAGE (CONCENTRATION): **18.5%**

PORTFOLIO TURNOVER: **5.38%**   BENCHMARK: **21.0%**

BETA COEFFICIENT: **1.00**

R-SQUARED (1 YEAR): **100%**

1-YEAR RETURN: **25.7%**   BENCHMARK: **25.9%**

3-YEAR RETURN: **0.89%**   BENCHMARK: **0.89%**

TRACKING ERROR (PRICE VS. NAV)   1 YEAR: **0.25%**   ASSET CLASS MEDIAN: **11.1%**

$10,000 Invested at inception	2006	2007	2008	2009	2010	2011
	$11,828	$12,465	$7,871	$9,446	$11,427	$12,314

What's Under the Hood

Symbol	Name	Percentage of fund
AAPL	Apple Inc.	3.06%
IBM	International Business Machines Corp.	1.86%
CVX	Chevron Corp.	1.77%
MSFT	Microsoft Corp.	1.72%
GE	General Electric Co.	1.61%
JNJ	Johnson & Johnson	1.50%
T	AT&T Inc.	1.47%
PG	Procter & Gamble Co.	1.45%
JPM	JPMorgan Chase and Co.	1.36%
KO	Coca Cola Co.	1.32%
GOOG	Google Inc.	1.29%
PFE	Pfizer Inc.	1.29%
WFC	Wells Fargo & Co.	1.25%
BRK/B	Berkshire Hathaway Inc.	1.09%
PM	Philip Morris International Inc.	1.07%
SLB	Schlumberger NV	1.04%
ORCL	Oracle Corp.	1.01%
INTC	Intel Corp.	1.00%
C	Citigroup Inc.	0.95

State Street Global Advisors
State Street Financial Center
1 Lincoln Street
Boston, MA 02111-2900
Phone: (617) 786-3000
Website: *www.spdrs.com*

PowerShares QQQ Trust, Series I

Ticker Symbol: QQQ ❑ Issuer: Invesco PowerShares Capital Management ❑ Description: Market Index Large Cap Core Blend ❑ Geography: Global ❑ Morningstar Rating: 3 stars ❑ Marco Polo XTF Rating: 9.0 ❑ Yield: 0.72% ❑ Expense Ratio: 0.20% (Benchmark: 0.60%)

Stated Purpose

The investment is a unit investment trust designed to correspond generally to the performance, before fees and expenses, of the NASDAQ-100 index. The fund holds all the stocks in the NASDAQ-100 index, which consists of the largest nonfinancial securities listed on the NASDAQ Stock Market. The fund issues and redeems shares of NASDAQ-100 Index Tracking Stock in multiples of 50,000 in exchange for the stocks in the NASDAQ-100 and cash.

Our Take

Like the SPDR S&P 500 Trust (SPY), the QQQ (or "cubes," in Wall Street parlance) has long been a bellwether in the ETF space. As indicated, it holds a cap-weighted mix of stocks designed to represent the NASDAQ-100 index (not the entire NASDAQ). As you can see from the list below, the NAS-DAQ-100 has many of the familiar names from the technology sector and from the more growth-oriented segments of the U.S. economy. Since it is a cap-weighted index, some of

Silicon Valley's biggest success stories have made their way to the top of the list, notably Apple and Google. This fund can be a good way to ingest a diet of such up-and-comers.

Incidentally, those who want to invest in strong NASDAQ growth stories but who would rather make it an all-in tech bet or an all-*not*-in tech bet might want to consider two other funds that didn't make our *100 Best ETF* list but have merit regardless. The First Trust NAS-DAQ100 Tech (QTEC) is based on the top 100 NASDAQ tech stocks, while the First Trust NASDAQ ex-Tech (QQXT) is a NASDAQ-100 blend that excludes tech stocks.

Why Should I Care?

The "cubes" have long been a way to spice up a portfolio with a more aggressive growth play without incurring the risks of investing in individual stocks. Since it's a cap-weighted fund, new buyers must be sure they want to accept the current weightings of the hugely successful top end of the list—notably Apple and Google.

Upside
- Strongest U.S. growth stories
- Low expense ratio
- Large and liquid

Downside
- Cap weighting requires careful buy-in
- Too much Apple and Google?
- Too much tech in general?

Just the Facts

INCEPTION DATE: May 10, 1999

TOTAL ASSETS: $243 billion

AVERAGE DAILY VOLUME: 51.3 million

TOTAL HOLDINGS: 101

PERCENT NORTH AMERICA HOLDINGS: 93.3%

TOP 10 HOLDINGS PERCENTAGE (CONCENTRATION): 51.5%

PORTFOLIO TURNOVER: 8.2%   BENCHMARK: 21.0%

BETA COEFFICIENT: 1.17

R-SQUARED (1 YEAR): 92.9%

1-YEAR RETURN: 29.9%   BENCHMARK: 30.69%

3-YEAR RETURN: 5.9%   BENCHMARK: -1.77%

TRACKING ERROR (PRICE VS. NAV)   1 YEAR: 5.64%   ASSET CLASS MEDIAN: 10.41%

$10,000 Invested at inception	2006	2007	2008	2009	2010	2011
	$7,518	$8,951	$5,221	$8,063	$9,565	$10,365

What's Under the Hood

Symbol	Name	Percentage of fund
AAPL	Apple Inc.	13.84%
MSFT	Microsoft Corp.	8.85%
ORCL	Oracle Corp.	5.93%
GOOG	Google Inc.	5.85%
INTC	Intel Corp.	4.54%
AMZN	Amazon.com Inc.	3.85%

Symbol	Name	Percentage of fund
QCOM	Qualcomm Inc.	3.50%
CSCO	Cisco Systems Inc.	3.37%
AMGN	Amgen Inc.	1.95%
CMCSA	Comcast Corp.	1.92%
EBAY	eBay Inc.	1.63%
BIDU	Baidu Inc.	1.63%
DTV	DirecTV	1.49%
COST	Costco Wholesale Corp.	1.31%
GILD	Gilead Sciences Inc.	1.28%
TEVA	Teva Pharmaceutical Industries Ltd.	1.26%
DELL	Dell Inc.	1.17%
SBUX	Starbucks Corp.	1.15%
NWSA	News Corp.	1.12%
ESRX	Express Scripts Inc.	1.10%

Invesco PowerShares Capital Management LLC
301 West Roosevelt Road
Wheaton, IL 60187
(800) 803-0903
Website: *www.invescopowershares.com*

100 BEST STRATEGY: **FOUNDATION**

100 BEST CATEGORY: **GENERAL EQUITY/INDEX**

iShares Russell 2000 Growth Index Fund

Ticker Symbol: IWO ◻ Issuer: BlackRock/iShares ◻ Description: Market Index Small Cap Selection ◻ Geography: U.S. ◻ Morningstar Rating: 3 stars ◻ Marco Polo XTF Rating: 8.2 ◻ Yield: 0.54% ◻ Expense Ratio: 0.25% (Benchmark: 0.60%)

Stated Purpose

The investment seeks to replicate, net of expenses, the Russell 2000 Growth index. The fund invests at least 90 percent of its assets in the securities of the index and in depositary receipts representing securities in the index. The index measures the performance of the small-capitalization sector of the U.S. equity broad market. It is a subset of the Russell Growth index and consists of stocks with higher price-to-book ratios and higher forecasted growth.

Our Take

The best way to understand the iShares Russell 2000 Growth Index Fund is to take in the index creator Russell Investment Group's explanation of its own index: "The Russell 2000 Growth Index measures the performance of the small-cap growth segment of the U.S. equity universe. It includes those Russell 2000 Index companies with higher price-to-value ratios and higher forecasted growth values. . . .

"The Russell 2000 Growth Index is constructed to provide a comprehensive and unbiased barometer for the small-cap growth segment. The Index is completely reconstituted annually to ensure larger stocks do not distort the performance and characteristics of the true small-cap opportunity set and that the represented companies continue to reflect growth characteristics."

We can't add a lot to that, except to say that the resulting fund, while diversified to the extreme at 1,156 component stocks, measures up to both performance metrics and our own sense of a good stock selection. While in a largely equal-weighted fund of 1,156 stocks the Top 20 picks don't matter much, we like most of what we see there.

Why Should I Care?

If you like the idea of investing in smaller, growing companies without the inherent risks of committing to one, ten, or even a hundred of them, this fund is for you, primarily as a foundation pick.

Upside

• Strong one-year and three-year performance for a diverse fund
• Won't pay too much for past performance
• Large, liquid, and lots of history

Downside

• Way too diverse for investors looking for focus
• Higher "price to value ratios" not always the best path
• Low yield

Just the Facts

INCEPTION DATE: **July 24, 2000**

TOTAL ASSETS: **$4.2 billion**

AVERAGE DAILY VOLUME: **1.9 million**

TOTAL HOLDINGS: **1,156**

PERCENT NORTH AMERICA HOLDINGS: **98.5%**

TOP 10 HOLDINGS PERCENTAGE (CONCENTRATION): **4.78%**

PORTFOLIO TURNOVER: **36.0%**   BENCHMARK: **20.0%**

BETA COEFFICIENT: **1.26**

R-SQUARED (1 YEAR): **81.2%**

1-YEAR RETURN: **43.4%**   BENCHMARK: **30.69%**

3-YEAR RETURN: **8.37%**   BENCHMARK: **3.34%**

TRACKING ERROR (PRICE VS. NAV)   1 YEAR: **9.0%**   ASSET CLASS MEDIAN: **10.41%**

$10,000 Invested at inception	2006	2007	2008	2009	2010	2011
	$12,515	$13,388	$8,238	$11,072	$14,290	$13,514

What's Under the Hood

Symbol	Name	Percentage of fund
CASH	Cash	0.83%
CPX	Complete Production Services Inc.	0.51%
IDCC	Interdigital Inc.	0.51%
BRY	Berry Petroleum Co.	0.49%
BID	Sotheby's	0.48%
ROSE	Rosetta Resources Inc.	0.46%
CROX	Crocs Inc.	0.44%
MAA	Mid-America Apartment Communities Inc.	0.43%
HME	Home Properties Inc.	0.42%
LUFK	Lufkin Industries Inc.	0.41%
PMTC	Parametric Technology Corp.	0.41%
CLH	Clean Harbors Inc.	0.41%
EXXI	Energy XXI Bermuda Ltd.	0.41%
JKHY	Jack Henry & Associates Inc.	0.41%
SBNY	Signature Bank	0.41%
TEN	Tenneco Inc.	0.40%
DRQ	Dril Quip Inc	0.40%
NETL	Netlogic Microsystems Inc.	0.39%
CPHD	Cepheid	0.39%
CVI	CVR Energy Inc.	0.39%

BlackRock iShares
525 Washington Boulevard, Suite 1405
Jersey City, NJ 07310
(800) 474-2737
Website: *www.ishares.com*

iShares S&P Midcap 400 Growth Index Fund

Ticker Symbol: IJK ❑ **Issuer: BlackRock/iShares** ❑ **Description: U.S. Mid-Cap Growth Selection** ❑ **Geography: U.S.** ❑ **Morningstar Rating: 4 stars** ❑ **Marco Polo XTF Rating: 9.2** ❑ **Yield: 0.56%** ❑ **Expense Ratio: 0.25% (Benchmark: 0.60%)**

Stated Purpose

The investment seeks to replicate, net of expenses, the S&P MidCap/ Citigroup 400 Growth index. The fund invests at least 90 percent of its assets in securities of the index and in depositary receipts representing securities in the index. The index measures the performance of the mid-capitalization growth sector of the U.S. equity market. It is a subset of the S&P 400 index and consists of stocks with the strongest growth characteristics within the index.

Our Take

We like the S&P 400 Midcap index as a place to be in general. Mid-cap companies (with a market cap between $750 million and $3 billion) seem like a good place to be as a starting point to capture the best growth opportunities in the U.S. economy. Add to that the fact that the S&P MidCap 400 Growth Index captures the strongest growing segment—growth stocks—within this index, based on "sales growth, earnings change to price and momentum," and you arrive at a compelling investment formula.

The iShares S&P Midcap 400 Growth Index fund goes further to use a sampling approach (which wasn't defined in the summary prospectus we looked at) to weight the portfolio. The resulting portfolio differs subtly from the Rydex S&P Midcap 400 Pure Growth Index fund (RFG, another *100 Best ETF*) and seems a bit more diversified away from technology and into more consumer-driven areas of the economy. While information technology stocks top the allocation at 22.4 percent, consumer discretionary comes in at 18.8 percent, health care at 15.4 percent, and financials at 12.2 percent. While the glamorous Green Mountain Coffee tops the list, other top holdings lack some of the glamour of the Rydex fund and may be less "priced for perfection" than some of the Rydex picks. Accordingly, the twelve-month return of 45 percent is a fair bit lower than the Rydex's 56 percent. As a consolation, expenses are lower (0.25 percent) as compared to the 0.35 percent expense ratio of the Rydex fund.

Why Should I Care?

This portfolio is a good way to play a broad cross section of growing stocks in the U.S. economy.

Upside

- Balanced portfolio
- Low expense ratio
- Large and liquid

Downside

- Allocation scheme not clear
- A bit overdiversified at 243 holdings
- Lower returns versus some comparable funds

Just the Facts

INCEPTION DATE: July 24, 2000

TOTAL ASSETS: $3.3 billion

AVERAGE DAILY VOLUME: 421,400

TOTAL HOLDINGS: 243

PERCENT NORTH AMERICA HOLDINGS: 99.8%

TOP 10 HOLDINGS PERCENTAGE (CONCENTRATION): 12.56%

PORTFOLIO TURNOVER: 47.0%   BENCHMARK: 20.0%

BETA COEFFICIENT: 1.01

R-SQUARED (ONE YEAR): 82.8%

1-YEAR RETURN: 45.17%   BENCHMARK: 30.69%

3-YEAR RETURN: 8.57%   BENCHMARK: 3.34%

TRACKING ERROR (PRICE VS. NAV)   1 YEAR: 6.37%   ASSET CLASS MEDIAN: 10.41%

$10,000 Invested at inception	2006	2007	2008	2009	2010	2011
	$13,167	$14,924	$9,308	$13,111	$17,078	$18,879

What's Under the Hood

Symbol	Name	Percentage of fund
GMCR	Green Mountain Coffee Roasters Inc.	2.24%
LZ	Lubrizol Corp.	1.49%
DLTR	Dollar Tree Inc.	1.40%
PRGO	Perrigo Co.	1.30%
MAC	Macerich Co.	1.20%
SLG	SL Green Realty Corp.	1.16%
FOSL	Fossil Inc.	1.08%
ALB	Albemarle Corp.	1.05%
ROVI	Rovi Corp.	1.03%
ATML	Atmel Corp.	0.95%
INFA	Informatica Corp.	0.93%
HANS	Hansen Natural Corp.	0.91%
BWA	BorgWarner Inc.	0.89%
VRTX	Vertex Pharmaceuticals Inc.	0.87%
ADS	Alliance Data Systems Corp.	0.87%
MTD	Mettler Toledo International Inc.	0.86%
PETM	PetSmart Inc.	0.84%
UHS	Universal Health Services Inc.	0.84%
EQIX	Equinix Inc.	0.84%
PVH	PVH Corp.	0.83%

BlackRock iShares
525 Washington Boulevard, Suite 1405
Jersey City, NJ 07310
(800) 474-2737
Website: *www.ishares.com*

Vanguard Midcap ETF

Ticker Symbol: VO ❑ Issuer: Vanguard ❑ Description: U.S. Mid Cap Blend ❑ Geography: U.S. ❑
Morningstar Rating: 3 stars ❑ Marco Polo XTF Rating: 9.6 ❑ Yield: 1.11% ❑ Expense Ratio: 0.12%
(Benchmark: 0.60%)

Stated Purpose

The investment seeks to replicate, net of expenses, the MSCI U.S. Mid Cap 450 Index. The fund generally invests all, or substantially all, of its assets in the stocks that make up the index, holding each stock in approximately the same proportion as its weighting in the index. The index measures the investment return of mid-capitalization stocks.

Our Take

The Vanguard Midcap ETF covers the range of mid-cap stock as defined by the MSCI U.S. Mid Cap 450 index. This index, rather than targeting a specific capitalization range as its S&P equivalent does, simply takes a sequential 450 issues from a 2,500-issue universe (large cap are the first 300, mid cap are the next 450, small cap are the final 1,750). The index is roughly equal-weighted.

The result is a fund that tracks the broadest definition of the mid-cap segment of the market without giving favor to any particular group, such as growth stars or companies whose shares have appreciated

recently. The portfolio is split wide across many sectors and industries, with many familiar and not-so-familiar names. The fund has 448 of the 450 holdings in the index, so is highly diversified albeit not focused. It is a pure play on the entire mid-cap segment, and the typically low Vanguard expense ratio of 0.12 percent makes it an inexpensive play.

Why Should I Care?

For those investors primarily looking for a no-brainer mid-cap play for a foundation portfolio to lock up for the long term, VO makes sense.

Upside

- Very low expenses
- Relatively safe with diversification, stronger during dips
- Equal weighted so you don't have to pay for past performance

Downside

- Overdiversified for some
- Twelve-month return of 39 percent less than rest of mid-cap group
- Not as exciting as other mid-cap funds

Just the Facts

INCEPTION DATE: **January 28, 2004**

TOTAL ASSETS: **$3.8 billion**

AVERAGE DAILY VOLUME: **219,300**

TOTAL HOLDINGS: **448**

PERCENT NORTH AMERICA HOLDINGS: **95.8%**

TOP 10 HOLDINGS PERCENTAGE (CONCENTRATION): **5.3%**

PORTFOLIO TURNOVER: **10.0%**   BENCHMARK: **20.0%**

BETA COEFFICIENT: **1.02**

R-SQUARED (1 YEAR): **95.4%**

1-YEAR RETURN: **38.67%**   BENCHMARK: **30.69%**

3-YEAR RETURN: **6.37%**   BENCHMARK: **3.34%**

TRACKING ERROR (PRICE VS. NAV)   1 YEAR: **3.14%**   ASSET CLASS MEDIAN: **10.41%**

$10,000 Invested at inception	2006	2007	2008	2009	2010	2011
	$15,204	$16,934	$9,382	$13,183	$16,385	$17,896

What's Under the Hood

Symbol	Name	Percentage of fund
EP	El Paso Corp	0.62%
NFLX	Netflix Inc.	0.58%
GMCR	Green Mountain Coffee Roasters Inc.	0.57%
CLF	Cliffs Natural Resources Inc.	0.56%
HUM	Humana Inc.	0.54%
GR	Goodrich Corp.	0.52%
CNX	CONSOL Energy Inc.	0.52%
AVB	Avalonbay Communities Inc.	0.50%
HK	Petrohawk Energy Corp.	0.50%
DOV	Dover Corp.	0.49%
CF	CF Industries Holdings Inc.	0.48%
FTI	FMC Technologies Inc.	0.47%
HST	Host Hotels and Resorts Inc.	0.47%
HOT	Starwood Hotels and Resorts Worldwide Inc.	0.46%
VRTX	Vertex Pharmaceuticals Inc.	0.46%
ALXN	Alexion Pharmaceuticals Inc.	0.45%

Symbol	Name	Percentage of fund
ABC	AmerisourceBergen Corp.	0.45%
LTD	Limited Brands Inc.	0.45%
RRC	Range Resources Corp.	0.45%
HOG	Harley Davidson Inc.	0.44%

Vanguard
P.O. Box 1110
Valley Forge, PA 19482–1110
(877) 241-1395
Website: *www.vanguard.com*

100 BEST STRATEGY: **FOUNDATION/ROTATIONAL**

100 BEST CATEGORY: **GENERAL EQUITY/INDEX**

Vanguard Midcap Growth Index ETF

Ticker Symbol: VOT ❑ Issuer: Vanguard ❑ Description: U.S. Mid Cap Growth Selection ❑ Geography: U.S. ❑ Morningstar Rating: 3 stars ❑ Marco Polo XTF Rating: 9.6 ❑ Yield: 0.48% ❑ Expense Ratio: 0.12% (Benchmark: 0.60%)

Stated Purpose

The investment seeks to track the performance of a benchmark index that measures the investment return of mid-capitalization growth stocks. The fund employs a "passive management"—or indexing—investment approach designed to track the performance of the MSCI U.S. Mid Cap Growth Index, a broadly diversified index of growth stocks of medium-sized U.S. companies. It attempts to replicate the target index by investing all, or substantially all, of its assets in the stocks that make up the index, holding each stock in approximately the same proportion as its weighting in the index.

Our Take

You may have noticed that we have three *100 Best ETF* picks in the "Mid-Cap Growth" space. Why so many dogs in the fight? Simply, each of the three takes a slightly different approach to indexing, or utilizing the indexes, to build the resulting portfolio. Not surprisingly, the resulting portfolios look different.

The Vanguard Midcap Growth Index fund is the most "different" of the three. It uses the MSCI Mid Cap Growth Index, while the others use the S&P Mid-Cap 400 Growth Index. This index is more or less equal-weighted, meaning that the best performers are sold and redeployed at rebalancing time. In addition, the MSCI index has 450 companies, not 400, and they are sequential by market cap among a broader universe of 2,500 stocks (large cap are the first 300, mid cap are the next 450, and small cap are the last 1,750) rather than being defined by a market-cap dollar range.

As a result, some of the big mid-cap performers such as Chipotle, Green Mountain, and Netflix are on the list but in diminished proportions; meanwhile, other less-glamorous issues get a stronger nod. As is typical for a Vanguard fund, the expense ratio of 0.12 percent gives you a good ride for your money.

Why Should I Care?
This portfolio should appeal to investors who want to buy into a solid mid-cap growth portfolio without paying too much for previous winners; the low expenses are also compelling.

Upside
- Very low expense ratio
- Equal weighting less risky for new purchases
- Relatively low turnover for an equal weighted portfolio

Downside
- Does it ride winners long enough?
- A bit overdiversified at 240 holdings
- Low yield

Just the Facts

INCEPTION DATE: **August 28, 2006**

TOTAL ASSETS: **$1.3 billion**

AVERAGE DAILY VOLUME: **138,600**

TOTAL HOLDINGS: **240**

PERCENT NORTH AMERICA HOLDINGS: **97.3%**

TOP 10 HOLDINGS PERCENTAGE (CONCENTRATION): **9.36%**

PORTFOLIO TURNOVER: **38.0%**   BENCHMARK: **20.0%**

BETA COEFFICIENT: **1.01**

R-SQUARED (1 YEAR): **89.3%**

1-YEAR RETURN: **45.65%**   BENCHMARK: **30.69%**

3-YEAR RETURN: **4.39%**   BENCHMARK: **3.34%**

TRACKING ERROR (PRICE VS. NAV)   1 YEAR: **4.86%**   ASSET CLASS MEDIAN: **10.41%**

$10,000 Invested at inception	2006	2007	2008	2009	2010	2011
	$10,754	$12,636	$6,692	$9,560	$12,343	$13,484

What's Under the Hood

Symbol	Name	Percentage of fund
EP	El Paso Corp.	1.21%
NFLX	Netflix Inc.	1.12%
GMCR	Green Mountain Coffee Roasters Inc.	1.11%
CNX	CONSOL Energy Inc.	1.02%
HK	Petrohawk Energy Corp.	0.97%
CF	CF Industries Holdings Inc.	0.93%
FTI	FMC Technologies Inc.	0.92%
VRTX	Vertex Pharmaceuticals Inc.	0.89%
RRC	Range Resources Corp.	0.88%
ABC	AmerisourceBergen Corp.	0.88%
HOT	Starwood Hotels and Resorts Worldwide Inc.	0.88%
ALXN	Alexion Pharmaceuticals Inc.	0.87%
HOG	Harley Davidson Inc.	0.86%
CMG	Chipotle Mexican Grill Inc.	0.84%
MYL	Mylan Inc.	0.83%
JOYG	Joy Global Inc.	0.82%
PXD	Pioneer Natural Resources Co.	0.82%
WFM	Whole Foods Market Inc.	0.82%
TIF	Tiffany and Co.	0.80%
CERN	Cerner Corp.	0.79%

Vanguard
P.O. Box 1110
Valley Forge, PA 19482–1110
(877) 241-1395
Website: *www.vanguard.com*

Rydex S&P 500 Pure Growth ETF

Ticker Symbol: RPG ❑ Issuer: Rydex Investments ❑ Description: U.S. Large Cap Growth Selection ❑ Geography: U.S. ❑ Morningstar Rating: 5 stars ❑ Marco Polo XTF Rating: 7.4 ❑ Yield: 0.38% ❑ Expense Ratio: 0.35% (Benchmark: 0.60%)

Stated Purpose

The investment seeks to replicate as closely as possible, before expenses, the performance of the S&P 500 Pure Growth Index. The fund uses a passive management strategy to track the performance of the underlying index. The advisor expects that, over time, the correlation between the fund's performance and that of the underlying index, before fees and expenses, may be 95 percent or better.

Our Take

This fund starts with the S&P 500 "universe" of stocks, which could be "bought" by buying the venerable SPDR S&P 500 Trust (SPY). But it adds a twist in that it selects, through the S&P 500 Pure Growth Index selection, a subset of 127 companies with the highest "sales growth, earnings change to price and momentum." The result is an interesting and dynamic set of companies with a market cap ranging between $2.1 billion to $271.3 billion.

So for the most part, you get a combination of large-cap size,

recognition, reputation, and stability with better-than-average growth prospects. Indeed, it has worked out fairly well over the past year, with twelve-month return of 49 percent before the August 2011 jitters. Those jitters did take a 20 percent whack out of the price of the fund, but it still rose north of 20 percent for the year even with the sharp downturn.

We like many of the top names in the portfolio, and many are found on our *100 Best* and *100 Best Aggressive* lists. That said, as a cap-weighted fund, some of the more glamorous and perhaps more vulnerable names such as Netflix and Chipotle—both of which we love but are priced for perfection—have found their way to the top of the list.

Why Should I Care?

This portfolio is great for an investor seeking large-cap stability with a dynamic growth component. It's a good rotational pick for a "bull" run and has the right amount of diversification to be relatively safer than individual stock picks in a downturn.

Upside
- Large cap with growth kicker
- Some favorite names on the list
- Safety: right amount of diversification

Downside
- Some of top names priced for perfection
- Cap-weighted, so entry point is important
- Relatively low yield

Just the Facts
INCEPTION DATE: **March 1, 2006**

TOTAL ASSETS: **$283 million**

AVERAGE DAILY VOLUME: **93,500**

TOTAL HOLDINGS: **127**

PERCENT NORTH AMERICA HOLDINGS: **99.54%**

TOP 10 HOLDINGS PERCENTAGE (CONCENTRATION): **16.98%**

PORTFOLIO TURNOVER: **31.0%**   BENCHMARK: **20.0%**

BETA COEFFICIENT: **0.95**

R-SQUARED (1 YEAR): **80.44%**

ONE-YEAR RETURN: **49.06%**   BENCHMARK: **30.69%**

3-YEAR RETURN: **11/56%**   BENCHMARK: **3.34%**

TRACKING ERROR (PRICE VS. NAV)   1 YEAR: **6.60%**   ASSET CLASS MEDIAN: **10.41%**

$10,000 Invested at inception	2006	2007	2008	2009	2010	2011
	$10,390	$11,048	$6,729	$10,107	$12,848	$14,138

What's Under the Hood

Symbol	Name	Percentage of fund
NFLX	Netflix Inc.	2.08%
CMG	Chipotle Mexican Grill Inc.	2.00%
PCLN	Priceline.com Inc.	1.96%
AMZN	Amazon.com Inc.	1.86%
AAPL	Apple Inc.	1.84%
COH	Coach Inc.	1.58%

Symbol	Name	Percentage of fund
EXPE	Expedia Inc	1.49%
CTSH	Cognizant Technology Solutions Corp.	1.47%
CI	CIGNA Corp.	1.43%
WYNN	Wynn Resorts Ltd.	1.42%
CRM	Salesforce.com Inc.	1.41%
WDC	Western Digital Corp.	1.41%
ISRG	Intuitive Surgical Inc.	1.39%
JOYG	Joy Global Inc.	1.39%
CF	CF Industries Holdings Inc.	1.30%
THC	Tenet Healthcare Corp.	1.29%
RHT	Red Hat Inc.	1.28%
WFM	Whole Foods Market Inc.	1.25%
AZO	Autozone Inc.	1.19%
BIIB	Biogen Idec Inc.	1.19%

Rydex SGI
P.O. Box 758567
Topeka, KS 66675–8567
(800) 820-0888
Website: *www.rydex-sgi.com*

100 BEST STRATEGY: **FOUNDATION/ROTATIONAL**

100 BEST CATEGORY: **GENERAL EQUITY/INDEX**

Rydex S&P Midcap 400 Pure Growth ETF

Ticker Symbol: RFG ▫ Issuer: Rydex Investments ▫ Description: U.S. Mid-Cap Growth Selection ▫ Geography: U.S. ▫ Morningstar Rating: 5 stars ▫ Marco Polo XTF Rating: 8.2 ▫ Yield: 0.09% ▫ Expense Ratio: 0.35% (Benchmark: 0.60%)

Stated Purpose

The investment seeks to replicate as closely as possible, before expenses, the performance of the S&P Mid-Cap 400 Pure Growth Index. The fund uses a passive management strategy to track the performance of the underlying index. The advisor expects that, over time, the correlation between the fund's performance and that of the underlying index, before fees and expenses, may be 95 percent or better.

Our Take

The Rydex S&P 400 Pure Growth ETF has occupied a "best of the best" niche in the markets over the past year and appears well positioned to continue that distinction. The index starts with the S&P MidCap 400 Index, which is comprised of companies with a market cap between $750 million and $3 billion. The S&P 400 MidCap Pure Growth Index takes a subset, which turn out to have a market cap between $892.1 million and $9.2 billion and have what S&P calls "growth characteristics"—highest sales "growth, earnings change to price and momentum." The result is a growth-oriented subset of 106 stocks (currently). This gives what we feel to be a right-sized play—diverse, but not too diverse, and focused on growth.

The fund and its index base are similar to the Rydex S&P 500 Pure Growth ETF (RPG)—another *100 Best ETF* pick—except that it aims at mid-cap, not large-cap, issues.

The resulting portfolio contains some of the most dynamic "mover-and-shaker" names out there—Green Mountain Coffee, Rackspace, Under Armour, Riverbed Technology, Tractor Supply. Many—but not a majority—of these names are found on our *100 Best Aggressive* list. Recent performance speaks for itself, with a 56 percent gain last year handily beating the S&P 500 benchmark.

Why Should I Care?

A fund like RFG allows you to participate in some of the most dynamic names out there without having to pick and choose among individual names.

Upside

- Strong and dynamic stock selection; you won't be bored
- Excellent recent performance *and* 3-year performance
- Right-sized, right amount of diversification

Downside

- Biggest names could be vulnerable to volatility
- Cap weighting requires careful buy-in
- Very low yield

Just the Facts

INCEPTION DATE: **March 1, 2006**

TOTAL ASSETS: **$678.2 million**

AVERAGE DAILY VOLUME: **126,000**

TOTAL HOLDINGS: **106**

PERCENT NORTH AMERICA HOLDINGS: **100%**

TOP 10 HOLDINGS PERCENTAGE (CONCENTRATION): **21.06%**

PORTFOLIO TURNOVER: **51.0%**   BENCHMARK: **20.0%**

BETA COEFFICIENT: **0.92**

R-SQUARED (1-YEAR): **57.42%**

1-YEAR RETURN: **56.42%**   BENCHMARK: **30.69%**

3-YEAR RETURN: **17.24%**   BENCHMARK: **3.34%**

TRACKING ERROR (PRICE VS. NAV)   1 YEAR: **11.01%**   ASSET CLASS MEDIAN: **10.41%**

$10,000 Invested at inception	2006	2007	2008	2009	2010	2011
	$9,819	$10,786	$6,965	$11,728	$14,991	$16,987

What's Under the Hood

Symbol	Name	Percentage of fund
GMCR	Green Mountain Coffee Roasters Inc.	4.76%
RAX	Rackspace Hosting Inc.	2.23%
DECK	Deckers Outdoor Corp.	2.20%
FOSL	Fossil Inc.	2.19%
NEU	Newmarket Cor.p	1.96%
MRX	Medicis Pharmaceutical Corp.	1.77%
ASNA	Ascena Retail Group Inc.	1.66%
UA	Under Armour Inc.	1.56%
INFA	Informatica Corp.	1.55%
DRC	Dresser Rand Group Inc.	1.53%
COO	The Cooper Companies Inc.	1.51%
TIBX	TIBCO Software Inc.	1.51%
HANS	Hansen Natural Corp.	1.44%
GES	Guess Inc.	1.43%
RVBD	Riverbed Technology Inc.	1.39%
CAKE	Cheesecake Factory Inc.	1.39%
BEAV	BE Aerospace Inc.	1.38%
TSCO	Tractor Supply Co.	1.37%
ATW	Atwood Oceanics Inc.	1.34%
CHSI	Catalyst Health Solutions Inc.	1.32%

Rydex SGI
P.O. Box 758567
Topeka, KS 66675–8567
(800) 820-0888
Website: *www.rydex-sgi.com*

100 BEST STRATEGY: **FOUNDATION**

100 BEST CATEGORY: **GENERAL EQUITY/INDEX**

Schwab U.S. Broad Market ETF

Ticker Symbol: SCHB ❑ Issuer: Charles Schwab & Co. ❑ Description: U.S. Broad Market Equity Blend ❑ Geography: U.S. ❑ Morningstar Rating: NR ❑ Marco Polo XTF Rating: 9.8 ❑ Yield: 1.64% ❑ Expense Ratio: 0.06% (Benchmark: 0.60%)

Stated Purpose

The ETF offers diversified exposure across large- and small-cap U.S. stocks. It seeks investment results that track performance, before fees and expenses, of the approximately 2,500-stock Dow Jones U.S. Broad Stock Market Index.

Our Take

For those investors who can't decide what segment of the market to buy, let alone which stock, the Schwab Broad Market ETF (Schwab B) probably makes sense. This ETF is a low-cost way to play the entire market.

What do we mean by "entire market"? Simply this, that the index this fund is based on, the Dow Jones U.S. Broad Stock Market Index, contains the top 2,500 companies in the United States by market capitalization. So why are there "only" 1,483 holdings in this fund?

The answer is, at the same time, simple and complex. The managers at Schwab are given the leeway to use what they call "statistical sampling"—which is really creating a sample portfolio that tracks the Dow Jones index as closely as possible, without owning all of its components. The reason to do this is to keep administration relatively straightforward and not to have to buy and sell up to 2,500 different issues at rebalancing time. That helps, and it is part of the story behind the very low 2.0 percent portfolio turnover. Makes sense, really. Also note that Schwab managers are only required to maintain 90 percent of the portfolio in congruence with this index, so they have a fair amount of leeway to adjust and modify holdings as they please. Not that any single holding will make that much difference on such a large portfolio, but . . .

The portfolio is cap weighted, and in such a broad universe, the cap weightings really come into play when going from largest to smallest. Even with almost 1,500 stocks, the top ten holdings represent 15.5 percent, and we see such familiar names as Apple, Exxon Mobil, GE, Microsoft, etc., dominating the top tiers of the list. So despite the breadth, this fund will act more like a large-cap fund just based on sheer percentages of the total holdings.

Why Should I Care?

This fund, with its breadth and low cost (0.06 percent) should only be considered as a way to buy the whole market for a foundation portfolio.

Upside

- Very low expenses
- Decent dividend
- Broad exposure, but slightly beat market in 2011

Downside

- Overdiversified
- Cap weighting moves expensive names to the top, so must find attractive entry points
- Almost impossible to beat the market

Just the Facts

INCEPTION DATE: **November 3, 2009**

TOTAL ASSETS: **$771.5 million**

AVERAGE DAILY VOLUME: **283,800**

TOTAL HOLDINGS: **1,483**

PERCENT NORTH AMERICA HOLDINGS: **97.9%**

TOP 10 HOLDINGS PERCENTAGE (CONCENTRATION): **15.5%**

PORTFOLIO TURNOVER: **2.0%**   BENCHMARK: **20.0%**

BETA COEFFICIENT: **1.01**

R-SQUARED (1 YEAR): **99.7%**

1-YEAR RETURN: **32.42%**   BENCHMARK: **30.69%**

3-YEAR RETURN: **NA**   BENCHMARK: **3.34%**

TRACKING ERROR (PRICE VS. NAV)   1 YEAR: **0.86%**   ASSET CLASS MEDIAN: **10.41%**

$10,000 Invested at inception	2006	2007	2008	2009	2010	2011
	$—	$—	$—	$10,280	$12,040	$12,819

What's Under the Hood

Symbol	Name	Percentage of fund
XOM	Exxon Mobil Corp.	2.72%
AAPL	Apple Inc.	2.47%
IBM	International Business Machines Corp.	1.53%
CVX	Chevron Corp.	1.44%
MSFT	Microsoft Corp.	1.41%
GE	General Electric Co.	1.32%
JNJ	Johnson & Johnson	1.23%
T	AT&T Inc.	1.20%
PG	Procter & Gamble Co.	1.19%
JPM	JPMorgan Chase and Co.	1.11%
PFE	Pfizer Inc.	1.07%
GOOG	Google Inc.	1.04%
KO	Coca Cola Co.	1.00%
BRK/B	Berkshire Hathaway Inc.	0.99%
WFC	Wells Fargo & Co.	0.96%
PM	Philip Morris International Inc.	0.87%
SLB	Schlumberger NV	0.86%
INTC	Intel Corp.	0.85%
ORCL	Oracle Corp.	0.81%
C	Citigroup Inc.	0.77%

Charles Schwab & Co.
200 California Street
San Francisco, CA 94111
(866) 855-9102
Website: *www.schwab.com*

100 BEST STRATEGY: **FOUNDATION**

100 BEST CATEGORY: **GENERAL EQUITY/INDEX**

Schwab U.S. Small Cap ETF

Ticker Symbol: SCHA ❑ Issuer: Charles Schwab & Co. ❑ Description: U.S. Small-Cap Blend ❑ Geography: U.S. ❑ Morningstar Rating: NR ❑ Marco Polo XTF Rating: 8.9 ❑ Yield: 1.06% ❑ Expense Ratio: 0.13% (Benchmark: 0.60%)

Stated Purpose

The ETF offers exposure to small-cap U.S. companies. It seeks investment results that track the performance, before fees and expenses, of the Dow Jones U.S. Small-Cap Total Stock Market Index SM made up of approximately 1,750 U.S. small-cap stocks.

Our Take

If you wanna buy an entire market segment, the "Schwab A" fund is one way to do it. Especially if what you're looking for is exposure to the small-cap segment of the market.

That segment is defined by Dow Jones, in this case, as 1,750 stocks in a 15,000-stock universe. But those stocks aren't in the sequence you might expect. "Large cap" comprises the largest 750 companies by total market capitalization. Then, the small cap makes up the next 1,750. Okay, you might ask, where are the mid caps? Great question. For Dow Jones, they overlap the other two groups, covering positions 501 through 1,000. Therefore, the largest 250 of the Dow Small Caps are also Dow Mid Caps.

As it turns out in real life, the details of index composition don't matter that much, because what you end up with is a highly diverse universe of 1,724 stock picks (at last count), and not very much of any of them. The picks are market-cap weighted, but only slightly, as the largest holding is only 0.48 percent of the portfolio. You don't end up paying a huge premium for a big recent performer like Apple or Chipotle or Google.

Why Should I Care?

This fund makes sense for a foundation portfolio where you don't want to think too much about what's under the hood. You get the entire segment and can lock it away for decent returns at low cost and not pay much attention to it.

Upside

- Total cap segment exposure to the max
- Low expense ratio, decent yield
- Safety in numbers; extreme diversification

Downside
- Overdiversified, won't beat more focused smaller-cap funds
- Boring compared to other small-cap picks
- Doesn't perform as well as other small-cap picks

Just the Facts
INCEPTION DATE: November 3, 2009

TOTAL ASSETS: $519.1 million

AVERAGE DAILY VOLUME: 195,100

TOTAL HOLDINGS: 1,724

PERCENT NORTH AMERICA HOLDINGS: 98.11%

TOP 10 HOLDINGS PERCENTAGE (CONCENTRATION): 3.88%

PORTFOLIO TURNOVER: 8.0%   BENCHMARK: 20.0%

BETA COEFFICIENT: 1.20

R-SQUARED (1 YEAR): 89.7%

1-YEAR RETURN: 39.85%   BENCHMARK: 30.69%

3-YEAR RETURN: NA   BENCHMARK: 3.34%

TRACKING ERROR (PRICE VS. NAV)   1 YEAR: 6.41%   ASSET CLASS MEDIAN: 10.41%

$10,000 Invested at inception	2006	2007	2008	2009	2010	2011
	$—	$—	$—	$10,797	$13,856	$14,911

What's Under the Hood

Symbol	Name	Percentage of fund
CASH	Cash	0.84%
HFC	HollyFrontier Corp.	0.48%
TPX	Tempur-Pedic International Inc.	0.30%
TSCO	Tractor Supply Co.	0.29%
CPT	Camden Property Trust	0.29%
AGNC	American Capital Agency Corp	0.29%
GDI	Gardner Denver Inc.	0.28%
ESS	Essex Property Trust Inc.	0.28%
VSEA	Varian Semiconductor Equipment Associates	0.28%
VRUS	Pharmasset Inc.	0.27%
OIS	Oil States International Inc.	0.26%
DRC	Dresser Rand Group Inc.	0.26%

Symbol	Name	Percentage of fund
WBC	WABCO Holdings Inc.	0.26%
ROC	Rockwood Holdings Inc.	0.25%
RKT	Rock Tenn Co.	0.25%
TUP	Tupperware Brands Corp.	0.24%
PII	Polaris Industries Inc.	0.24%
MCRS	Micros Systems Inc.	0.24%
SLH	Solera Holdings Inc.	0.24%
DECK	Deckers Outdoor Corp.	0.24%

Charles Schwab & Co.
200 California Street
San Francisco, CA 94111
(866) 855-9102
Website: *www.schwab.com*

100 BEST STRATEGY: **FOUNDATION/ROTATIONAL**

100 BEST CATEGORY: **GENERAL EQUITY/INDEX**

iShares S&P Small Cap 600 Growth Index Fund

Ticker Symbol: IJT ▫ Issuer: BlackRock/iShares ▫ Description: U.S. Small Cap Growth Selection ▫ Geography: U.S. ▫ Morningstar Rating: 4 stars ▫ Marco Polo XTF Rating: 9.1 ▫ Yield: 0.77% ▫ Expense Ratio: 0.25% (Benchmark: 0.60%)

Stated Purpose

The investment seeks to replicate, net of expenses, the S&P Small Cap 600/Citigroup Growth index. The fund generally invests at least 90 percent of its assets in securities of the index and in depositary receipts representing securities of the index. The index measures the performance of the small-capitalization growth sector of the U.S. equity market. It is a subset of the S&P 600 index and consists of stocks with a market capitalization between $200 million and $1 billion.

Our Take

The iShares S&P Small Cap Growth Index Fund takes the same market-cap defined segment of stocks as the parent/cousin iShares S&P Small Cap Index Fund (symbol IJR, also a *100 Best ETF*) and applies growth criteria ("sales growth, earnings change to price and momentum") to boil it down further into the 363 issues most likely to grow.

The result is a portfolio with few recognizable names, at least for most of us.

Why Should I Care?

If you can handle the bumps in the road represented by "small cap" and "growth" this fund can be a good place to stash some slightly more aggressive cash.

Upside

- Good returns for this segment, but not quite as good as the Vanguard entry

- Decent yield for this segment
- Large, liquid, and lots of history

Downside

- Expense ratio a bit higher, higher than Vanguard
- Relatively high portfolio turnover
- Did not do well in recent downturns

Just the Facts

INCEPTION DATE: **July 24, 2000**

TOTAL ASSETS: **$2 billion**

AVERAGE DAILY VOLUME: **229,600**

TOTAL HOLDINGS: **363**

PERCENT NORTH AMERICA HOLDINGS: **100%**

TOP 10 HOLDINGS PERCENTAGE (CONCENTRATION): **10.03%**

PORTFOLIO TURNOVER: **46.0%**   BENCHMARK: **20.0%**

BETA COEFFICIENT: **1.07**

R-SQUARED (1 YEAR): **78.55%**

1-YEAR RETURN: **42.40%**   BENCHMARK: **30.69%**

3-YEAR RETURN: **8.88%**   BENCHMARK: **3.34%**

TRACKING ERROR (PRICE VS. NAV)   1 YEAR: **7.80%**   ASSET CLASS MEDIAN: **10.41%**

$10,000 Invested at inception	2006	2007	2008	2009	2010	2011
	$16,688	$17,664	$11,846	$15,147	$19,362	$21,524

What's Under the Hood

Symbol	Name	Percentage of fund
REGN	Regeneron Pharmaceuticals Inc.	1.64%
CROX	Crocs Inc.	1.15%
HS	HealthSpring Inc.	1.15%
SBNY	Signature Bank	1.12%

Symbol	Name	Percentage of fund
SKT	Tanger Factory Outlet Centers Inc.	0.98%
SLXP	Salix Pharmaceuticals Ltd.	0.94%
HMSY	HMS Holdings Corp.	0.89%
CBST	Cubist Pharmaceuticals Inc.	0.85%
SF	Stifel Financial Corp.	0.85%
DAR	Darling International Inc.	0.82%
QCOR	Questcor Pharmaceuticals Inc.	0.80%
CRI	Carters Inc.	0.80%
WXS	Wright Express Corp.	0.79%
VSAT	ViaSat Inc.	0.78%
THS	Treehouse Foods Inc.	0.76%
QSII	Quality Systems Inc.	0.73%
CVLT	CommVault Systems Inc.	0.71%
ICON	Iconix Brand Group Inc.	0.71%
HAE	Haemonetics Corp.	0.70%
EZPW	EZCORP Inc.	0.69%

BlackRock/iShares
525 Washington Boulevard, Suite 1405
Jersey City, NJ 07310
(800) 474-2737
Website: *www.ishares.com*

100 BEST STRATEGY: **FOUNDATION/ROTATIONAL**

100 BEST CATEGORY: **GENERAL EQUITY/INDEX**

iShares S&P Small Cap 600 Value Index Fund

Ticker Symbol: IJS ❑ Issuer: BlackRock/iShares ❑ Description: U.S. Small Cap Value Selection ❑ Geography: U.S. ❑ Morningstar Rating: 3 stars ❑ Marco Polo XTF Rating: 7.5 ❑ Yield: 1.18% ❑ Expense Ratio: 0.25% (Benchmark: 0.60%)

Stated Purpose

The investment seeks to replicate, net of expenses, the S&P Small Cap 600/Citigroup Value index. The fund generally invests at least 90 percent of its securities in the index and in depositary receipts representing securities in the index. The index measures the performance of the small-capitalization value sector of the U.S. equity market. It is a subset of the S&P and consists of stocks with a market capitalization between $200 million and $1 billion.

Our Take

The iShares S&P Small Cap 600 Value Index Fund captures a value-oriented subset of the *100 Best ETFs*-listed S&P Small Cap 600 Index Fund, symbol IJR. Without giving a lot of detail, the folks at S&P use "book value to price ratio, sales to price ratio and dividend yield" to segment the portfolio into this "style" selection.

The result is a portfolio of mostly no-name companies, for in the value segment you even lose the more glamorous "name" stocks like Crocs that appear at the top of the S&P Small Cap 600 and S&P Small Cap 600 Growth selections. With some of the growth and glamour, though, also go some of the returns, and this fund barely beat the market yardsticks over the past twelve months. The good news: It did better during the weak markets of 2008–2009 and actually doubled the market benchmark.

That said, this one didn't hold up as well as we might have expected during the August 2011 turbulence, so how much safer is this fund than its growth-oriented brethren? At least there's a 1.18 percent dividend, healthy for a small-cap selection.

Why Should I Care?

For the more nervous investors who want to venture into small-cap stocks but still want a value orientation, this portfolio makes sense.

Upside

- Reasonably good yield for this segment
- Safety in numbers (450 issues) and value orientation
- Large, liquid, and lots of history

Downside

- Returns a bit muted for a small-cap portfolio
- Relatively safe, but not always
- Too diverse to really beat market?

Just the Facts

INCEPTION DATE: **July 24, 2000**

TOTAL ASSETS: **$1.8 billion**

AVERAGE DAILY VOLUME: **113,500**

TOTAL HOLDINGS: **430**

PERCENT NORTH AMERICA HOLDINGS: **99.6%**

TOP 10 HOLDINGS PERCENTAGE (CONCENTRATION): **8.23%**

PORTFOLIO TURNOVER: **31.0%**   BENCHMARK: **20.0%**

BETA COEFFICIENT: **1.21**

R-SQUARED (ONE YEAR): **88.3%**

1-YEAR RETURN: **31.41%**   BENCHMARK: **30.69%**

3-YEAR RETURN: **7.02%**   BENCHMARK: **3.34%**

TRACKING ERROR (PRICE VS. NAV)   1 YEAR: **6.84%**   ASSET CLASS MEDIAN: **10.41%**

$10,000 Invested at inception	2006	2007	2008	2009	2010	2011
	$20,866	$19,674	$13,875	$17,026	$21,189	$22,017

What's Under the Hood

Symbol	Name	Percentage of fund
CASH	Cash	1.16%
INT	World Fuel Services Corp.	1.09%
PRA	ProAssurance Corp.	0.87%
TDY	Teledyne Technologies Inc.	0.81%
MOG/A	Moog Inc.	0.77%
EME	Emcor Group Inc.	0.76%
NJR	New Jersey Resources Corp.	0.74%
AXE	Anixter International Inc.	0.73%
CACI	CACI International Inc.	0.73%
BRS	Bristow Group Inc.	0.72%
LYV	Live Nation Entertainment Inc.	0.71%
SWX	Southwest Gas Corp.	0.70%
CASY	Casey's General Stores Inc.	0.70%
ATU	Actuant Corp.	0.69%
CNC	Centene Corp.	0.67%
UIL	UIL Holdings Corp.	0.66%
BRC	Brady Corp.	0.64%
CW	Curtiss Wright Corp.	0.61%
ARRS	ARRIS Group Inc.	0.61%
DFG	Delphi Financial Group Inc.	0.61%

BlackRock/iShares
525 Washington Boulevard, Suite 1405
Jersey City, NJ 07310
(800) 474-2737
Website: *www.ishares.com*

Vanguard Small Cap Index ETF

Ticker Symbol: VB ▫ Issuer: Vanguard ▫ Description: U.S. Small Cap Blend ▫ Geography: U.S. ▫ Morningstar Rating: 4 stars ▫ Marco Polo XTF Rating: 9.0 ▫ Yield: 1.08% ▫ Expense Ratio: 0.17% (Benchmark: 0.60%)

Stated Purpose

The investment seeks to replicate, net of expenses, the MSCI U.S. Small Cap 1750 Index. The fund generally invests all, or substantially all, of its assets in the stocks that make up the index, holding each stock in approximately the same proportion as its weighting in the index. The index measures the investment return of small capitalization stocks.

Our Take

Interested in climbing on board with the next IBM? Google? Apple? Or another small-cap rocket ship destined for takeoff?

Of course you are. Problem is, you just don't know which of the 2,000 or so so-called small-cap stocks is gonna do it for you. We're not talking "micro-cap" stocks— stocks of companies with their corporate headquarters next door to your local convenience store. These are still companies with a market cap north of $50 million or so. In fact, the MSCI U.S. Small Cap Index captures 1,750 of the largest 2,500 companies in the United States. (Large cap is the top 300, mid cap

is the next 450, by MSCI's definition.) All 2,500 stocks together represent 98.5 percent of the total U.S. market capitalization.

What does that mean? You'll have heard of some of these companies—perhaps Tempur-Pedic and ETrade Financial—but you won't have heard of most of them. But who cares; you'll own 1,720 of them, so you couldn't keep track anyway.

With this fund, we get a broad exposure to a mysterious group of companies at a very low cost (0.17 percent) and with decent market performance exceeding one-year and three-year benchmarks.

Why Should I Care?

For those wanting a broad small-cap exposure that still beats the market averages, all at modest cost, this fund makes sense, primarily for a foundation portfolio.

Upside

- Broad small-cap exposure with decent returns
- Low expense ratio
- Safety in numbers—diversification

Downside
- So broad, it's hard, but not impossible, to beat market indexes
- Fairly boring, won't make you rich quick
- You'll own the next IBM, just not enough of it

Just the Facts

INCEPTION DATE: **January 26, 2004**

TOTAL ASSETS: **$4.4 billion**

AVERAGE DAILY VOLUME: **375,500**

TOTAL HOLDINGS: **1,720**

PERCENT NORTH AMERICA HOLDINGS: **97.5%**

TOP 10 HOLDINGS PERCENTAGE (CONCENTRATION): **2.71%**

PORTFOLIO TURNOVER: **12.0%**   BENCHMARK: **20.0%**

BETA COEFFICIENT: **1.20**

R-SQUARED (1 YEAR): **90.5%**

1-YEAR RETURN: **39.49%**   BENCHMARK: **30.69%**

3-YEAR RETURN: **9.38%**   BENCHMARK: **3.34%**

TRACKING ERROR (PRICE VS. NAV)   1 YEAR: **6.14%**   ASSET CLASS MEDIAN: **10.41%**

$10,000 Invested at inception	2006	2007	2008	2009	2010	2011
	$14,365	$14,546	$9,299	$12,678	$16,215	$17,449

What's Under the Hood

Symbol	Name	Percentage of fund
TPX	Tempur-Pedic International Inc.	0.30%
AGNC	American Capital Agency Corp.	0.29%
PLCM	Polycom Inc.	0.29%
CPT	Camden Property Trust	0.28%
VSEA	Varian Semiconductor Equipment Assoc.	0.28%
VRUS	Pharmasset Inc.	0.27%
ESS	Essex Property Trust Inc.	0.27%
GDI	Gardner Denver Inc.	0.27%
TDG	TransDigm Group Inc.	0.26%
BEAV	BE Aerospace Inc.	0.25%

Symbol	Name	Percentage of fund
GNTX	Gentex Corp.	0.25%
OIS	Oil States International Inc.	0.25%
WBC	WABCO Holdings Inc.	0.25%
SLH	Solera Holdings Inc.	0.24%
MCRS	Micros Systems Inc.	0.24%
ROC	Rockwood Holdings Inc.	0.24%
ETFC	E*Trade Financial Corp.	0.24%
CPO	Corn Products International Inc.	0.24%
BRE	BRE Properties Inc.	0.23%
DECK	Deckers Outdoor Corp.	0.23%

Vanguard
P.O. Box 1110
Valley Forge, PA 19482–1110
(877) 241-1395
Website: *www.vanguard.com*

100 BEST STRATEGY: **FOUNDATIONAL/ROTATIONAL**

100 BEST CATEGORY: **GENERAL EQUITY/INDEX**

Vanguard Small Cap Growth Index ETF

Ticker Symbol: VBK ❑ Issuer: Vanguard ❑ Description: U.S. Small Cap Growth Selection ❑ Geography: U.S. ❑ Morningstar Rating: 4 stars ❑ Marco Polo XTF Rating: 9.2 ❑ Yield: 0.43% ❑ Expense Ratio: 0.12% (Benchmark: 0.60%)

Stated Purpose

The investment seeks to replicate, net of expenses, the MSCI U.S. Small Cap Growth Index. The fund generally invests all, or substantially all, of its assets in the stocks that make up the index, holding each stock in approximately the same proportion as its weighting in the index. The index measures the investment return of small capitalization growth stocks.

Our Take

To understand the Vanguard Small Cap Growth Index ETF, it probably makes sense to start with its close cousin, the Vanguard Small Cap Index, symbol VB and another *100 Best ETF*. That index simply takes the bottom 1,720 of the top 2,500 U.S. stocks, the so-called "small-cap" stocks determined by the MSCI index people. That fund has 1,720 stocks; this "growth" fund selection has 953 of those 1,720 stocks, still a broad selection.

MSCI segments these growth stocks on the following factors:

- Long-term forward earnings per share (EPS) growth rate
- Short-term forward EPS growth rate
- Current internal growth rate
- Long-term historical EPS growth trend
- Long-term historical sales per share (SPS) growth trend

What you end up with is a broad-based small-cap fund with a little more zip and higher return (46 percent versus 39 percent) than its Vanguard VB cousin. Many of the top twenty companies are the same, but many others, such as Deckers, Waste Connections, and Level 3 Communications, have a decidedly more growth-oriented profile.

Why Should I Care?

For those looking to play the more aggressive, growth-oriented side of the small-cap segment, with some pizzazz but still a high degree of diversification and a low-cost profile, this fund makes sense. It could work in a foundation and some rotational portfolios.

Upside

- Captures broad section of fast-growing market segment
- Very low expenses for this segment
- Safety in numbers—diversification counteracts individual company risk

Downside

- Too diversified and diluted for some growth investors
- Small weightings of winners hurts performance (top holding only 0.64 percent)
- Growth criteria based on EPS, not cash flow

Just the Facts

INCEPTION DATE: **January 26, 2004**

TOTAL ASSETS: **$2.2 billion**

AVERAGE DAILY VOLUME: **249,200**

TOTAL HOLDINGS: **953**

PERCENT NORTH AMERICA HOLDINGS: **97.8%**

TOP 10 HOLDINGS PERCENTAGE (CONCENTRATION): **5.12%**

PORTFOLIO TURNOVER: **34.0%**   BENCHMARK: **20.0%**

BETA COEFFICIENT: **1.24**

R-SQUARED (1 YEAR): **86.9%**

1-YEAR RETURN: **46.62%**   BENCHMARK: **30.69%**

3-YEAR RETURN: **7.42%**   BENCHMARK: **3.34%**

TRACKING ERROR (PRICE VS. NAV)   1 YEAR: **7.49%**   ASSET CLASS MEDIAN: **10.41%**

$10,000 Invested at inception	2006	2007	2008	2009	2010	2011
	$13,449	$14,758	$8,862	$12,587	$16,473	$18,149

What's Under the Hood

Symbol	Name	Percentage of fund
TPX	Tempur-Pedic International Inc.	0.61%
PLCM	Polycom Inc.	0.58%
VSEA	Varian Semiconductor Equipment Assoc.	0.56%
GDI	Gardner Denver Inc.	0.54%
TDG	TransDigm Group Inc.	0.52%
GNTX	Gentex Corp.	0.49%
ROC	Rockwood Holdings Inc.	0.48%
SLH	Solera Holdings Inc.	0.48%
MCRS	Micros Systems Inc.	0.48%
PII	Polaris Industries Inc	0.47%
DECK	Deckers Outdoor Corp.	0.47%
LVLT	Level 3 Communications Inc.	0.45%
GRA	W R Grace and Co.	0.45%
SIG	Signet Jewelers Ltd.	0.45%
BEXP	Brigham Exploration Co.	0.45%
ITC	ITC Holdings Corp.	0.44%
WCN	Waste Connections Inc.	0.43%
PNRA	Panera Bread Co.	0.42%
BMRN	BioMarin Pharmaceutical Inc.	0.42%
IEX	Idex Corp.	0.42%

Vanguard
P.O. Box 1110
Valley Forge, PA 19482–1110
(877) 241-1395
Website: *www.vanguard.com*

100 BEST STRATEGY: **FOUNDATION/ROTATIONAL**

100 BEST CATEGORY: **GENERAL EQUITY/INDEX**

iShares S&P Small Cap 600 Index Fund

Ticker Symbol: IJR ❑ Issuer: BlackRock/iShares ❑ Description: U.S. Small-Cap Blend ❑ Geography: U.S. ❑ Morningstar Rating: 3 stars ❑ Marco Polo XTF Rating: 8.8 ❑ Yield: 1.02% ❑ Expense Ratio: 0.20% (Benchmark: 0.60%)

Stated Purpose

The investment seeks to replicate, net of expenses, the S&P Small Cap 600 Index. The fund generally invests at least 90 percent of its assets in securities and in depositary receipts representing securities of the index. The index measures the performance of the small-capitalization sector of the U.S. equity market. The stocks in the index have a market capitalization between $300 million and $1 billion.

Our Take

We at *100 Best* like to have choices, and we like to offer choices to our readers and investors when it makes sense, too. We decided that the small-cap segment was important enough to individual stock investors, who are trying to beat typical market returns, to warrant two broad small-cap ETFs which take in the small-cap universe.

The two we selected do it quite differently. The Vanguard Small Cap Index Fund, ticker symbol VB, is the other. How do they differ? The Vanguard fund casts a wider net.

Employing the MSCI U.S. Small Cap 1750 index, VB has 1,720 stocks in its small-cap universe, meaning that essentially you're buying the whole segment.

This iShares entry into the small-cap fray employs the S&P Small Cap 600 Index, which as the number in the name implies, is more selective. Companies in the $300 million to $1 billion range qualify, so a lot of the smaller stuff in the other index is left out. What's left in is a relatively attractive and diverse set of names; 594 of them to be exact, which are big enough to have already enjoyed some success.

Yet, things aren't always what they seem—the much more diverse VB actually enjoyed slightly better returns. It may be that some of the larger small caps had been mid caps previously (like Crocs for instance), and their size and decline negatively influenced the index (although Crocs has done better of late). Still, we like this fund for its relative focus while still bringing a smorgasbord of smaller companies from across the business landscape.

Why Should I Care?

The iShares S&P Small Cap 600 Index Fund is a good way to deploy foundation or some rotational cash into a high-energy sector, with a bit more concentration than some comparable funds.

Upside

- More focused, doesn't buy the universe
- Moderately low expenses, decent yield
- Large, liquid, and lots of history

Downside

- Not as good a performer as some
- More expensive than some, notably Vanguard
- Still pretty diversified, won't get rich quick

Just the Facts

INCEPTION DATE: **May 22, 2000**

TOTAL ASSETS: **$7.5 billion**

AVERAGE DAILY VOLUME: **1.6 million**

TOTAL HOLDINGS: **594**

PERCENT NORTH AMERICA HOLDINGS: **99.8%**

TOP 10 HOLDINGS PERCENTAGE (CONCENTRATION): **5.62%**

PORTFOLIO TURNOVER: **21.0%**　　BENCHMARK: **20.0%**

BETA COEFFICIENT: **1.14**

R-SQUARED (1 YEAR): **85.4%**

1-YEAR RETURN: **36.81%**　　BENCHMARK: **30.69%**

3-YEAR RETURN: **4.5%**　　BENCHMARK: **3.34%**

TRACKING ERROR (PRICE VS. NAV)　　1 YEAR: **6.86%**　　ASSET CLASS MEDIAN: **10.41%**

$10,000 Invested at inception	2006	2007	2008	2009	2010	2011
	$19,013	$18,928	$13,043	$16,366	$20,646	$22,189

What's Under the Hood

Symbol	Name	Percentage of fund
REGN	Regeneron Pharmaceuticals Inc.	0.82%
CASH	Cash	0.67%
HS	Healthspring Inc.	0.57%
CROX	Crocs Inc.	0.57%
SBNY	Signature Bank	0.55%
INT	World Fuel Services Corp.	0.55%
BMR	Biomed Realty Trust Inc.	0.53%
HME	Home Properties Inc.	0.53%
MAA	Mid-America Apartment Communities Inc.	0.53%
LUFK	Lufkin Industries Inc.	0.51%
SKT	Tanger Factory Outlet Centers Inc.	0.49%
SLXP	Salix Pharmaceuticals Ltd.	0.47%
CLC	CLARCOR Inc.	0.46%
KRC	Kilroy Realty Corp.	0.46%
CKH	SEACOR Holdings Inc.	0.45%
EPR	Entertainment Properties Trust	0.45%
RBN	Robbins & Myers Inc.	0.45%
HMSY	HMS Holdings Corp	0.44%
PPS	Post Properties Inc.	0.44%
PRA	ProAssurance Corp.	0.44%

BlackRock iShares
525 Washington Boulevard, Suite 1405
Jersey City, NJ 07310
(800) 474-2737
Website: *www.ishares.com*

International Equity/Index

Looking to round out your portfolio with some international exposure? The seven funds in this group are designed to give you a broad exposure to overseas companies. They are highly diversified, so they will move with the markets in these regions. The S&P Global 100 Index fund has the top 100 companies worldwide, so is blended with a number of larger U.S. companies. The others mainly cover Asia or the so-called "EAFE" (Europe-Australasia-Far East) region. More targeted ETFs targeting specific countries like Japan or smaller regions like Latin America can be found in the Strategy/Sector group. Expense ratios are a bit higher than the General Equities group, ranging from 0.12 to 0.40 percent.

100 BEST STRATEGY: **FOUNDATION**

100 BEST CATEGORY: **INTERNATIONAL EQUITY/INDEX**

iShares S&P Global 100 Index Fund

Ticker Symbol: 100 ◻ Issuer: BlackRock/iShares ◻ Description: International Equity Blend ◻ Geography: Global ◻ Morningstar Rating: 3 stars ◻ Marco Polo XTF Rating: 7.8 ◻ Yield: 2.56% ◻ Expense Ratio: 0.40% (Benchmark: 0.60%)

Stated Purpose

The investment seeks results that correspond generally to the price and yield performance, before fees and expenses, of the S&P Global 100 Index (the "underlying index"). The fund generally invests at least 90 percent of assets in securities of the underlying index and in depositary receipts representing securities of the underlying index. It may invest the remainder of its assets in securities not included in the underlying index. The underlying index is designed to measure the performance of 100 large-capitalization global companies.

Our Take

Suppose you wish to invest in the broader market and have already considered investing in the S&P 500 through the SPDR S&P 500 Trust ETF (SPY). But you have this nagging feeling, this notion, that the U.S. economy isn't so much "where it's at" anymore, and you'd like to have a few more international stocks in this portfolio. You want the breadth and mainstreamed-ness of the SPY portfolio, but the SPY portfolio is 99.5 percent U.S. companies. What do you do?

The iShares S&P Global 100 Index Fund is a pretty good product to fill that need. As you can see below, the familiar Exxon Mobils, the Microsofts, the GEs, the IBMs, and Johnson & Johnsons of the world are right there, front and center at the top of the list. But so also do you have Nestlé, Novartis, and HSBC. So you've achieved a bit of international diversification while still maintaining the comfort of a "best of the best" type of portfolio. Unlike the SPY fund, this fund is more concentrated in large-cap holdings with 107 total issues in the portfolio. Finally, with 47.9 percent of the holdings in North America, you've gotten a good portion of international exposure without having it become the entire meal.

We should also note that the larger U.S. companies do much if not most of their business overseas, so the international exposure is actually larger than this figure indicates.

Why Should I Care?

This portfolio would work well for an investor looking for large-cap safety and growth with a dose, but not a dominance, of international stocks.

Upside

- Attractive blend of United States and international
- Relatively focused
- Attractive yield

Downside

- Lackluster returns
- Still too much U.S. large cap?
- "International" is mostly Europe (Europe 44 percent, Asia 8 percent)

Just the Facts

INCEPTION DATE: **December 5, 2000**

TOTAL ASSETS: **$1 billion**

AVERAGE DAILY VOLUME: **118,500**

TOTAL HOLDINGS: **107**

PERCENT NORTH AMERICA HOLDINGS: **47.9%**

TOP 10 HOLDINGS PERCENTAGE (CONCENTRATION): **28.14%**

PORTFOLIO TURNOVER: **6.0%**   BENCHMARK: **21.0%**

BETA COEFFICIENT: **0.92**

R-SQUARED (1 YEAR): **98.2%**

1-YEAR RETURN: **30.23%**   BENCHMARK: **30.38%**

3-YEAR RETURN: **0.85%**   BENCHMARK: **-1.77%**

TRACKING ERROR (PRICE VS. NAV)   1 YEAR: **3.27%**   ASSET CLASS MEDIAN: **10.41%**

$10,000 Invested at inception	2006	2007	2008	2009	2010	2011
	$11,599	$12,586	$8,107	$10,257	$10,803	$11,493

What's Under the Hood

Symbol	Name	Percentage of fund
XOM	Exxon Mobil Corp.	5.17%
NESN:CH	Nestle SA	2.91%
IBM	International Business Machines Corp.	2.90%
CVX	Chevron Corp.	2.75%
MSFT	Microsoft Corp.	2.68%
GE	General Electric Co.	2.50%
JNJ	Johnson & Johnson	2.34%
NOVN:CH	Novartis AG	2.30%
HSBA:GB	HSBC Holdings PLC	2.28%
PG	Procter & Gamble Co.	2.26%
JPM	JPMorgan Chase and Co.	2.12%
KO	Coca Cola Co.	2.05%
PFE	Pfizer Inc.	2.00%
BHP:AU	BHP Billiton Ltd.	1.93%
VOD:GB	Vodafone Group PLC	1.90%
BP_:GB	BP PLC	1.88%
RDSA:GB	Royal Dutch Shell Plc	1.73%
FP:FR	Total SA	1.68%
PM	Philip Morris International Inc.	1.66%
INTC	Intel Corp.	1.56%

BlackRock/iShares
525 Washington Boulevard, Suite 1405
Jersey City, NJ 07310
(800) 474-2737
Website: *www.ishares.com*

iShares MSCI ACWI Ex-U.S. Index Fund

Ticker Symbol: ACWX ◻ Issuer: BlackRock/iShares ◻ Description: International Equity Blend ◻ Geography: Global ◻ Morningstar Rating: 3 stars ◻ Marco Polo XTF Rating: 6.5 ◻ Yield: 2.58% ◻ Expense Ratio: 0.35% (Benchmark: 0.60%)

Stated Purpose

The investment seeks to replicate, net of expenses, the MSCI All Country World Index Ex-U.S. The fund generally invests at least 90 percent of its assets in securities of the index and in depositary receipts representing securities of the index. The index is a free float-adjusted market capitalization index that measures the combined equity market performance of developed and emerging markets countries, excluding the United States.

Our Take

At first glance, this fund and the index it's based on probably resemble the alphabet soup of acronyms you might encounter working in a computer networking or software firm. Maybe so, but there is a real meaning behind the abbreviations.

First, MSCI is the name of the company (actually MSCI Barra) in business to design, maintain, and sell the index and its brethren as a "decision support tool" (a DST, we would suppose) to the institutional investment community. The second acronym, ACWI, is the real key.

ACWI stands for "All Country World Index," and it is defined by MSCI as a "free float-adjusted market capitalization weighted index that is designed to measure the equity market performance of developed and emerging markets. The MSCI ACWI consists of 45 country indices comprising 24 developed and 21 emerging market country indices. The developed market country indices included are: Australia, Austria, Belgium, Canada, Denmark, Finland, France, Germany, Greece, Hong Kong, Ireland, Israel, Italy, Japan, Netherlands, New Zealand, Norway, Portugal, Singapore, Spain, Sweden, Switzerland, and the United Kingdom. The emerging market country indices included are: Brazil, Chile, China, Colombia, Czech Republic, Egypt, Hungary, India, Indonesia, Korea, Malaysia, Mexico, Morocco, Peru, Philippines, Poland, Russia, South Africa, Taiwan, Thailand, and Turkey."

Okay, that's a lot of countries, and notable is the "Ex-U.S." part— the United States is excluded from the index. You'll also note that 9.9

percent of the holdings are North America–based, mostly Canada.

Enough about the index—we like the resulting fund for its broad international exposure and decent yield at a decent level of expenses. Large-cap names dominate the list, but there are smaller companies too. Japan, Canada, and Australia are among the top five countries.

Why Should I Care?

This fund is good for a broad international exposure covering the range of company sizes and investing styles.

Upside

• Broadest international exposure
• Attractive yield
• Reasonable cost

Downside

• Recent performance so-so
• Hit hard during 2008 downturn
• Very correlated to market—U.S. investments safer vis-à-vis returns?

Just the Facts

INCEPTION DATE: **March 26, 2008**

TOTAL ASSETS: **$983.2 million**

AVERAGE DAILY VOLUME: **145,100**

TOTAL HOLDINGS: **894**

PERCENT NORTH AMERICA HOLDINGS: **9.9%**

TOP 10 HOLDINGS PERCENTAGE (CONCENTRATION): **9.1%**

PORTFOLIO TURNOVER: **10.0%**   BENCHMARK: **21.0%**

BETA COEFFICIENT: **0.92**

R-SQUARED (1 YEAR): **97.4%**

1-YEAR RETURN: **28.82%**   BENCHMARK: **30.38%**

3-YEAR RETURN: **-1.80%**   BENCHMARK: **-1.77%**

TRACKING ERROR (PRICE VS. NAV)   1 YEAR: **3.61%**   ASSET CLASS MEDIAN: **10.41%**

$10,000 Invested at inception	2006	2007	2008	2009	2010	2011
	$—	$—	$5,963	$8,392	$9,207	$9,521

What's Under the Hood

Symbol	Name	Percentage of fund
NESN:CH	Nestle SA	1.37%
HSBA:GB	HSBC Holdings PLC	1.05%
BHP:AU	BHP Billiton Ltd.	1.00%
VOD:GB	Vodafone Group PLC	0.88%
NOVN:CH	Novartis AG	0.86%
BP_:GB	BP PLC	0.84%
ROG:CH	Roche Holding AG	0.79%
7203:JP	Toyota Motor Corp.	0.75%
GSK:GB	GlaxoSmithKline PLC	0.73%
SMSN	Samsung Electronics Co Ltd.	0.67%
RDSA:GB	Royal Dutch Shell Plc	0.67%
CASH	Cash	0.66%
CHT	Chunghwa Telecom Co Ltd.	0.66%
SIE:DE	Siemens AG	0.65%
RIO:GB	Rio Tinto PLC	0.64%
FP:FR	Total SA	0.62%
BAS:DE	BASF SE	0.60%
TSM	Taiwan Semiconductor Manufacturing Co. Ltd.	0.58%
CBA:AU	Commonwealth Bank of Australia	0.58%
BATS:GB	British American Tobacco PLC	0.56%

BlackRock/iShares
525 Washington Boulevard, Suite 1405
Jersey City, NJ 07310
(800) 474-2737
Website: *www.ishares.com*

iShares MSCI EAFE Small Cap Index Fund

Ticker Symbol: SCZ ❑ Issuer: BlackRock/iShares ❑ Description: International Equity Small Cap Blend ❑ Geography: Global ❑ Morningstar Rating: 2 stars ❑ Marco Polo XTF Rating: 6.8 ❑ Yield: 3.47% ❑ Expense Ratio: 0.40% (Benchmark: 0.60%)

Stated Purpose

The investment seeks results that correspond generally to the price and yield performance, before fees and expenses, of the MSCI EAFE Small Cap Index. The fund invests at least 90 percent of its assets in the securities of its underlying index or in ADRs, GDRs, or EDRs representing securities in the underlying index. The underlying index targets 40 percent of the eligible small-cap universe in each industry group of each country represented by the MSCI EAFE Index.

Our Take

One of the best reasons to use ETFs, or any kind of fund for that matter, as an investment vehicle is that it gives you exposure to parts of the economy and parts of the business landscape that you would otherwise never be able to research or comprehend on your own. The iShares MSCI EAFE Small Cap Index Fund is just that sort of fund.

As in most cases, understanding the underlying index goes a long way toward understanding the fund. First, MCSI stands for MCSI Barra, a New York–headquartered company in business to provide "decision support tools for institutional investors"—that is, to provide investment analytics and indices such as this one.

Second, EAFE (which is pronounced "EEF-ah" in the jungles of Wall Street) stands for "Europe, Australasia, and the Far East." The index is comprised of stocks in the markets of twenty-one developed countries in these regions, specifically excluding the United States and Canada. The "small-cap" part is determined by a percentile ranking; specifically, the index contains companies between the eighty-fifth and ninety-ninth percentile in these countries by total market capitalization. Interestingly, the EAFE indexes are the oldest truly international stock indexes, having been in existence since December 31, 1969.

What attracted us to this fund is the international exposure, recent performance, yield, and relatively low cost compared to many other international funds. In addition, there is a relatively large exposure to Japan (24.8 percent) and Australia (8.5 percent), while many other funds in this space tend to be more weighted toward Europe. We also note the small exposure to China— 0.30 percent—which takes some of the risk out of the equation.

Why Should I Care?
This fund will work well for a broad-based and moderately aggressive international exposure.

Upside
- Favorable country mix
- Attractive yield
- Strong recovery

Downside
- Vulnerable in downturns, like 2008
- Too many stocks?
- Weak dollar won't help

Just the Facts

INCEPTION DATE: **December 10, 2007**

TOTAL ASSETS: **$1.6 billion**

AVERAGE DAILY VOLUME: **153,800**

TOTAL HOLDINGS: **1255**

PERCENT NORTH AMERICA HOLDINGS: **4.0%**

TOP 10 HOLDINGS PERCENTAGE (CONCENTRATION): **6.81%**

PORTFOLIO TURNOVER: **15.0%**   BENCHMARK: **20.0%**

BETA COEFFICIENT: **1.00**

R-SQUARED (1 YEAR): **92.7%**

1-YEAR RETURN: **36.15%**   BENCHMARK: **30.38%**

3-YEAR RETURN: **2.65%**   BENCHMARK: **-1.77%**

TRACKING ERROR (PRICE VS. NAV)   1 YEAR: **5.20%**   ASSET CLASS MEDIAN: **10.41%**

$10,000 Invested at inception	2006	2007	2008	2009	2010	2011
	$—	$10,000	$5,213	$7,626	$9,329	$9,696

What's Under the Hood

Symbol	Name	Percentage of fund
CASH	Cash	2.87%
PSPN:CH	PSP Swiss Property AG	0.36%
GBF:DE	Bilfinger Berger Se	0.36%
CPR:IT	Davide Campari Milano SpA	0.34%
NWG:GB	Northumbrian Water Group PLC	0.33%
GKN:GB	Gkn PLC	0.33%
TATE:GB	Tate and Lyle PLC	0.33%
IMI:GB	IMI PLC	0.33%
T82U:SG	Suntec Real Estate Investment Trust	0.33%
HLMA:GB	Halma PLC	0.32%
PNN:GB	Pennon Group PLC	0.32%
GALN:CH	Galenica AG	0.32%
APA:AU	Apa Group	0.31%
INF:GB	Informa Plc	0.31%
EKTA_B:SE	Elekta AB (Publ)	0.31%
S08:SG	Singapore Post Ltd.	0.31%
SXS:GB	Spectris PLC	0.30%
MTX:DE	MTU Aero Engines Holding AG	0.30%
REC:IT	Recordati Industria Chimica e Farmaceutica	0.30%
GTO:FR	Gemalto NV	0.30%

BlackRock iShares
525 Washington Boulevard, Suite 1405
Jersey City, NJ 07310
(800) 474-2737
Website: *www.ishares.com*

iShares MSCI EAFE Value Index Fund

Ticker Symbol: EFV ❑ Issuer: BlackRock/iShares ❑ Description: International Equity Value Selection ❑ Geography: Global ❑ Morningstar Rating: 2 stars ❑ Marco Polo XTF Rating: 6.6 ❑ Yield: 3.9% ❑ Expense Ratio: 0.40% (Benchmark: 0.60%)

Stated Purpose

The investment seeks to replicate, net of expenses, the MSCI EAFE Value Index. The fund invests at least 90 percent of its assets in the securities of the index or in depositary receipts representing securities in the index. The index is a subset of the MSCI EAFE Index and consists of securities classified by MSCI as most representing the value style.

Our Take

If you've already looked at some of our other international *100 Best ETF* picks, you've picked up that MSCI is the name of the company that develops indexing tools (decision support tools) and EAFE is "Europe, Australasia, and the Far East." (For a more in-depth treatment of these acronyms, see our write-up for the iShares MSCI EAFE Small Cap Index Fund.)

Now, in the iShares MSCI EAFE Value Index Fund, "value" is added as a selection criterion to the mix. The folks at MSCI employ a formula that includes book value to price ratio, twelve-month forward earnings to price ratio, and dividend

yield. Based on this formula, they select about 496 stocks from a much larger twenty-one-country universe. The resulting company list is heavily weighted toward large-cap dividend-paying heavyweights like Royal Dutch Shell and Total SA, giving a fund with an attractive balance of growth and current yield.

Why Should I Care?

This portfolio is good as a way to get relatively less risky international exposure with a high current yield and decent long-term growth prospects.

Upside

- Dividends *and* some growth potential
- Relatively stable large names
- Japan tops country list

Downside

- A bit more vulnerable to bad markets than one would expect
- Big oil and big pharma dominate the list (that may not be bad)
- Next three countries, after Japan, are Germany, France, United Kingdom

Just the Facts

INCEPTION DATE: **August 1, 2003**

TOTAL ASSETS: **$1.4 billion**

AVERAGE DAILY VOLUME: **101,300**

TOTAL HOLDINGS: **496**

PERCENT NORTH AMERICA HOLDINGS: **0.9%**

TOP 10 HOLDINGS PERCENTAGE (CONCENTRATION): **20.36%**

PORTFOLIO TURNOVER: **30.0%**   BENCHMARK: **21.0%**

BETA COEFFICIENT: **1.08**

R-SQUARED (1 YEAR): **97.4%**

1-YEAR RETURN: **29.11%**   BENCHMARK: **30.38%**

3-YEAR RETURN: **-1.80%**   BENCHMARK: **-1.47%**

TRACKING ERROR (PRICE VS. NAV)   1 YEAR: **4.69%**   ASSET CLASS MEDIAN: **10.41%**

$10,000 Invested at inception	2006	2007	2008	2009	2010	2011
	$14,099	$14,904	$8,362	$11,180	$11,599	$12,190

What's Under the Hood

Symbol	Name	Percentage of fund
VOD:GB	Vodafone Group PLC	2.60%
NOVN:CH	Novartis AG	2.56%
BP_:GB	BP PLC	2.53%
RDSA:GB	Royal Dutch Shell Plc	2.34%
GSK:GB	GlaxoSmithKline PLC	2.06%
FP:FR	Total SA	2.04%
RDSB:GB	Royal Dutch Shell Plc	1.75%
TEF:ES	Telefonica SA	1.63%
SAN:ES	Banco Santander SA	1.59%
SAN:FR	Sanofi SA	1.55%
CBA:AU	Commonwealth Bank of Australia	1.49%
BAS:DE	BASF SE	1.49%
NESN:CH	Nestle SA	1.37%
7203:JP	Toyota Motor Corp.	1.31%
WBC:AU	Westpac Banking Corp.	1.20%
AZN:GB	AstraZeneca PLC	1.20%

Symbol	Name	Percentage of fund
8306:JP	Mitsubishi UFJ Financial Group Inc.	1.16%
BNP:FR	BNP Paribas SA	1.12%
ALV:DE	Allianz Se	1.06%
ANZ:AU	Australia and New Zealand Banking Group	1.06%

BlackRock iShares
525 Washington Boulevard, Suite 1405
Jersey City, NJ 07310
(800) 474-2737
Website: *www.ishares.com*

100 BEST STRATEGY: **FOUNDATION/ROTATIONAL**

100 BEST CATEGORY: **INTERNATIONAL EQUITY/INDEX**

Vanguard Pacific Stock Index Fund

Ticker Symbol: VPL ❑ Issuer: Vanguard ❑ Description: Regional Equity Blend ❑ Geography: Global ❑ Morningstar Rating: 2 stars ❑ Marco Polo XTF Rating: 6.4 ❑ Yield: 4.0% ❑ Expense Ratio: 0.14% (Benchmark: 0.60%)

Stated Purpose

The investment seeks to track the performance of a benchmark index that measures the investment return of stocks issued by companies located in the major markets of the Pacific region. The fund employs a "passive management"—or indexing—investment approach by investing all, or substantially all, of its assets in the common stocks included in the MSCI Pacific Index. The MSCI Pacific Index consists of approximately 494 common stocks of companies located in Japan, Australia, Hong Kong, Singapore, and New Zealand.

Our Take

In this instance, the fund issuer's "stated purpose" pretty much covers it. This fund is focused on the core companies in the core countries in the Asia-Pacific region and is concentrated most heavily in the countries where we currently think the best opportunities are: Japan is 61.4 percent of the portfolio while Australia is 23.7 percent. The resulting portfolio is dominated by resources giant BHP, Toyota, Canon, and a few financial institutions.

The result is a decent play in Japan, which we think will

eventually see a fairly strong recovery, and the currently booming Australia. This fund largely eschews China (0.36 percent) which we think is a good thing; China is a far riskier play that should be dealt with more directly and strategically (see our Country/Region picks, CHIM and CHIQ). So, bottom line, this fund touches all the right bases and has an attractive yield and very low costs (typical Vanguard) to boot.

Why Should I Care?

This fund provides relatively less risky international exposure with good current yield, low expenses, and decent long-term growth potential.

Upside

- Attractive and focused country mix
- Very low expenses
- Stable, attractive yield and decent long-term growth potential

Downside

- If you don't believe in Japan, stay away
- Weak dollar will hurt businesses but may help investment values
- Recent returns not stellar

Just the Facts

INCEPTION DATE: March 4, 2005

TOTAL ASSETS: $1.6 billion

AVERAGE DAILY VOLUME: 7,900

TOTAL HOLDINGS: 391

PERCENT NORTH AMERICA HOLDINGS: nil

TOP 10 HOLDINGS PERCENTAGE (CONCENTRATION): 19.2%

PORTFOLIO TURNOVER: 3.0%   BENCHMARK: 21.0%

BETA COEFFICIENT: 0.73

R-SQUARED (1 YEAR): 77.8%

1-YEAR RETURN: 22.90%   BENCHMARK: 30.38%

3-YEAR RETURN: -0.74%   BENCHMARK: -1.77%

TRACKING ERROR (PRICE VS. NAV) 1 YEAR: 8.7%   ASSET CLASS MEDIAN: 10.41%

$10,000 Invested at inception	2006	2007	2008	2009	2010	2011
	$13,995	$14,671	$9,636	$11,683	$13,533	$13,372

What's Under the Hood

Symbol	Name	Percentage of fund
BHP:AU	BHP Billiton Ltd.	3.75%
7203:JP	Toyota Motor Corp.	2.79%
CBA:AU	Commonwealth Bank of Australia	2.17%
WBC:AU	Westpac Banking Corp.	1.70%
8306:JP	Mitsubishi UFJ Financial Group Inc.	1.61%
7267:JP	Honda Motor Co. Ltd.	1.61%
ANZ:AU	Australia and New Zealand Banking Group	1.51%
NAB:AU	National Australia Bank Ltd.	1.46%
7751:JP	Canon Inc.	1.36%
8316:JP	Sumitomo Mitsui Financial Group Inc.	1.05%
6954:JP	Fanuc Corp.	1.00%
RIO:AU	Rio Tinto Ltd.	0.98%
4502:JP	Takeda Pharmaceutical Co Ltd.	0.92%
WOW:AU	Woolworths Ltd.	0.90%
8058:JP	Mitsubishi Corp.	0.89%
NCM:AU	Newcrest Mining Ltd.	0.84%
8411:JP	Mizuho Financial Group Inc.	0.82%
9984:JP	Softbank Corp.	0.82%
WES:AU	Wesfarmers Ltd.	0.82%
8031:JP	Mitsui & Co Ltd.	0.79%

Vanguard
P.O. Box 1110
Valley Forge, PA 19482–1110
(877) 241-1395
Website: *www.vanguard.com*

Vanguard Emerging Markets Index Fund

Ticker Symbol: VWO ❑ Issuer: Vanguard ❑ Description: International Equity Blend ❑ Geography: Global ❑ Morningstar Rating: 4 stars ❑ Marco Polo XTF Rating: 8.1 ❑ Yield: 1.73% ❑ Expense Ratio: 0.22% (Benchmark: 0.60%)

Stated Purpose

The investment seeks to track the performance of a benchmark index that measures the investment return of stocks issued by companies located in emerging market countries. The fund employs a "passive management"— or indexing—investment approach by investing substantially all (normally about 95 percent) of its assets in the common stocks included in the MSCI Emerging Markets Index, while employing a form of sampling to reduce risk. The index includes approximately 748 common stocks of companies located in emerging markets around the world.

Our Take

Besides looking at history and a fund's portfolio, one of the best ways to understand an ETF is to get a clear view of the index on which the fund is based. The Vanguard Emerging Markets Fund is based on the MSCI Emerging Markets Index. Here's how index provider MSCI defines its Emerging Markets Index:

"The MSCI Emerging Markets Index is a free float-adjusted market capitalization index that is designed to measure equity market performance of emerging markets. The MSCI Emerging Markets Index consists of the following 21 emerging market country indices: Brazil, Chile, China, Colombia, Czech Republic, Egypt, Hungary, India, Indonesia, Korea, Malaysia, Mexico, Morocco, Peru, Philippines, Poland, Russia, South Africa, Taiwan, Thailand, and Turkey."

The resulting portfolio has an attractive country balance:

- China: 15.7 percent
- Brazil: 13.5 percent
- Taiwan: 11.1 percent
- Russia: 7.1 percent
- India: 6.8 percent

This mix really makes the fund sort of a "BRICs plus" (Brazil, Russia, India, China), a nice place to be if you want an international exposure that's heavy in growth-oriented economies and light in the traditional favorites such as Europe and Japan. In fact, Europe is only 6.4 percent of this portfolio.

Why Should I Care?

This fund gives solid and diverse international exposure in the up-and-coming segments of the international economy.

Upside

- Attractive country blend
- Low expense ratio

- Diversified, but not too diversified

Downside

- Weak dollar won't help
- Recent performance not stellar
- Smaller, may not be liquid in some situations

Just the Facts

INCEPTION DATE: **March 4, 2005**

TOTAL ASSETS: **$49.3 million**

AVERAGE DAILY VOLUME: **1.85 million**

TOTAL HOLDINGS: **543**

PERCENT NORTH AMERICA HOLDINGS: **nil**

TOP 10 HOLDINGS PERCENTAGE (CONCENTRATION): **18.2%**

PORTFOLIO TURNOVER: **12.0%**   BENCHMARK: **21.0%**

BETA COEFFICIENT: **0.78**

R-SQUARED (1 YEAR): **63.5%**

1-YEAR RETURN: **23.79%**   BENCHMARK: **30.38%**

3-YEAR RETURN: **4.77%**   BENCHMARK: **-1.77%**

TRACKING ERROR (PRICE VS. NAV)   1 YEAR: **11.44%**   ASSET CLASS MEDIAN: **10.41%**

$10,000 Invested at inception	2006	2007	2008	2009	2010	2011
	$16,848	$23,432	$11,849	$19,474	$23,164	$23,366

What's Under the Hood

Symbol	Name	Percentage of fund
SMSN	Samsung Electronics Co Ltd	2.21%
PBR/A	Petroleo Brasileiro SA Petrobras	2.17%
VALE/P	Vale SA	2.10%
OGZD:GB	Gazprom OAO	2.04%

Symbol	Name	Percentage of fund
PBR	Petroleo Brasileiro SA Petrobras	1.86%
VALE	Vale SA	1.71%
ITUB	Itau Unibanco Holding SA	1.64%
941:HK	China Mobile Ltd.	1.55%
TSM	Taiwan Semiconductor Manufacturing Co Ltd.	1.55%
BBD	Banco Bradesco SA	1.36%
AMX_L:MX	America Movil SAB de CV	1.24%
1398:HK	Industrial and Commercial Bank of China	1.16%
LKOD:GB	NEFTYANAYA KOMPANIYA LUKOIL OAO	1.09%
883:HK	CNOOC Ltd.	1.04%
939:HK	China Construction Bank Corp.	0.97%
MTN:SA	MTN Group Limited	0.92%
CIB	Bancolombia SA	0.92%
ABV	Companhia De Bebidas Das Americas	0.85%
A005380:KR	Hyundai Motor Co	0.85%
857:HK	PetroChina Co Ltd.	0.80%

Vanguard
P.O. Box 1110
Valley Forge, PA 19482–1110
(877) 241-1395
Website: *www.vanguard.com*

100 BEST STRATEGY: **FOUNDATION/ROTATIONAL**

100 BEST CATEGORY: **INTERNATIONAL EQUITY/INDEX**

Vanguard Europe Pacific ETF

Ticker Symbol: VEA ❑ Issuer: Vanguard ❑ Description: International Equity Blend ❑ Geography: Global ❑ Morningstar Rating: 3 stars ❑ Marco Polo XTF Rating: 8.7 ❑ Yield: 2.46% ❑ Expense Ratio: 0.12% (Benchmark: 0.60%)

Stated Purpose

The investment seeks to provide a tax-efficient investment return consisting of long-term capital appreciation. The fund invests in stocks included in the MSCI EAFE Index, which is made up of approximately 970 common stocks of companies located in twenty-two countries in Europe, Australia, Asia, and the Far East. The fund advisor uses statistical methods to "sample" the index, aiming to closely track its investment performance while limiting investments in index securities that have undesirable tax characteristics in an attempt to minimize taxable income distributions.

Our Take

The Vanguard Europe Pacific ETF is pretty much what the name describes—a broad selection of mostly large-cap names in some of the more developed international regions of the world. What the title doesn't say is that about two-thirds of the holdings are in Europe, while about one-third are in the Asia-Pacific region, with only tiny amounts in Latin America (no surprise) and the Middle East.

So if you like a "world" fund dominated by Europe, this one may be calling your name. Ordinarily, we'd prefer a more even balance with Asia, but we also like the European companies that float to the top of this list, like Nestlé, Vodaphone, Novartis, and Royal Dutch Shell.

These are truly worldwide firms, and not so dependent on the European economy. Essentially, this fund gives you exposure to the true blue chips of the world that happen not to be headquartered in the United States. And in typical Vanguard fashion, you get this exposure at a very low cost with a decent dividend yield.

Why Should I Care?

This portfolio would be appropriate as a safety-oriented international pick for a foundation portfolio or perhaps a longish rotational run, with a decent balance between current yield and longer-term growth prospects.

Upside
- Very low expenses
- Bluest international blue chips
- Large and liquid

Downside
- Too much Europe?
- Recent returns don't excite
- Too correlated to market?

Just the Facts

INCEPTION DATE: **July 20, 2007**
TOTAL ASSETS: **$7.1 billion**
AVERAGE DAILY VOLUME: **1.9 million**
TOTAL HOLDINGS: **661**
PERCENT NORTH AMERICA HOLDINGS: **nil**
TOP 10 HOLDINGS PERCENTAGE (CONCENTRATION): **12.8%**
PORTFOLIO TURNOVER: **6.0%**   BENCHMARK: **21.0%**

BETA COEFFICIENT: **1.07**

R-SQUARED (1 YEAR): **99.74%**

1-YEAR RETURN: **32.08%**   BENCHMARK: **30.38%**

3-YEAR RETURN: **-1.34%**   BENCHMARK: **-1.77%**

TRACKING ERROR (PRICE VS. NAV)   1 YEAR: **2.36%**   ASSET CLASS MEDIAN: **10.41%**

$10,000 Invested at inception	2006	2007	2008	2009	2010	2011
	$—	$10,241	$6,007	$7,709	$8,360	$8,795

What's Under the Hood

Symbol	Name	Percentage of fund
NESN:CH	Nestlé SA	1.97%
HSBA:GB	HSBC Holdings PLC	1.48%
BHP:AU	BHP Billiton Ltd.	1.32%
VOD:GB	Vodafone Group PLC	1.30%
NOVN:CH	Novartis AG	1.23%
RDSA:GB	Royal Dutch Shell PLC	1.22%
BP_:GB	BP PLC	1.18%
ROG:CH	Roche Holding AG	1.14%
GSK:GB	GlaxoSmithKline PLC	1.04%
7203:JP	Toyota Motor Corp.	1.01%
FP:FR	Total SA	0.98%
SIE:DE	Siemens AG	0.96%
RIO:GB	Rio Tinto PLC	0.94%
RDSB:GB	Royal Dutch Shell PLC	0.87%
BATS:GB	British American Tobacco PLC	0.83%
TEF:ES	Telefonica SA	0.83%
SAN:ES	Banco Santander SA	0.78%
BAS:DE	BASF SE	0.76%
CBA:AU	Commonwealth Bank of Australia	0.75%
BG_:GB	BG Group PLC	0.74%

Vanguard
P.O. Box 1110
Valley Forge, PA 19482–1110
(877) 241-1395
Website: *www.vanguard.com*

Dividend

We believe it's good to earn some current income from your investments as part of your overall return on investment and as a sign that management has your best interests in mind. We particularly like a scenario where the dividends increase, as often as yearly, effectively giving you a "raise" to keep up with inflation and increase the reward for tying up your capital for longer periods. There are several individual stocks you can buy paying 3, 4, even 5 percent; a healthy return as 2012 unfolds. But there are risks in buying individual dividend-paying stocks—what if something happens and the dividend is cut? In that spirit, we offer seven high-dividend general equity ETFs that pay 3 to 4 percent while offering safety through diversification. We added diverse international utility and telecom funds for those wanting to take a little more risk for returns in the 5 to 7 percent range. Expense ratios for these funds range from 0.35 to 0.50 percent.

100 BEST STRATEGY: FOUNDATION

100 BEST CATEGORY: DIVIDEND

SPDR S&P Dividend ETF

Ticker Symbol: SDY ◻ **Issuer: State Street Global Advisors** ◻ **Description: U.S. Large Cap Dividend-Oriented Fund** ◻ **Geography: U.S.** ◻ **Morningstar Rating: 4 stars** ◻ **Marco Polo XTF Rating: 9.7** ◻ **Yield: 3.3%** ◻ **Expense Ratio: 0.35% (Benchmark: 0.60%)**

Stated Purpose

The SPDR S&P Dividend ETF seeks to match the return of the S&P High Yield Dividend Aristocrats Index. The fund issuer, State Street Global Advisors, intends to provide low portfolio turnover, accurate tracking, and relatively low costs.

Our Take

The current yield of 3.3 percent is not bad, especially for a portfolio as diversified as this one. Even if one or two companies ran into tough times and suspended their dividends, it wouldn't affect overall yield performance very much. The top holdings come from an assortment of sectors—health care, household goods, real estate investment trusts—and have for the most part steered clear of the financial services industry. In fact, the only financial in its Top 20 holdings is Cincinnati Financial, a solid individual stock play found on our *100 Best Stocks 2012* list.

We like the fact that many of these stocks are not just pure dividend plays like utilities—they have reasonably good growth prospects as well—Johnson & Johnson, Procter & Gamble, McDonald's, Clorox, and Abbott Labs in particular. The fund is up more than 20 percent since its 2005 inception, not a bad record for a dividend-oriented fund. Most of these companies have been raising dividends as well, which contributes to the growth prospects. Of the top 20 holdings, eleven can be found on our *100 Best Stocks 2012 List*.

Why Should I Care?

This portfolio would be appropriate for a foundation portfolio, with a decent balance between current yield and longer-term growth prospects.

Upside
- Dividends *and* growth
- Low expense ratio
- Safety: right amount of diversification

Downside
- Vulnerable to interest rate hikes
- Relatively high portfolio turnover
- Trading near all-time high

Just the Facts

INCEPTION DATE: **November 8, 2005**

TOTAL ASSETS: **$5.9 billion**

AVERAGE DAILY VOLUME: **651,500**

TOTAL HOLDINGS: **61**

PERCENT NORTH AMERICA HOLDINGS: **100%**

TOP 10 HOLDINGS PERCENTAGE (CONCENTRATION): **29.2%**

PORTFOLIO TURNOVER: **44.0%**   BENCHMARK: **21.0%**

BETA COEFFICIENT: **0.99**

R-SQUARED (1 YEAR): **88.5%**

1-YEAR RETURN: **22.2%**   BENCHMARK: **30.69%**

3-YEAR RETURN: **5.3%**   BENCHMARK: **3.34%**

TRACKING ERROR (PRICE VS. NAV)   1 YEAR: **5.3%**   ASSET CLASS MEDIAN: **10.41%**

$10,000 Invested at inception	2006	2007	2008	2009	2010	2011
	$11,767	$11,002	$9,482	$10,100	$11,750	$12,623

What's Under the Hood

Symbol	Name	Percentage of fund
PBI	Pitney Bowes Inc.	3.79%
CTL	CenturyLink Inc.	3.63%
HCP	HCP Inc.	3.32%
ED	Consolidated Edison Inc.	3.04%
CINF	Cincinnati Financial Corp.	3.01%
KMB	Kimberly Clark Corp.	2.66%
STR	Questar Corp.	2.54%
ABT	Abbott Laboratories	2.44%
LEG	Leggett and Platt Inc.	2.38%
CLX	Clorox Co.	2.34%
JNJ	Johnson & Johnson	2.21%
GPC	Genuine Parts Co.	2.16%
MCD	McDonald's Corp.	2.15%
VFC	VF Corp.	2.01%
CVX	Chevron Corp.	1.99%
PG	Procter & Gamble Co.	1.95%
KO	Coca Cola Co.	1.94%
BMS	Bemis Co Inc.	1.87%
NNN	National Retail Properties Inc.	1.82%
PEP	Pepsico Inc.	1.77%

State Street Global Advisors
State Street Financial Center
1 Lincoln Street
Boston, MA 02111-2900
Phone: (617) 786-3000
Website: *www.spdrs.com*

WisdomTree Equity Income Fund

Ticker Symbol: DHS ❑ Issuer: WisdomTree Investments ❑ Description: U.S. Equity Dividend-Oriented Fund ❑ Geography: U.S. ❑ Morningstar Rating: 2 stars ❑ Marco Polo XTF Rating: 5.2 ❑ Yield: 3.49% ❑ Expense Ratio: 0.38% (Benchmark: 0.60%)

Stated Purpose

The investment seeks to replicate, net of expenses, the WisdomTree Equity Income Index. The fund normally invests at least 95 percent of its total assets in the securities of the index. The index is a fundamentally weighted index that measures the performance of companies with high dividend yields selected from the WisdomTree Dividend index. The fund is nondiversified.

Our Take

Like most WisdomTree funds, the WisdomTree Equity Income Fund uses a creative approach to selecting and weighting stocks via its index. Unlike most indexes that are equal weighted or cap weighted, the WisdomTree Dividend Index makes annual adjustments of weightings based on the relative amount of dividends paid for each stock; that is, the stock with the highest proportion of total dividends paid out of a select group of companies will rise to the top weighting. The Equity Income Index is an extract of the Dividend index for companies with a market cap of at least $200 million and

trading volumes of at least $200,000 per day. So the resulting list emphasizes high-large and mid-cap dividend payers.

So much for the mechanics—the resulting stock list is a who's who of blue chip dividend payers—AT&T, Verizon, Johnson & Johnson, Altria, and so forth. In fact, twelve of the top twenty stocks are also found on our *100 Best Stocks* list. We're not sure why they need to have 332 issues in this fund; it seems like fifty or 100 of the top dividend players would do the trick. We'd like to see them cut the breadth and lower expenses. But in this figure, there's plenty of diversity, and if a single company hits the skids it won't hurt much. Also noteworthy is the fact that there are no financial stocks on the top twenty list; they've been adjusted out based on recent dividend cuts and are not part of the current risk equation.

Why Should I Care?

This portfolio makes a lot of sense for investors looking for a solid and steady dividend return with modest risk and some price growth and dividend growth potential.

Upside
- Steady dividend players
- Dividend growth potential
- Safety in numbers

Downside
- Too many stocks?
- Could yield be a little higher?
- Could costs be a little lower?

Just the Facts

INCEPTION DATE: June 15, 2006

TOTAL ASSETS: $200.4 million

AVERAGE DAILY VOLUME: 37,000

TOTAL HOLDINGS: 332

PERCENT NORTH AMERICA HOLDINGS: 100%

TOP 10 HOLDINGS PERCENTAGE (CONCENTRATION): 28.95%

PORTFOLIO TURNOVER: 8.0%   BENCHMARK: 21.0%

BETA COEFFICIENT: 0.61

R-SQUARED (1 YEAR): 72.4%

1-YEAR RETURN: 32.45%   BENCHMARK: 30.69%

3-YEAR RETURN: 0.61%   BENCHMARK: 3.34%

TRACKING ERROR (PRICE VS. NAV)   1 YEAR: 8.21%   ASSET CLASS MEDIAN: 10.41%

$10,000 Invested at inception	2006	2007	2008	2009	2010	2011
	$11,519	$6,993	$6,644	$7,855	$9,242	$10,202

What's Under the Hood

Symbol	Name	Percentage of fund
T	AT&T Inc.	7.56%
CVX	Chevron Corp.	5.19%
PFE	Pfizer Inc.	4.93%
JNJ	Johnson & Johnson	4.66%
VZ	Verizon Communications Inc.	4.26%
PM	Philip Morris International Inc.	4.21%
PG	Procter & Gamble Co.	3.95%
MRK	Merck & Co Inc.	3.30%
INTC	Intel Corp.	3.20%
COP	ConocoPhillips	2.71%

Symbol	Name	Percentage of fund
MO	Altria Group Inc.	2.56%
ABT	Abbott Laboratories	2.19%
LLY	Eli Lilly and Co.	1.87%
BMY	Bristol Myers Squibb Co.	1.78%
KFT	Kraft Foods Inc.	1.67%
SO	Southern Co.	1.21%
DD	E I Du Pont De Nemours And Co.	1.18%
EXC	Exelon Corp.	1.14%
DUK	Duke Energy Corp.	1.04%
RAI	Reynolds American Inc.	0.94%

WisdomTree Investments
380 Madison Avenue, 21st Floor
New York, NY 10017
(866) 909-9473
Website: *www.wisdomtree.com*

100 BEST STRATEGY: **FOUNDATION**

100 BEST CATEGORY: **DIVIDEND**

First Trust Morningstar Dividend Leaders Index Fund

Ticker Symbol: FDL ▫ Issuer: First Trust ▫ Description: U.S. Large Cap Dividend-Oriented Fund ▫ Geography: U.S. ▫ Morningstar Rating: 3 stars ▫ Marco Polo XTF Rating: 9.5 ▫ Yield: 3.59% ▫ Expense Ratio: 0.45% (Benchmark: 0.60%)

Stated Purpose

The investment seeks results that correspond generally to the price and yield (before the fund's fees and expenses) of an equity index called the Morningstar Dividend Leaders Index. The fund normally invests at least 90 percent of total assets in common stocks that comprise the index. The objective of the index is to offer investors a benchmark for dividend portfolios as well as a means to invest in a portfolio of stocks that have a consistent record of growing dividends as well as the ability to sustain them.

Our Take

The Morningstar Dividend Leaders Index is one of the standard dividend-weighted indexes. What is a dividend-weighted index? In this case, in Morningstar's words, it "captures the performance of the 100 highest-yielding stocks that have a consistent record of dividend payment and have the ability to sustain their dividend payments. Stocks in the index are weighted in proportion to the total pool of dividends available to investors."

What that means is companies that pay a healthy dividend and especially that raise their dividends over time will rise to the top weightings in the index. Not surprisingly, we find some of the "gold standard" dividend players at the top of the portfolio, including AT&T, Verizon, Johnson & Johnson, and Kimberly Clark. In fact, eleven of the Top 20 issues are also on our *100 Best Stocks* list, and many more are found further down the list.

Funds such as this will do well over time because the companies in them raise their dividends over time, and in fact, the three-year performance is attractive. Even though this is an income-oriented fund, it does fall when the markets fall, and finding a good entry point will not only reduce risk but also increase the effective yield. During the August 2011 market jitters, for example, the price was off about 12 percent, raising the effective yield from 3.6 percent to 3.9 percent. We should also note that this fund has only 101 issues, compared to the 332 issues in our comparable WisdomTree pick (DHS).

Why Should I Care?

This fund makes a lot of sense for investors looking for solid yield, long-term-yield growth and muted response to market swings (beta is 0.69). It's a good alternative to fixed income investments.

Upside
- Index rewards dividend growth
- Decent long-term performance
- More focused than DHS

Downside
- Could yield be higher?
- Could expenses be lower?
- Why is turnover so high?

Just the Facts

INCEPTION DATE: **March 9, 2006**

TOTAL ASSETS: **$171.7 million**

AVERAGE DAILY VOLUME: **83,400**

TOTAL HOLDINGS: **101**

PERCENT NORTH AMERICA HOLDINGS: **100%**

TOP 10 HOLDINGS PERCENTAGE (CONCENTRATION): **58.6%**

PORTFOLIO TURNOVER: **30.0%**   BENCHMARK: **21.0%**

BETA COEFFICIENT: **0.69**

R-SQUARED (1 YEAR): **69.70%**

1-YEAR RETURN: **31.06%**   BENCHMARK: **30.69%**

3-YEAR RETURN: **9.84%**   BENCHMARK: **3.34%**

TRACKING ERROR (PRICE VS. NAV)   1 YEAR: **7.46%**   ASSET CLASS MEDIAN: **10.41%**

$10,000 Invested at inception	2006	2007	2008	2009	2010	2011
	$11,946	$10,676	$7,241	$8,330	$9,667	$10,423

What's Under the Hood

Symbol	Name	Percentage of fund
T	AT&T Inc.	9.64%
VZ	Verizon Communications Inc.	9.03%
JNJ	Johnson & Johnson	8.94%
MRK	Merck & Co Inc.	7.39%
COP	ConocoPhillips	5.74%
ABT	Abbott Laboratories	4.88%
BMY	Bristol Myers Squibb Co.	3.88%
LLY	Eli Lilly and Co.	3.24%
KFT	Kraft Foods Inc.	3.11%
SO	Southern Co.	2.61%
EXC	Exelon Corp.	2.40%
D	Dominion Resources Inc.	1.92%
KMB	Kimberly Clark Corp.	1.81%
FE	Firstenergy Corp.	1.55%
NEE	NextEra Energy Inc.	1.51%
AEP	American Electric Power Co Inc.	1.43%
PPL	PPL Corp.	1.33%
LMT	Lockheed Martin Corp.	1.31%
PGN	Progress Energy Inc.	1.18%
PEG	Public Service Enterprise Group Inc.	1.18%

First Trust Portfolios LP
120 E. Liberty Drive, Suite 400
Wheaton, IL 60187
(800) 621-1675
Website: *www.ftportfolios.com*

iShares Dow Jones Select Dividend Index Fund

Ticker Symbol: DVY ◻ Issuer: BlackRock/iShares ◻ Description: U.S. Equity Enhanced Index Dividend Selection ◻ Geography: U.S. ◻ Morningstar Rating: 3 stars ◻ Marco Polo XTF Rating: 9.9 ◻ Yield: 3.6% ◻ Expense Ratio: 0.40% (Benchmark: 0.60%)

Stated Purpose

The investment seeks to replicate, net of expenses, the Dow Jones Select Dividend Index. The fund generally invests at least 90 percent of its assets in securities of the index and in depositary receipts representing in the index. The index is comprised of 100 of the highest dividend-yielding securities (excluding real estate investment trusts) in the Dow Jones U.S. Index.

Our Take

Those of you who have read our *100 Best Stocks You Can Buy* know that we like stocks that combine a healthy current yield with above-average growth prospects—in the stock price *and* in the dividend. It's a fairly simple and typically foolproof investing premise so long as the fund doesn't stretch too far to get those dividends—into shaky financial sector stocks, for instance.

The iShares Dow Jones Select Dividend Index Fund and its underlying index selects a group of high-yielding stocks and weights it according to the indicated annual dividend. Index components are screened by dividend growth rate (a plus), trading volume, and payout ratio (the ratio of dividends paid to earnings per share).

The result is an attractive yield with minimal risk due to diversification; there is above-average dividend growth potential in this group also. We like the fact that the fund avoids most financial and tobacco stocks, at least at the top of the list.

Why Should I Care?

This portfolio balances current yield, yield, and long-term share price growth potential into an attractive blend for a foundation portfolio.

Upside

• Dividends *and* growth
• Large, liquid, and experienced
• Safety: right amount of diversification

Downside

• Vulnerable to interest rate hikes
• Expenses could be lower for a relatively simple fund
• Long-term growth record okay but not stellar

Just the Facts

INCEPTION DATE: **November 3, 2003**

TOTAL ASSETS: **$6.4 billion**

AVERAGE DAILY VOLUME: **1.4 million**

TOTAL HOLDINGS: **98**

PERCENT NORTH AMERICA HOLDINGS: **98.55%**

TOP 10 HOLDINGS PERCENTAGE (CONCENTRATION): **23.55%**

PORTFOLIO TURNOVER: **5.06%**   BENCHMARK: **21.0%**

BETA COEFFICIENT: **0.76**

R-SQUARED (1 YEAR): **86.85%**

1-YEAR RETURN: **26.22%**   BENCHMARK: **30.69%**

3-YEAR RETURN: **4.78%**   BENCHMARK: **0.9%**

TRACKING ERROR (PRICE VS. NAV)   1 YEAR: **5.1%**   ASSET CLASS MEDIAN: **11.1%**

$10,000 Invested at inception	2006	2007	2008	2009	2010	2011
	$15,313	$14,489	$9,720	$10,788	$12,697	$13,309

What's Under the Hood

Symbol	Name	Percentage of fund
LO	Lorillard Inc.	4.27%
CASH	Cash	3.25%
VFC	VF Corp.	2.30%
CVX	Chevron Corp.	2.23%
ETR	Entergy Corp.	2.09%
KMB	Kimberly Clark Corp.	1.99%
MCD	McDonald's Corp.	1.95%
TEG	Integrys Energy Group Inc.	1.93%
FE	Firstenergy Corp.	1.85%
DTE	DTE Energy Co.	1.69%
OKE	Oneok Inc.	1.67%
CLX	Clorox Co.	1.61%
CTL	CenturyLink Inc.	1.58%
EXC	Exelon Corp.	1.57%
PNW	Pinnacle West Capital Corp.	1.55%
NEE	NextEra Energy Inc.	1.51%

Symbol	Name	Percentage of fund
D	Dominion Resources Inc.	1.50%
MCY	Mercury General Corp.	1.43%
LLY	Eli Lilly and Co.	1.42%
AEP	American Electric Power Co. Inc.	1.38%

BlackRock iShares
525 Washington Boulevard, Suite 1405
Jersey City, NJ 07310
(800) 474-2737
Website: *www.ishares.com*

100 BEST STRATEGY: **FOUNDATION/ROTATIONAL**

100 BEST CATEGORY: **DIVIDEND/INTERNATIONAL SECTOR**

iShares MSCI ACWI Ex-U.S. Health Care Sector Index Fund

Ticker Symbol: AXHE ▫ Issuer: iShares ▫ Description: Ex-U.S. Sector Specific Dividend-Oriented Equity Fund ▫ Geography: Global ▫ Morningstar Rating: NR ▫ Marco Polo XTF Rating: 2.2 ▫ Yield: 3.94% ▫ Expense Ratio: 0.48% (Benchmark: 0.60%)

Stated Purpose

The investment seeks to replicate, net of expenses, the MSCI All Country World Ex-U.S. Health Care Index. The fund generally invests at least 80 percent of its assets in securities of the index and in depositary receipts representing securities of the index. The index is a free float-adjusted market capitalization index, which measures the performance of the health care sector of developed and emerging markets countries, excluding the United States.

Our Take

If you're looking for a solid current return and believe that health care has a bright or at least a safe future and believe further that international plays make sense and that a weak dollar will bring favorable currency conversions, this fund's for you. Now that's a lot of stuff to believe in—it might seem like having to call the first four horses in a race in order. But if you think all of the above have a much better than average chance of coming true, then you might as well be in this market sweet spot. The portfolio, not too surprisingly, contains a lot of overseas "big pharma" companies. Such picks, like Bayer and Novartis and GlaxoSmithKline and AstraZeneca, are hardly risky. With a fund of only fifty-six holdings and two-thirds of the holdings in the top ten issues, this fund is oriented toward these pharma stalwarts; there are likely to be few surprises down this list.

The nature of the holdings adds a measure of safety; in fact, the August 2011 jitters brought only a 10 percent correction, compared to about 16 percent for the broader market. That correction raised the effective yield to 4.22 percent. Buyers should look for entry points like this to buy in.

Why Should I Care?

This fund is a good way to boost dividends beyond what can be earned in comparable U.S.-only funds. It provides international exposure and targets a "healthy" sector.

Upside

- Solid returns
- Focused, few surprises
- Safe picks

Downside

- Small, untested, may be illiquid
- Relatively high expenses
- Expenses in foreign currencies could hurt some of these companies

Just the Facts

INCEPTION DATE: July 13, 2010

TOTAL ASSETS: $3.0 million

AVERAGE DAILY VOLUME: 2,500

TOTAL HOLDINGS: 56

PERCENT NORTH AMERICA HOLDINGS: 0%

TOP 10 HOLDINGS PERCENTAGE (CONCENTRATION): 67.6%

PORTFOLIO TURNOVER: 1.0%   BENCHMARK: 21.0%

BETA COEFFICIENT: NA

R-SQUARED (1 YEAR): NA

1-YEAR RETURN: 23.21%   BENCHMARK: 30.69%

3-YEAR RETURN: NA   BENCHMARK: 3.34%

TRACKING ERROR (PRICE VS. NAV)   1 YEAR: NA   ASSET CLASS MEDIAN: 10.41%

$10,000 Invested at inception	2006	2007	2008	2009	2010	2011
	$—	$—	$—	$—	$11,303	$12,393

What's Under the Hood

Symbol	Name	Percentage of fund
NOVN:CH	Novartis AG	12.37%
ROG:CH	Roche Holding AG	11.99%
GSK:GB	GlaxoSmithKline PLC	11.18%
SAN:FR	Sanofi SA	7.86%
BAYN:DE	Bayer AG	5.03%
NOVO_B:DK	Novo Nordisk A/S	4.86%
AZN:GB	AstraZeneca PLC	4.52%
4502:JP	Takeda Pharmaceutical Co Ltd.	3.76%
TEVA:IL	Teva Pharmaceutical Industries Ltd.	3.66%
SHP:GB	Shire PLC	2.50%
SHP:GB	Shire PLC	2.50%
CSL:AU	Csl Ltd.	1.98%
EI:FR	Essilor International	1.94%
4503:JP	Astellas Pharma Inc.	1.92%
FME:DE	Fresenius Medical Care AG & Co Kgaa	1.84%
VRX:CA	Valeant Pharmaceuticals International Inc.	1.64%
FRE:DE	Fresenius SE & Co KGaA	1.51%
SYST:CH	Synthes Inc.	1.50%
4568:JP	Daiichi Sankyo Co Ltd.	1.49%
4523:JP	Eisai Co Ltd.	1.20%

BlackRock iShares
525 Washington Boulevard, Suite 1405
Jersey City, NJ 07310
(800) 474-2737
Website: *www.ishares.com*

iShares MSCI ACWI Ex-U.S. Utilities Sector Index Fund

Ticker Symbol: AXUT ▫ Issuer: iShares ▫ Description: Ex-U.S. Sector Specific Dividend-Oriented Fund ▫ Geography: Global ▫ Morningstar Rating: NR ▫ Marco Polo XTF Rating: 2.7 ▫ Yield: 7.12% ▫ Expense Ratio: 0.48% (Benchmark: 0.60%)

Stated Purpose

The investment seeks to replicate, net of expenses, the MSCI All Country World Ex-U.S. Utilities Index. The fund generally invests at least 80 percent of its assets in securities of the index and in depositary receipts representing securities of the index. The index is a free float-adjusted market capitalization index, which measures the performance of the utilities sector of developed and emerging markets countries, excluding the United States.

Our Take

When you invest for a specific purpose, sometimes you want to go "all in" for that purpose, at least for that part of your portfolio. In that spirit, we bring you the iShares MSCI ACWI Ex-U.S. Utilities Sector Index Fund.

This fund invests in utilities, which we yield seekers were all taught to do. But here's the twist—all of the utilities are overseas, specifically in the ACWI group of twenty-one developed non-U.S. economies as defined

by index provider MSCI. Unless you own a home in France, Germany, Italy, or Japan, you probably won't have heard of most of these names. But if you did, they'd be familiar.

The result is a very attractive yield of 7.12 percent on a well-diversified portfolio of seventy-six companies. The regional split is about 59 percent Europe and 30 percent Asia. One caveat: The fund is very new (July 2010) and hasn't developed the size or the trading volume to ensure trading liquidity.

Why Should I Care?

This fund makes sense to boost overall yield for a yield-seeking portion of a foundation portfolio.

Upside

• Strong yield
• Strong country mix
• Will benefit from weak dollar

Downside

• Vulnerable to interest rate hikes
• New, small, and thinly traded
• Some nuclear exposure

Just the Facts

INCEPTION DATE: **July 13, 2010**

TOTAL ASSETS: **$2.6 million**

AVERAGE DAILY VOLUME: **2,700**

TOTAL HOLDINGS: **76**

PERCENT NORTH AMERICA HOLDINGS: **0%**

TOP 10 HOLDINGS PERCENTAGE (CONCENTRATION): **45.3%**

PORTFOLIO TURNOVER: **0%**   BENCHMARK: **21.0%**

BETA COEFFICIENT: **NA**

R-SQUARED (1 YEAR): **NA**

1-YEAR RETURN: **8.7%**   BENCHMARK: **30.39%**

3-YEAR RETURN: **NA**   BENCHMARK: **3.34%**

TRACKING ERROR (PRICE VS. NAV)   1 YEAR: **NA**   ASSET CLASS MEDIAN: **10.41%**

$10,000 Invested at inception	2006	2007	2008	2009	2010	2011
	$—	$—	$—	$—	$10,577	$10,639

What's Under the Hood

Symbol	Name	Percentage of fund
EOAN:DE	EON AG	7.07%
GSZ:FR	Gdf Suez SA	6.45%
ENEL:IT	Enel SpA	5.94%
IBE:ES	Iberdrola SA	5.34%
NG	National Grid PLC	5.14%
CNA:GB	Centrica PLC	3.93%
RWE:DE	Rwe AG	3.14%
SSE:GB	Scottish and Southern Energy PLC	3.12%
2:HK	CLP Holdings Ltd.	2.97%
CASH	Cash	2.61%
6:HK	Power Assets Holdings Ltd.	2.00%
3:HK	The Hong Kong and China Gas Co Ltd.	1.97%
9531:JP	Tokyo Gas Co Ltd.	1.92%
9503:JP	Kansai Electric Power Co Inc.	1.83%
FUM1V:FI	Fortum Oyj	1.78%
9502:JP	Chubu Electric Power Co Inc.	1.73%

Symbol	Name	Percentage of fund
GAID:GB	Gail India Ltd.	1.38%
VIE:FR	Veolia Environnement Ve SA	1.35%
CIG	Energy Co of Minas Gerais	1.34%
SRG:IT	Snam Rete Gas SpA	1.32%

BlackRock iShares
525 Washington Boulevard, Suite 1405
Jersey City, NJ 07310
(800) 474-2737
Website: *www.ishares.com*

100 BEST STRATEGY: **FOUNDATION**

100 BEST CATEGORY: **DIVIDEND**

SPDR S&P International Telecommunication Sector ETF

Ticker Symbol: IST □ Issuer: State Street Global Assets □ Description: □ Ex-U.S. Sector Specific Dividend-Oriented Fund □ Geography: Global □ Morningstar Rating: NR □ Marco Polo XTF Rating: 4.1 □ Yield: 5.3% □ Expense Ratio: 0.50% (Benchmark: 0.60%)

Stated Purpose

The investment seeks to replicate, net of expenses, the S&P Developed Ex-U.S. BMI Telecommunication Services Sector Index. The fund generally invests substantially all, but at least 80 percent, of its assets in the securities comprising the index. The index represents the non-U.S. telecommunications sub-industry of developed countries included in the BMI Global index.

Our Take

For most of the history of stock investing, if you wanted a steady dividend with modest growth and a bit of protection created by a monopolistic market position, you bought shares of AT&T, put the stock certificate in your safe-deposit box, cashed your healthy dividend checks four times a year, and forgot about it.

Times have changed a bit—AT&T still pays the nice dividend but gets most of its revenue and profit from the highly competitive and rapidly evolving (and capital-consuming) wireless business. The "monopoly" is more a matter of sheer size and competitive moat than of regulation and extreme first-mover advantage. Regardless, we still like "T," and recommend it in our *100 Best Stocks* portfolio.

But if you'd rather get your dividends from a diverse basket of stocks, get some international exposure, and play the growth of telecom in world markets at the same time, the SPDR S&P International Telecommunications Sector ETF just might be your next call. The fund pays 5.3 percent and carries an assortment of names from different nations, some in the wireless business (like Vodafone) and some in broad-traditional monopoly providers in their countries. Europe accounts for about 68 percent of this portfolio; Asia about 24 percent.

This fund does take dips in weak markets. It doesn't hurt to look for an inexpensive entry point—the fund shares dropped about 15 percent to produce a yield of 5.7 percent during the August 2011 market jitters.

Why Should I Care?

This portfolio would be appropriate to capture a bit higher yield for a foundation portfolio, with a longer-term growth prospect added in.

Upside
- Dividends *and* growth
- Safety in numbers: 47 companies
- Should do well if dollar weakens

Downside
- Telecom competition in some markets
- Expense ratio a bit high
- Too much Vodafone?

Just the Facts

INCEPTION DATE: **July 16, 2008**

TOTAL ASSETS: **$9 million**

AVERAGE DAILY VOLUME: **4,300**

TOTAL HOLDINGS: **47**

PERCENT NORTH AMERICA HOLDINGS: **0%**

TOP 10 HOLDINGS PERCENTAGE (CONCENTRATION): **66.4%**

PORTFOLIO TURNOVER: **6.0%**   BENCHMARK: **21.0%**

BETA COEFFICIENT: **0.89**

R-SQUARED (1 YEAR): **50.91%**

1-YEAR RETURN: **32.71%**   BENCHMARK: **30.69%**

3-YEAR RETURN: **NA**   BENCHMARK: **3.34%**

TRACKING ERROR (PRICE VS. NAV)   1 YEAR: **NA**   ASSET CLASS MEDIAN: **10.41%**

$10,000 Invested at inception	2006	2007	2008	2009	2010	2011
	$—	$—	$8,254	$9,568	$10,314	$11,277

What's Under the Hood

Symbol	Name	Percentage of fund
VOD:GB	Vodafone Group PLC	20.22%
TEF:ES	Telefonica SA	12.41%
DTE:DE	Deutsche Telekom AG	6.40%
9984:JP	Softbank Corp.	4.86%
FTE:FR	France Telecom SA	4.54%
BT_A:GB	BT Group PLC	3.91%
9432:JP	Nippon Telegraph And Telephone Corp.	3.83%
9437:JP	NTT Docomo Inc.	3.71%
9433:JP	Kddi Corp.	3.46%
KPN:NL	Koninklijke KPN NV	3.44%
Z74:SG	Singapore Telecommunications Ltd.	3.02%
RCI	Rogers Communications Inc.	2.70%
TLSN:SE	Teliasonera AB	2.41%
TIT:IT	Telecom Italia SpA	1.88%
TEL:NO	Telenor ASA	1.83%
SCMN:CH	Swisscom AG	1.61%
BCE	BCE Inc.	1.60%
TLS:AU	Telstra Corp Ltd.	1.34%
TU	Telus Corp.	1.31%
MIC_SDB:SE	Millicom International Cellular SA	1.30%

State Street Global Advisors
State Street Financial Center
1 Lincoln Street
Boston, MA 02111–2900
Phone: (617) 786-3000
Website: *www.spdrs.com*

Fixed Income

The dividend funds in the last section were chosen to provide a reasonably strong and growing yield as a solid base for a foundation portfolio. But some investors, for at least a portion of that portfolio, may want to eliminate two risks: first, the risk of stock market declines and second, the risk that dividends may be reduced or cut altogether. Bond issuers cannot cut yields outside of insolvency and bankruptcy, and many bonds are *inversely correlated* to the markets, meaning they may actually rise in a "flight to quality" movement if the markets falter. So bonds provide an additional measure of safety even if they fail to exceed the yields of dividend stocks. On the other hand, bonds and bond funds can suffer if inflation rises or if interest rates rise (reducing the relative worth of a bond portfolio). With that tradeoff in mind, we present seven fixed-income ETFs mainly operating in the intermediate and long-term bond spaces. As buying individual bonds is difficult and expensive, bond ETFs offer ordinary investors a way to participate in the relatively obscure and mysterious bond market.

We did not present any municipal tax-exempt bond ETFs as they are normally geography-specific; that is, a fund of New York municipal bonds would be advantageous only to New York residents. But investors should consider municipal and government alternatives. Expense ratios are modest, ranging from 0.15 percent to 0.45 percent for the actively managed PIMCO Build America Bond Strategy Portfolio.

> 100 BEST STRATEGY: **FOUNDATION**

> 100 BEST CATEGORY: **FIXED INCOME**

Vanguard Long Term Corporate Bond ETF

Ticker Symbol: VCLT ❑ Issuer: Vanguard ❑ Description: Long-Term Corporate Bond Fund ❑ Geography: U.S. ❑ Debt Type Objective: Corporate Debt ❑ Maturity Objective: Long Term ❑ Credit Grade Objective: Investment Grade ❑ Morningstar Rating: NR ❑ Marco Polo XTF Rating: 5.3 ❑ Distribution Yield: 5.49% ❑ Average Maturity: 24 years ❑ Expense Ratio: 0.15% (Benchmark: 0.30%)

Stated Purpose

The investment seeks to track the performance of a market-weighted corporate bond index with a long-term dollar-weighted average maturity. The fund tracks the performance of the Barclays Capital U.S. 10+ Year Corporate Bond Index. It invests at least 80 percent of the assets in the index.

Our Take

Bond funds are fairly simple, and this one is one of the simpler of the bunch. The portfolio is mostly a who's who of corporate America, and the bonds are long in maturation with a stated maturity goal of ten years and an actual average maturity of twenty-four years. So if you believe in bonds for the long term, this fund gives you the long term and a reasonable amount of diversity with fifty-five issues. The result is an attractive distribution yield of 5.49 percent.

That yield comes with a surprising safety buffer. During the August 2011 market turmoil, the "flight to quality" trend actually drove up the price of this portfolio about 5 percent —one of the few types of investments to benefit from this turbulent period. That said, more than most because of its long maturities, this fund will be vulnerable to signs of inflation and interest-rate hikes over the long term. Such a fund should always be evaluated against dividend-paying stocks, which have the added potential to benefit from corporate earnings and dividend growth.

Why Should I Care?

This fund makes sense as a way to gain long-term bond exposure in a foundation portfolio.

Upside

- Solid yield
- "Flight to quality" destination
- Right amount of diversification

Downside

- Vulnerable to interest rate hikes
- High portfolio turnover
- Some exposure to financial industry

Just the Facts

INCEPTION DATE: **November 10, 2009**

TOTAL ASSETS: **$164.1 million**

AVERAGE DAILY VOLUME: **26,100**

TOTAL HOLDINGS: **55**

PERCENT NORTH AMERICA HOLDINGS: **88.1%**

TOP 10 HOLDINGS PERCENTAGE (CONCENTRATION): **28.0%**

PORTFOLIO TURNOVER: **72.0%**   BENCHMARK: **27.0%**

BETA COEFFICIENT: **2.08**

R-SQUARED (1 YEAR): **59.99%**

1-YEAR RETURN: **5.66%**   BENCHMARK: **3.90%**

3-YEAR RETURN: **NA**   BENCHMARK: **6.46%**

TRACKING ERROR (PRICE VS. NAV)   1 YEAR: **5.77%**   ASSET CLASS MEDIAN: **3.62%**

$10,000 Invested at inception	2006	2007	2008	2009	2010	2011
	$—	$—	$—	$9,839	$10,939	$11,221

What's Under the Hood

Symbol	Name	Percentage of fund
T 4 5/8 07/31/12	U.S. Treasury Note	4.41%
C 8 1/8 07/15/39	Citigroup Inc.	3.28%
T 8 3/4 03/01/31	AT&T Wireless Svcs Inc.	3.16%
T 8 11/15/31	AT&T Inc.	2.98%
BBT 6.82 06/12/57	BB&T Capital Trust IV	2.87%
WMT 6 1/2 08/15/37	Wal-Mart Stores Inc.	2.70%
GE 6 3/4 03/15/32	General Elex Cap Corp.	2.51%
PRU 5 5/8 05/12/41	Prudential Financial Inc.	2.51%
EXC 6 1/4 10/01/39	Exelon Generation Co. LLC	2.40%
NXYCN 7 1/2 07/30/39	—	2.27%
HSBC 5 7/8 11/01/34	HSBC Bank USA	2.22%
SO 5.95 02/01/39	Georgia Power Company	2.11%
BRK 6 1/8 04/01/36	MidAmerican Energy Hldgs	2.11%
ED 5.7 06/15/40	CTS Crestview Bible Ch	2.09%
K 7.45 04/01/31	Kellogg Co.	2.07%
KPN 8 3/8 10/01/30	8.375 KPN 30 Nts	2.07%
TRICN 5.85 04/15/40	—	2.07%
TCKCN 6 08/15/40	—	1.94%
JNJ 5.95 08/15/37	Johnson & Johnson	1.88%
MMC 5 7/8 08/01/33	Marsh & McClennan Cos. Inc.	1.87%

Vanguard
P.O. Box 1110
Valley Forge, PA 19482–1110
(877) 241-1395
Website: *www.vanguard.com*

100 BEST STRATEGY: **FOUNDATION**

100 BEST CATEGORY: **FIXED INCOME**

SPDR Barclays Capital Long Term Corporate Bond ETF

Ticker Symbol: LWC ❑ Issuer: State Street Global Advisors (SSGA) ❑ Description: Long-Term Corporate Bond Fund ❑ Geography: U.S. ❑ Debt Type Objective: Corporate Debt ❑ Maturity Objective: Long Term ❑ Credit Grade Objective: Investment Grade ❑ Morningstar Rating: NR ❑ Marco Polo XTF Rating: 2.3 ❑ Distribution Yield: 7.83% ❑ Average Maturity: 24.5 years ❑ Expense Ratio: 0.15% (Benchmark: 0.30%)

Stated Purpose

The investment seeks to replicate, net of expenses, the Barclays Capital U.S. Long Corporate Index. The fund invests at least 80 percent of asset securities that comprise the index. The index measures the performance of the long-term sector of the U.S. investment bond market, which includes investment grade corporate debt and sovereign, supranational, local authority, and non-U.S. agency bonds that are dollar denominated and have a remaining maturity of greater than or equal to ten years. The fund is nondiversified.

Our Take

The SPDR Barclays Capital Long Term Corporate Bond ETF is similar in nature to our bellwether Vanguard Long Term Corporate Bond ETF (VCLT). However, it is smaller, newer, and has a somewhat higher yield—the distribution yield was 7.83 percent in the most recent period.

It offers most of the same advantages as the VCLT fund—steady returns, low cost, and a "flight to quality" destination in times of market turmoil. The portfolio is much more diverse, with 257 issues compared to VCLT's fifty-five, so if you like safety in numbers, you might find it here. Similarly, this fund is a bit less vested in the financial sector, although some exposure is still there. As you can see from the list below, the fund is invested in some of the bluest blue-chip names out there.

Some of the risks are the same—the average maturity is 24.5 years, which means you're exposed to inflation risk, interest rate risk, and even corporate survival (credit) risk, a bigger deal these days as fewer companies survive for the long term without big changes. That said, for long-term corporates, this fund should be about as steady as they get.

Why Should I Care?
This fund makes sense as a way to gain long-term bond exposure in a foundation portfolio.

Upside
• Blue chips
• "Flight to quality" beneficiary

• Safety in numbers—highly diversified

Downside
• Vulnerable to inflation, interest rate hikes
• Smaller, newer, and less liquid
• Average price premium to NAV 0.45 percent—pretty high

Just the Facts
INCEPTION DATE: **March 10, 2009**

TOTAL ASSETS: **$35.6 million**

AVERAGE DAILY VOLUME: **6,800**

TOTAL HOLDINGS: **257**

PERCENT NORTH AMERICA HOLDINGS: **86.9%**

TOP 10 HOLDINGS PERCENTAGE (CONCENTRATION): **14.24%**

PORTFOLIO TURNOVER: **42.0%**   BENCHMARK: **27.0%**

BETA COEFFICIENT: **2.04**

R-SQUARED (1 YEAR): **65.13%**

1-YEAR RETURN: **5.22%**   BENCHMARK: **3.90%**

3-YEAR RETURN: **NA**   BENCHMARK: **6.46%**

TRACKING ERROR (PRICE VS. NAV)   1 YEAR: **5.82%**   ASSET CLASS MEDIAN: **3.62%**

$10,000 Invested at inception	2006	2007	2008	2009	2010	2011
	$—	$—	$—	$12,285	$13,489	$13,821

What's Under the Hood

Symbol	Name	Percentage of fund
CASH	Cash	3.83%
HSBC 6 1/2 09/15/37	—	1.28%
PFE 7.2 03/15/39	Pfizer Inc.	1.26%
C 6 7/8 03/05/38	Citigroup Inc.	1.24%
T 5.35 09/01/40	AT&T Inc.	1.22%
TWC 7.3 07/01/38	Time Warner Cable Inc.	1.14%
GE 5 7/8 01/14/38	General Elec Cap Corp.	1.12%
WMT 5 7/8 04/05/27	Wal-Mart Stores Inc.	1.12%
GS 6 3/4 10/01/37	Goldman Sachs Group Inc.	1.10%
GE 6 3/4 03/15/32	General Elec Cap Corp.	1.08%
VZ 8.95 03/01/39	Verizon Communications	1.01%
WMT 5 1/4 09/01/35	Wal-Mart Stores	1.00%
IBM 5.6 11/30/39	IBM Corp.	0.91%
AIG 8.175 05/15/58	American Intl Group	0.89%
DUK 6.45 04/01/39	Duke Energy Indiana Inc.	0.84%
NWSA 6.4 12/15/35	News America Inc.	0.84%
CMCSA 6.95 08/15/37	Comcast Corp.	0.80%
VALEBZ 6 7/8 11/21/36	—	0.79%
T 6.55 02/15/39	AT&T Inc.	0.78%
UTX 6 1/8 07/15/38	United Technologies Corp.	0.78%

State Street Global Advisors
State Street Financial Center
1 Lincoln Street
Boston, MA 02111-2900
Phone: (617) 786-3000
Website: *www.spdrs.com*

100 BEST STRATEGY: **FOUNDATION**

100 BEST CATEGORY: **FIXED INCOME**

Guggenheim Enhanced Core Bond ETF

Ticker Symbol: GIY ❑ Issuer: Guggenheim ❑ Description: U.S. Higher Yielding Government, Agency, and Corporate Bonds ❑ Geography: U.S. ❑ Debt Type Objective: Blend ❑ Maturity Objective: Intermediate ❑ Credit Grade Objective: Investment Grade ❑ Morningstar Rating: 2 stars ❑ Marco Polo XTF Rating: NR ❑ Distribution Yield: 5.95% ❑ Average Maturity: 7 years ❑ Expense Ratio: 0.32% (Benchmark: 0.30%)

Stated Purpose

The investment seeks results that correspond to the performance, before fees and expenses, of the Capital Markets Bond Index. The fund normally invests at least 80 percent of total assets in fixed income securities that comprise the index. It also will normally invest at least 80 percent of net assets in U.S. fixed income securities.

Our Take

This fund, originally conceived as a fairly traditional intermediate-term fixed income fund, underwent a transition on June 1, 2011, to become fairly unique in the ETF and especially the fixed income space as an actively managed fund. As WisdomTree itself states, the idea is to "combin[e] the portfolio management expertise of an actively managed strategy with the transparency of the ETF structure."

In its actively managed approach, the fund, again in WisdomTree's own words, "utilizes quantitative security selection, fundamental credit analysis and the Investment Adviser's views of

particular sectors to construct a portfolio through a process that employs a rigorous risk management framework. The Investment Adviser utilizes a quantitative strategy which attempts to identify relative mispricing among the instruments of a given asset class and estimate future returns which may arise from the eventual correction of the relative mispricing."

It isn't clear how all of this active management will work out, but in the meantime, GIY has offered better than average returns in the intermediate term space, with a seven-year average maturity. As an actively managed fund, the expense ratio is a bit higher—0.32 percent versus 0.15 percent for most—time will tell if the extra fees are worthwhile.

Why Should I Care?

This fund is a good place to go for those of us who really don't understand or want to shop bonds, but want some bond market exposure managed by people who are experts in the field.

Upside

- Active management may boost yields and reduce risk
- Attractive yield already for mid-term portfolio
- "Flight to quality" appeal

Downside

- Don't know how active management will turn out
- A bit heavy on financial companies
- Not diverse enough?

Just the Facts

INCEPTION DATE: **February 12, 2008**

TOTAL ASSETS: **$5.3 million**

AVERAGE DAILY VOLUME: **1,000**

TOTAL HOLDINGS: **28**

PERCENT NORTH AMERICA HOLDINGS: **94.85%**

TOP 10 HOLDINGS PERCENTAGE (CONCENTRATION): **79.77%**

PORTFOLIO TURNOVER: **458%**   BENCHMARK: **27.0%**

BETA COEFFICIENT: **0.99**

R-SQUARED (1 YEAR): **98.14%**

1-YEAR RETURN: **2.89%**   BENCHMARK: **3.90%**

3-YEAR RETURN: **5.85%**   BENCHMARK: **6.46%**

TRACKING ERROR (PRICE VS. NAV)   1 YEAR: **NA**   ASSET CLASS MEDIAN: **3.62%**

$10,000 Invested at inception	2006	2007	2008	2009	2010	2011
	$—	$—	$10,293	$10,802	$11,457	$11,682

What's Under the Hood

Symbol	Name	Percentage of fund
FNCI 5.5 9/11	FNMA T05509GC05 50%	25.69%
CASH	Cash	18.59%
T 6 02/15/26	U.S. Treasury Bond	12.47%
FHLMC 5 1/4 04/18/16	Federal Home Ln Mtg Corp.	8.66%
T 4 3/8 05/15/40	U.S. Treasury Bond	5.06%
MS 7.3 05/13/19	Morgan Stanley	2.86%
C 8 1/8 07/15/39	Citigroup Inc.	1.65%
CB 5 3/4 05/15/18	Chubb Corp.	1.46%
BAC 7 5/8 06/01/19	Bank Of America Corp.	1.44%
PRE 6 7/8 06/01/18	Partnerre Finance	1.42%
OKE 5.2 06/15/15	ONEOK Inc.	1.38%
CEG 4.55 06/15/15	Constellation Energy Grp.	1.36%
CBS 8 7/8 05/15/19	CBS Corp.	1.32%
AFG 9 7/8 06/15/19	American Financial Group	1.30%
TWX 4 3/4 03/29/21	Time Warner Inc. New	1.29%
AXS 5 7/8 06/01/20	Axis Specialty Finance	1.29%
GS 5 3/8 03/15/20	Goldman Sachs Group Inc.	1.29%
CYN 5 1/4 09/15/20	CTS Centennial Cmmnty Ch	1.27%
ACE 2.6 11/23/15	Amphenol Corporation	1.26%
EQT 8 1/8 06/01/19	EQT Corp.	1.24%

Guggenheim Funds Distributors, Inc.
2455 Corporate West Drive
Lisle, IL 60532
(888) 949-3837
Website: *www.guggenheimfunds.com*

Vanguard Intermediate Term Corporate Bond ETF

Ticker Symbol: VCIT ❑ Issuer: Vanguard ❑ Description: Intermediate Term Corporate Bond Fund ❑ Geography: U.S. ❑ Debt Type Objective: Corporate Debt ❑ Maturity Objective: Intermediate Term—1 to 5 Years ❑ Credit Grade Objective: Investment Grade ❑ Morningstar Rating: NR ❑ Marco Polo XTF Rating: 7.4 ❑ Distribution Yield: 4.46% ❑ Average Maturity: 8 years ❑ Expense Ratio: 0.15% (Benchmark: 0.30%)

Stated Purpose

The investment seeks to replicate, net of expenses, the performance of Barclays Capital U.S. 5–10 Year Corporate Index. The fund employs a "passive management"—or indexing —investment approach designed to track the performance of the Barclays Capital U.S. 1–5 Year Corporate Index. This index includes U.S. dollar-denominated, investment-grade, fixed-rate, taxable securities issued by industrial, utility, and financial companies, with maturities between one and five years.

Our Take

One of our cornerstone "fixed income" recommendations is the Vanguard Long Term Corporate Bond ETF (VCLT), with a current distribution yield of 5.49 percent and a well-diversified longer maturity (average twenty-four years) corporate bond portfolio.

But in this day and age, you couldn't be blamed for being nervous about waiting an average of twenty-four years to get your money back, with so many companies born and dead within that time span. Who woulda thunk twenty-four years ago about the dire situation of Eastman Kodak, for instance? Most airlines? Fannie Mae and Freddie Mac?

It is in this vein that we bring you the "little brother" to the Vanguard long-term portfolio—the Vanguard Intermediate Term Corporate Bond ETF. Now, to bring the average maturity down to eight years, you give up about 1 percent in current distribution yield—to 4.46 percent. For many of us, that might not be such a bad tradeoff. In fact, many of the core holdings mature in the one- to five-year range.

And by the way, this fund really isn't the "little brother"—it has about three times the assets of its VCLT sibling.

Why Should I Care?
This fund makes sense as a way to gain corporate bond exposure in a foundation portfolio while avoiding the risks of longer maturity bonds.

Upside
- Solid yield for the maturity range
- A bit less interest rate risk

- Right amount of diversification

Downside
- Still vulnerable to interest rate hikes
- High portfolio turnover
- Some exposure to financial industry

Just the Facts

INCEPTION DATE: **November 19, 2009**

TOTAL ASSETS: **$561.8 million**

AVERAGE DAILY VOLUME: **76,800**

TOTAL HOLDINGS: **52**

PERCENT NORTH AMERICA HOLDINGS: **85.1%**

TOP 10 HOLDINGS PERCENTAGE (CONCENTRATION): **31.76%**

PORTFOLIO TURNOVER: **61.0%**   BENCHMARK: **27.0%**

BETA COEFFICIENT: **1.58**

R-SQUARED (1 YEAR): **89.76%**

1-YEAR RETURN: **7.41%**   BENCHMARK: **3.90%**

3-YEAR RETURN: **NA**   BENCHMARK: **6.46%**

TRACKING ERROR (PRICE VS. NAV)   1 YEAR: **2.38%**   ASSET CLASS MEDIAN: **3.62%**

$10,000 Invested at inception	2006	2007	2008	2009	2010	2011
	$—	$—	$—	$9,889	$10,940	$11,325

What's Under the Hood

Symbol	Name	Percentage of fund
KFT 6 1/2 08/11/17	Kraft Foods Inc.	4.47%
GS 5 3/4 10/01/16	Goldman Sachs Group Inc.	4.11%
JPM 6 01/15/18	JP Morgan Chase & Co.	3.85%
C 8 1/2 05/22/19	Citigroup Inc.	3.14%
AXP 6.15 08/28/17	American Express	2.86%
T 4 5/8 07/31/12	U.S. Treasury Note	2.65%
CVS 4 3/4 05/18/20	CVS Caremark Corp.	2.64%
PNC 4 3/8 08/11/20	Palo Alto Community Ch	2.57%
TCKCN 3.15 01/15/17	—	2.56%
DB 6 09/01/17	—	2.48%
GE 6 08/07/19	General Elec Cap Corp.	2.45%
EXC 4 10/01/20	Eastern Edison Co.	2.45%
BAC 6 1/2 08/01/16	Bank of America Corp.	2.42%
CP 7 1/4 05/15/19	—	2.29%
BMY 5.45 05/01/18	Bristol-Myers Squibb	2.16%
LLY 5.2 03/15/17	Eli Lilly & Co,	2.15%
NOVNVX 5 1/8 02/10/19	—	2.13%
ORCL 5 07/08/19	Oracle Corp.	2.11%
EMBRA 6 3/8 01/15/20	—	2.02%
AON 5 09/30/20	AAR Corporation	1.97%

Vanguard
P.O. Box 1110
Valley Forge, PA 19482–1110
(877) 241-1395
Website: *www.vanguard.com*

100 BEST STRATEGY: **FOUNDATION**

100 BEST CATEGORY: **FIXED INCOME**

PowerShares Build America Bond Portfolio

Ticker Symbol: BAB ❑ Issuer: Invesco ❑ Description: U.S. Build America Bond Fund ❑ Geography: U.S. ❑ Debt Type Objective: State/Municipal Bonds ❑ Maturity Objective: Various ❑ Credit Grade Objective: Investment Grade ❑ Morningstar Rating: NR ❑ Marco Polo XTF Rating: 4.5 ❑ Distribution Yield: 5.53% ❑ Average Maturity: NA ❑ Expense Ratio: 0.29% (Benchmark: 0.30%)

Stated Purpose

The investment seeks results that correspond to the price and yield of the Merrill Lynch Build America Bond Index. The fund normally invests at least 80 percent of the total assets in taxable municipal securities eligible to participate in the Build America Bonds program created under the American Recovery and Reinvestment Act of 2009 or other legislation providing for the issuance of taxable municipal securities on which the issuer receives federal support of the interest paid. It normally invests at least 80 percent of total assets in the securities that comprise the underlying index. The fund is nondiversified.

Our Take

You want to buy corporate bonds— or a corporate bond ETF—to enjoy interest rates north of 5 percent for a long-term portfolio. But you're just not so sure corporate bonds are safe or as "investment grade" as the ratings agency says they are. You've seen the business changes at GM, Eastman Kodak, and others wreak havoc on the safety, security, and ultimately, the price of corporate bonds. You seek the yield, but want the relatively safety of a government or government agency behind it.

For you and other such investors like you, the economic downturn gave us a new federal program in 2009 under that year's American Recovery and Reinvestment Act: the Build America Bond. Build America Bonds, or "BABs," are state or municipal securities where the interest is subsidized by the federal government, allowing them to pay rates approaching corporate rates within the safety framework of a state or local government or government agency. Unfortunately, however, the interest is taxable at all levels, so these are probably better suited for retirement accounts for most of us.

The PowerShares Build America Bond Portfolio is typical for such funds, with a decent yield and a diverse set of holdings. Among other reasons, we like it better than some because it is less exposed to California issues, although we think the threat of municipal defaults altogether is somewhat overblown.

Why Should I Care?

This BAB portfolio is probably best suited for the foundation portion of tax-deferred or tax-free retirement accounts.

Upside

• Yield and safety

• Geographic diversity
• Large and liquid

Downside

• Munis not quite as safe as they once were
• Interest rate and inflation risk
• Expenses a bit high

Just the Facts

INCEPTION DATE: **November 17, 2009**

TOTAL ASSETS: **$658.6 million**

AVERAGE DAILY VOLUME: **158,700**

TOTAL HOLDINGS: **315**

PERCENT NORTH AMERICA HOLDINGS: **100%**

TOP 10 HOLDINGS PERCENTAGE (CONCENTRATION): **13.52%**

PORTFOLIO TURNOVER: **5.0%**   BENCHMARK: **27.0%**

BETA COEFFICIENT: **2.21**

R-SQUARED (1 YEAR): **66.3%**

1-YEAR RETURN: **6.58%**   BENCHMARK: **3.90%**

3-YEAR RETURN: **NA**   BENCHMARK: **6.46%**

TRACKING ERROR (PRICE VS. NAV)   1 YEAR: **5.89%**   ASSET CLASS MEDIAN: **3.62%**

$10,000 Invested at inception	2006	2007	2008	2009	2010	2011
	$—	$—	$—	$9,681	$10,576	$11,399

What's Under the Hood

Symbol	Name	Percentage of fund
CASH	Cash	2.49%
167593AN2	Chicago Ill O'Hare Intl.	2.28%
13063A7D0	California St.	1.50%
64966HYM6	Oregon St. Alt Energy	1.47%
13063BFR8	Los Angeles CA Pens OBG	1.38%
650014TF0	Trenton, NJ RFDG	1.34%
59333NSD6	Miami-Dade Cnty FL SPL	1.18%
223777CN1	Cowlitz Co WA PUD NO 1	1.09%
66285WFS0	Michigan High Ed Stud Ln	1.00%
66285WFT8	American Museum DT MO RV	0.99%
646136XS5	New Jersey St Trans Tr	0.94%
139369AA0	Cape Coral FL Gas Tax	0.88%
452152FZ9	Illinois St Taxable	0.88%
072024NT5	Bay Area Toll Auth CA	0.88%
592125AM0	Metro Govt. Nashville	0.85%
18085PLL6	Clark Cnty Nev Arpt Rev	0.85%
838530NL3	South Jersey Port Corp.	0.85%
887440BG9	Timpanogos SPL SVC DT UT	0.85%
59259YDF3	Metropolitan Transn Auth	0.84%
59067ACT8	Mesa CLG COLO ENTR RV	0.84%

Invesco PowerShares Capital Management LLC
301 West Roosevelt Road
Wheaton, IL 60187
(800) 803-0903
Website: *www.invescopowershares.com*

PIMCO Build America Bond Strategy Fund

Ticker Symbol: BABZ ▫ Issuer: PIMCO ▫ Description: U.S. Higher Yielding Build America Bond Fund ▫ Geography: U.S. ▫ Debt Type Objective: State/Municipal Bonds ▫ Maturity Objective: Various ▫ Credit Grade Objective: Investment Grade ▫ Morningstar Rating: NR ▫ Marco Polo XTF Rating: NA ▫ Distribution Yield: 5.90% ▫ Average Maturity: NA ▫ Expense Ratio: 0.45% (Benchmark: 0.30%)

Stated Purpose

The investment seeks maximum income, consistent with preservation of capital. The fund invests at least 80 percent of assets in taxable municipal debt securities publicly issued under the Build America Bond program. The Build America Bond program was created as part of the American Recovery and Reinvestment Act of 2009 and is expected to continue through extensions of the Act or through other legislation providing for the issuance of taxable municipal securities on which the issuer receives U.S. government support for the interest paid.

Our Take

Build America Bonds are designed to help state and local governments and agencies finance projects to boost employment and improve infrastructure. They make this possible by subsidizing the interest rate up to levels typically paid by corporate bond issuers, making them attractive to investors while still holding costs

down for the issuing public entity. Unlike conventional municipal bonds, however, interest is not tax free to investors, so they make the most sense for nontaxable accounts.

The PIMCO Build America Bond Strategy Fund takes the standard "BAB" fund concept, exemplified by our *100 Best ETF* pick PowerShares Build America Bond Portfolio (symbol BAB), a step further by adding a level of active management. In this fund, the fund manager is allowed to take a closer look to avoid issuers with deteriorating credit quality (a popular theme in today's municipal market) and to eke out higher returns where opportunities exist.

The result (at least so far) has been a fund with a somewhat higher-distribution yield, but with a bit more risk especially in California securities—which the fund manager has apparently determined is a good risk/reward tradeoff. We do not necessarily disagree—investors just need to know what they're getting into.

Why Should I Care?

This fund makes sense as a slightly more aggressive bond play for foundation portfolios especially in a tax-free or tax-deferred account.

Upside

- Strong yield vis-à-vis risk
- Active management

- Constituent issuers are mostly larger public entities

Downside

- Relatively high expenses
- Not very diverse, too much California?
- Active management could backfire

Just the Facts

INCEPTION DATE: **April 20, 2010**

TOTAL ASSETS: **$37.5 million**

AVERAGE DAILY VOLUME: **9,600**

TOTAL HOLDINGS: **32**

PERCENT NORTH AMERICA HOLDINGS: **100%**

TOP 10 HOLDINGS PERCENTAGE (CONCENTRATION): **52.13%**

PORTFOLIO TURNOVER: **23.0%**   BENCHMARK: **27.0%**

BETA COEFFICIENT: **NA**

R-SQUARED (1 YEAR): **NA**

1-YEAR RETURN: **NA**   BENCHMARK: **3.90%**

3-YEAR RETURN: **NA**   BENCHMARK: **6.46%**

TRACKING ERROR (PRICE VS. NAV)   1 YEAR: **NA**   ASSET CLASS MEDIAN: **3.62%**

$10,000 Invested at inception	2006	2007	2008	2009	2010	2011
	$—	$—	$—	$—	$9,398	$10,179

What's Under the Hood

Symbol	Name	Percentage of fund
13063BJB9	California St. Taxable	9.66%
CASH	Cash	6.46%
59259YGG8	Metropolitan Transn Auth	5.43%
02765UEK6	American Mun Pwr Ohio	5.38%
66285WFS0	Michigan High Ed Stud Ln	4.76%
54438CPA4	Los Angeles Calif Cmnty	4.32%
13063BFV9	Ill HSG Dev Auth Rev	4.24%
54473ENS9	Los Angeles Co CA Pub	4.10%
68428TAD9	Orange Cnty Calif Santn	3.90%
072024NV0	Bay Area Toll Auth CA	3.78%
626207YM0	Municipal Elec Auth GA	3.68%
79739GBD7	San Diego Co CA RGL Arpt	3.64%
66285WFB7	North Tex Twy Auth Rev	3.63%
167593AN2	Chicago IL O'Hare Intl.	3.48%
64972FY26	New York NYC Mun WFA	2.84%
544435C32	Los Angeles CA Dept	2.82%
592643AA8	Metropolitan Wash DC AR AR	2.68%
167593AM4	Chicago IL O'Hare Intl	2.52%
452252FH7	Illinois St Toll Hwy AT	2.48%
59266TEC1	Metro WTR DT SO CA WWKS	2.01%

Pacific Investment Management Company LLC
840 Newport Center Drive, Suite 100
Newport Beach, CA 92660
(800) 400-4383
Website: *www.pimcoetfs.com*

Commodity—General

In a world with a growing population making use of a relatively fixed base of materials, that is, commodities, it makes sense to have at least some exposure to this important sector. You can do that through individual companies or funds that specialize in commodity producers. Or you may choose to eliminate the management layers, competitive threats, capital equipment costs, and so forth by instead owning commodities directly or through funds investing in futures contracts. The following five funds are designed to give you exposure to large groups of commodities, giving some diversification in case you don't know when the next big hailstorm is going to flatten Iowa corn or Ohio soybeans.

Note that all but one of these funds are Exchange Traded Notes—ETNs—designed to minimize the negative effects of trading and "rolling over" futures contracts into a new month, but incurring the general credit risk of the issuer. They aren't necessarily bad; you just need to know what you own.

100 BEST STRATEGY: **FOUNDATION/ROTATIONAL**

100 BEST CATEGORY: **COMMODITY—GENERAL**

iPATH S&P GSCI Total Return Index ETN

Ticker Symbol: GSP ❑ Issuer: Barclays ❑ Description: General Commodity Blend ❑ Geography: Global ❑ Morningstar Rating: NR ❑ Marco Polo XTF Rating: NR ❑ Yield: NM ❑ Expense Ratio: 0.75% (Benchmark: 0.75%)

Stated Purpose

The investment is linked to the GSCI Total Return index and provides investors with exposure to the returns potentially available through an unleveraged investment in the contracts comprising the GSCI plus the Treasury bill rate of interest that could be earned on funds committed to the trading of the underlying contracts. The commodities represented in the GSCI Total Return Index are production-weighted to reflect their relative significance to the world economy. Crude oil is currently the dominant commodity in this index. The fund is nondiversified.

Our Take

The iPath S&P CSCI Total Return Index fund is designed to capture price movements for the broadest and most diversified set of commodities of any fund on our *100 Best ETFs* list.

It's based on the S&P GSCI (which used to stand for Goldman Sachs Commodity Index until acquired by S&P)—a broad-based index covering twenty-four commodities, which today includes six energy products, five industrial metals, eight agricultural products, three livestock products, and two precious metals

The S&P GSCI index is recognized as a leading measure of general price movements and inflation in the world economy. Weighting is important with commodity indexes, and is complex because there is no real "market cap" equivalent. The GSCI is calculated on what's known as a "world production-weighted basis" of the world's principal physical commodities. As such, the quantity of each commodity in the index is determined by the average quantity of production in the last five years of available data. So if oil and corn production are up, they will get a greater weight in the index.

We think the resulting mix reflects more or less what you would want to have if you had the ability to create a storehouse of your own commodities for eventual use or sale.

That, plus the diversification, makes this an attractive play for investors looking for generalized commodity exposure. That said, the weighting scheme gives a lot of weight to energy, which has been somewhat of an erratic bet over the past few years.

Why Should I Care?

This ETN provides general, diverse, and relatively simple exposure to commodities for long-term holding in a foundation portfolio or possible rotation for commodity cycles.

Upside

• Compelling weighting scheme, diverse but still concentrated
• Experienced; one of the oldest generalized commodity ETNs
• Diversified, doesn't matter so much which commodity spikes

Downside

• Not all commodities move in lockstep; returns can be attenuated
• If you're bearish on energy, watch out
• ETN expenses and credit risk

Just the Facts

INCEPTION DATE: June 6, 2006
TOTAL ASSETS: $117.8 million
AVERAGE DAILY VOLUME: 24,500
TOTAL HOLDINGS: 24
PERCENT NORTH AMERICA HOLDINGS: NM
TOP 10 HOLDINGS PERCENTAGE (CONCENTRATION): 85.56%

PORTFOLIO TURNOVER: **NM**   BENCHMARK: **NM**

BETA COEFFICIENT: **NA**

R-SQUARED (1 YEAR): **NA**

1-YEAR RETURN: **26.36%**   BENCHMARK: **38.15%**

3-YEAR RETURN: **-22.51%**   BENCHMARK: **-9.8%**

TRACKING ERROR (PRICE VS. NAV)   1 YEAR: **7.68%**   ASSET CLASS MEDIAN: **20.35%**

$10,000 Invested at inception	2006	2007	2008	2009	2010	2011
	$8,037	$10,608	$5,543	$6,273	$6,812	$6,977

What's Under the Hood

Symbol	Name	Percentage of fund
CL	Sweet Light Crude Oil (WTI)	37.68%
CO	Brent Crude Oil	13.51%
NG	Natural Gas	6.49%
HO	Heating Oil	4.88%
W	Wheat	4.79%
QS	Gas Oil	4.78%
XB	Gasoline RBOB	4.36%
C	Corn	3.53%
HG	Copper Future	3.13%
LA	Aluminum	2.41%
S	Soybean	2.40%
LC	Live Cattle	2.15%
GC	Gold 100 Oz.	2.05%
MW	Red Wheat	1.15%
FSB	Sugar	1.09%
LH	Lean Hogs	1.07%
LN	Nickel	0.97%
FCT	Cotton	0.90%
LX	Zinc	0.64%
FCC	Coffee	0.62%

iPATH/Barclays
1 Churchill Place
London E14 5HP, England
(877) 764-7284
Website: *www.ipathetn.com*

Elements Rogers International Commodity Index Total Return ETN

Ticker Symbol: RJI ❑ Issuer: Swedish Export Credit Corporation ❑ Description: General Commodity Blend ❑ Geography: Global ❑ Morningstar Rating: NR ❑ Marco Polo XTF Rating: NR ❑ Yield: NM ❑ Expense Ratio: 0.75% (Benchmark: 0.75%)

Stated Purpose

The investment seeks to replicate, net of expenses, the Rogers International Commodity Index—Total Return Index. The index represents the value of a basket of thirty-five commodity futures contracts.

Our Take

Jim Rogers designed a generalized commodity index known as the Rogers International Commodity Index (RICI) in 1996–1997 and started using it as a basis for commodity funds in 1998. The index is the broadest based among those in use by *100 Best ETF* commodity funds. It is calculated from a list of thirty-five commodities with volumes and trading data from thirteen international exchanges. The weighting is determined by a central "RICI Committee" and is largely based on commodity trading volumes, open interest, and liquidity.

The result is a list of commodities not surprisingly weighted toward oil, wheat, and corn but also containing lead, palladium, wool, and tin. The resulting mix is approximately 44 percent energy, 34 percent agriculture, 10 percent industrial metals, 7 percent precious metals, and 5 percent "other." The fund did well in the past year due mostly to agriculture and precious metal price increases. For investors, this is the true "general store" of commodity funds, with the most commonly shopped items arranged at the front of every aisle.

Why Should I Care?

This ETN portfolio makes sense to get generalized, across-the-board commodity exposure with a bit less risk than some.

Upside

• Attractive commodity mix
• Diversification, safety, not too concentrated in any single commodity or group
• Relatively large and relatively liquid

Downside

• Downs in some commodities will attenuate gains in others
• Overdiversified?
• ETN credit risk

Just the Facts

INCEPTION DATE: **October 17, 2007**

TOTAL ASSETS: **$941.5 million**

AVERAGE DAILY VOLUME: **664,100**

TOTAL HOLDINGS: **35**

PERCENT NORTH AMERICA HOLDINGS: **NM**

TOP 10 HOLDINGS PERCENTAGE (CONCENTRATION): **67.8%**

PORTFOLIO TURNOVER: **NM**   BENCHMARK: **NM**

BETA COEFFICIENT: **0.87**

R-SQUARED (1 YEAR): **64.70%**

1-YEAR RETURN: **41.64%**   BENCHMARK: **38.15%**

3-YEAR RETURN: **-10.35%**   BENCHMARK: **-9.8%**

TRACKING ERROR (PRICE VS. NAV)   1 YEAR: **4.13%**   ASSET CLASS MEDIAN: **20.35%**

$10,000 Invested at inception	2006	2007	2008	2009	2010	2011
	$—	$10,239	$5,961	$7,464	$8,813	$9,501

What's Under the Hood

Symbol	Name	Percentage of fund
CL	Sweet Light Crude Oil (WTI)	21.00%
CO	Brent Crude Oil	14.00%
W	Wheat	7.00%
C	Corn	4.75%
FCT	Cotton	4.05%
HG	Copper Future	4.00%
LA	Aluminum	4.00%
S	Soybean	3.00%
XB	Gasoline RBOB	3.00%
GC	Gold 100 Oz.	3.00%
NG	Natural Gas	3.00%
LX	Zinc	2.00%
SI	Silver	2.00%
LC	Live Cattle	2.00%
LL	Lead	2.00%
FSB	Sugar	2.00%

Symbol	Name	Percentage of fund
BO	Soybean Oil	2.00%
FCC	Coffee	2.00%
HO	Heating Oil	1.80%
PL	Platinum	1.80%

ELEMENTS
Swedish Export Credit Corporation
Vasta Tradgardsgatan 11B
10327 Stockholm, Sweden
(877) 386-2384
Website: *www.sek.se/en/*

100 BEST STRATEGY: **FOUNDATION/ROTATIONAL**

100 BEST CATEGORY: **COMMODITY—GENERAL**

GreenHaven Continuous Commodity Index Fund

Ticker Symbol: GCC ❑ Issuer: GreenHaven Commodity Services LLC ❑ Description: General Commodity Blend ❑ Geography: Global ❑ Morningstar Rating: NR ❑ Marco Polo XTF Rating: NR ❑ Yield: NM ❑ Expense Ratio: 0.85% (Benchmark: 0.75%)

Stated Purpose

The investment seeks to reflect the performance of the index, over time, less the expenses of the operations of the fund and the master fund. The fund invests substantially all of its assets in the master fund, which invests in a portfolio of exchange-traded futures on the commodities comprising the index, or the index commodities. Its managing owner may adjust the portfolio on a daily basis to conform to periodic changes in the identity and/or relative weighting of the index commodities.

Our Take

We don't write the "stated purpose" statements, and if we did, it wouldn't turn out like the one above. Aside from that editorial, the GreenHaven Continuous Commodity Fund is a favorite among commodity fund investors looking for a focused, and efficiently managed, true commodity ETF.

Because of the so-called "contango" effect, commodity ETFs, which actually own futures contracts as opposed to tracking them as an index through a debt security as ETNs do, are fairly rare. But this one uses a creative and fairly real-time approach, through daily index adjustments and varied futures expirations, to minimize the negatives of contango. Further, it weights components equally, so you aren't overexposed to any given commodity sector. The result is a portfolio that weights lean hogs the same as Brent Crude, and if that is the way you see the world, it makes sense. What also makes sense is that even with this fund's relative simplicity, it matches its sector benchmarks (and its own index) almost exactly.

Why Should I Care?

This fund makes sense for generalized and evenly weighted commodity exposure for foundation or rotational portfolios. Investors should consider adding specialty funds to capture movements and cycles in specific sectors.

Upside

- Performance closely tracks commodity benchmark performance
- Large and liquid, relatively simple
- Avoids ETN credit risk

Downside

- Still some contango and other complexities
- Higher than average expense ratio
- You may want more weight on "hot" sectors

Just the Facts

INCEPTION DATE: **January 24, 2008**

TOTAL ASSETS: **$733.8 million**

AVERAGE DAILY VOLUME: **218,000**

TOTAL HOLDINGS: **17**

PERCENT NORTH AMERICA HOLDINGS: **NM**

TOP 10 HOLDINGS PERCENTAGE (CONCENTRATION): **32.35%**

PORTFOLIO TURNOVER: **NM**   BENCHMARK: **NM**

BETA COEFFICIENT: **0.94**

R-SQUARED (1 YEAR): **93.77%**

1-YEAR RETURN: **34.77%**   BENCHMARK: **38.15%**

3-YEAR RETURN: **-3.08%**   BENCHMARK: **-8.80%**

TRACKING ERROR (PRICE VS. NAV)   1 YEAR: **4.22%**   ASSET CLASS MEDIAN: **20.35%**

$10,000 Invested at inception	2006	2007	2008	2009	2010	2011
	$—	$—	$6,425	$8,284	$10,388	$10,612

What's Under the Hood

Symbol	Name	Percentage of fund
SI	Silver	3.25%
PL	Platinum	3.24%
JO	Orange Juice (FCOJ)	3.24%
C	Corn	3.24%
CT	Cotton No. 2	3.23%
NG	Natural Gas	3.23%
SB	Sugar No. 11	3.23%
W	Wheat	3.23%
CC	Cocoa	3.23%
LC	Live Cattle	3.23%
LH	Lean Hogs	3.23%
HO	Heating Oil	3.23%
S	Soybean	3.23%
HG	Copper Future	3.23%
CL	Sweet Light Crude Oil (WTI)	3.23%
KC	Coffee 'C'	3.22%
GC	Gold 100 Oz.	3.22%

GreenHaven LLC
3340 Peachtree Road #1910
Atlanta, GA 30326
(800) 845-8103
Website: *www.greenhavenfunds.com*

ELEMENTS S&P Commodity Trends Indicator Total Return ETN

Ticker Symbol: LSC ▫ Issuer: HSBC Investment Funds ▫ Description: General Commodity Specialty Index Blend ▫ Geography: Global ▫ Morningstar Rating: NR ▫ Marco Polo XTF Rating: NR ▫ Yield: NM ▫ Expense Ratio: 0.75% (Benchmark: 0.75%)

Stated Purpose

The investment seeks to replicate, net of expenses, the S&P Commodity Trends Indicator Total Return Index. The index is a composite of sixteen highly liquid commodity futures grouped into six sectors. It positions each of the sectors either long or short (except energy) based on its price behavior relative to its moving average.

Our Take

Those of you who have followed our *100 Best Stocks* and other entries in the *100 Best* series over the years know that we, fundamentally as value investors, like to understand what it is that we're investing in. The Elements S&P Commodity Trends Indicator Total Return ETN brings a unique approach to indexing a commodity portfolio, one that, frankly, tests the limits of our ability (and willingness) to understand a heavily financially engineered index.

According to S&P, their Commodity Trends Indicator (CTI) index is "a diversified composite of traditional, physical commodity futures designed to measure the extent and duration of price movements and volatility among the component sectors." Like the indexes that guide some of our other generalized commodity ETNs, the CTI tracks a diverse base of sixteen commodities grouped into six sectors, with a built-in "internal noncorrelation" to make the CTI a "well diversified and low volatility" indicator.

So far, so good, and not unlike our other funds. But now it gets more exciting. The CTI is further designed to track the price movements of each commodity against its own moving average, and will weight the index accordingly. The upshot: If corn and wheat go up, they will get a heavier weighting. If soybeans go down, they will get a lighter weighting, and the index/fund may even go short on them; that is, effectively, sell them into the market. One further complexity: The fund does not go short on energy because of its "continuous consumption with supply and concentration risk."

So we end up with a fund that favors what is favored and avoids what isn't, which sounds like a good thing if it is nimble enough. And on that last note, we're not sure, because the one-year return was fairly subpar. The three-year return was better. We think, because the fund quickly discards what is not in favor, that it might be a bit safer and less volatile than some others, as advertised. But it hasn't really been around long enough to prove much to us. So we'll include it—with fair warning—as an untested sports car to be driven carefully at first.

Why Should I Care?

This fund probably makes sense for a well-watched rotational portfolio to capture the latest commodity trends.

Upside

- Index approach sounds compelling
- Attractively diverse portfolio
- Goes short on weak hands

Downside

- Unproven formula
- Poor one-year return
- ETN credit risk

Just the Facts

INCEPTION DATE: **October 10, 2008**

TOTAL ASSETS: **$42.7 million**

AVERAGE DAILY VOLUME: **44,500**

TOTAL HOLDINGS: **16**

PERCENT NORTH AMERICA HOLDINGS: **NM**

TOP 10 HOLDINGS PERCENTAGE (CONCENTRATION): **83.5%**

PORTFOLIO TURNOVER: **NM**   BENCHMARK: **NM**

BETA COEFFICIENT: **0.60**

R-SQUARED (1 YEAR): **14.72%**

1-YEAR RETURN: **7.46%**   BENCHMARK: **38.15%**

3-YEAR RETURN: **-4.24%**   BENCHMARK: **-8.80%**

TRACKING ERROR (PRICE VS. NAV)   1 YEAR: **19.15%**   ASSET CLASS MEDIAN: **20.35%**

$10,000 Invested at inception	2006	2007	2008	2009	2010	2011
	$—	$—	$10,497	$9,400	$8,739	$8,780

What's Under the Hood

Symbol	Name	Percentage of fund
CL	Sweet Light Crude Oil (WTI)	17.00%
HG	Copper Future	17.00%
S	Soybean	10.00%
NG	Natural Gas	10.00%
C	Corn	8.50%
GC	Gold 100 Oz.	8.00%
HO	Heating Oil	7.00%
LC	Live Cattle	6.00%
XB	Gasoline RBOB	6.00%
W	Wheat	6.00%
LH	Lean Hogs	5.00%
SI	Silver	4.00%
KC	Coffee 'C'	3.50%
CC	Cocoa	3.00%
CT	Cotton No. 2	2.00%
FSB	Sugar	2.00%
FSB	Sugar	2.00%

HSBC Bank USA, N.A.
P.O. Box 2013
Buffalo, NY 14240
UK—(44) 945-607-6144
Website: *www.etf.hsbc.com*

100 BEST STRATEGY: **FOUNDATION/ROTATIONAL**

100 BEST CATEGORY: **COMMODITY—GENERAL**

UBS ETRACS DJ UBS Commodity Index Total Return ETN

Ticker Symbol: DJCI ▫ Issuer: UBS Global Asset Management ▫ Description: General Commodity Blend ▫ Geography: Global ▫ Morningstar Rating: NR ▫ Marco Polo XTF Rating: NR ▫ Yield: NM ▫ Expense Ratio: 0.80% (Benchmark: 0.75%)

Stated Purpose

The investment seeks to replicate, net of expenses, the DJ–UBS Commodity Index Total Return Index. The index measures the collateralized returns from a basket of nineteen commodity futures contracts representing the energy, precious metals, industrial metals, grains, softs, and livestock sectors. In addition, the index is rebalanced once a year to ensure that no commodity sector may constitute more than 33 percent of the index as of the date of such rebalancing.

Our Take

Of all the general commodity ETFs we looked at, this fund and its underlying index is probably the simplest and lowest cost of the bunch, a compelling position in this somewhat jungly and heavily financially engineered space.

Like most of the commodity indexes, this one produces a result that puts crude oil at the top, which isn't a bad place to be in today's world of long-term energy consumption and supply problems. But we like the sector cap, which keeps energy from becoming too dominant. We also like the resulting mix that, while well diversified, pushes agriculture to the top (at 35 percent, but will soon be rebalanced downward we suspect, as those prices have risen recently) and gives good weight to precious metals at 13.7 percent. (The others are energy at 33 percent, industrial metals at 10.3 percent, and "uncategorized" at 7.5 percent, in case you're interested.)

In today's inflation-wary environment, this seems like a good mix and a way to insulate against the volatility of the energy sector, which could be played more cyclically in another specialized fund. We like the departure from the traditional 0.75 percent expense ratio, and this fund has made money over its relatively short "long term."

Why Should I Care?

This is a good no-nonsense commodity ETN for a foundation or rotational portfolio.

Upside

- Agriculture/precious metal emphasis, less energy than most
- Lower expense ratio than some

- Safety: right amount of diversification

Downside

- New, small, and largely untested
- Difficult to get precise info about the index
- ETN credit risk, not a U.S. institution

Just the Facts

INCEPTION DATE: **October 29, 2008**

TOTAL ASSETS: **$24.8 million**

AVERAGE DAILY VOLUME: **4,000**

TOTAL HOLDINGS: **19**

PERCENT NORTH AMERICA HOLDINGS: **NM**

TOP 10 HOLDINGS PERCENTAGE (CONCENTRATION): **75.65%**

PORTFOLIO TURNOVER: **NM**   BENCHMARK: **NM**

BETA COEFFICIENT: **1.03**

R-SQUARED (1 YEAR): **87.93%**

1-YEAR RETURN: **25.37%**   BENCHMARK: **38.15%**

3-YEAR RETURN: **NA**   BENCHMARK: **-8.80%**

TRACKING ERROR (PRICE VS. NAV)   1 YEAR: **4.12%**   ASSET CLASS MEDIAN: **20.35%**

$10,000 Invested at inception	2006	2007	2008	2009	2010	2011
	$—	$—	$—	$10,848	$12,273	$11,926

What's Under the Hood

Symbol	Name	Percentage of fund
CL	Sweet Light Crude Oil (WTI)	14.71%
NG	Natural Gas	11.22%
GC	Gold 100 Oz.	10.45%
S	Soybean	7.86%
HG	Copper Future	7.54%
C	Corn	6.98%
LA	Aluminum	5.20%
W	Wheat	4.61%
HO	Heating Oil	3.58%
XB	Gasoline RBOB	3.50%
LC	Live Cattle	3.36%
FSB	Sugar	3.33%
SI	Silver	3.29%
BO	Soybean Oil	2.94%
LX	Zinc	2.85%
KC	Coffee 'C'	2.36%
LN	Nickel	2.25%
CT	Cotton No. 2	2.00%
LH	Lean Hogs	2.00%

UBS AG
Bahnhofstr. 45
P.O. Box CH-8098
Zurich, Switzerland
(877) 387-2275
Website: *www.ubs.com/etracs*

Commodity—Specialized

Instead of the "general" approach to commodity fund investing offered in the last section, suppose you prefer to invest in a specific commodity or a closely related group of commodities like "energy" (usually oil and gas), or perhaps gold or precious metals? The eight ETFs and ETNs in this group will make that possible.

100 BEST STRATEGY: **FOUNDATION/ROTATIONAL**

100 BEST CATEGORY: **COMMODITY—SPECIALIZED**

UBS ETRACS UBS Bloomberg CMCI Food Trust ETN

Ticker Symbol: FUD ❑ Issuer: UBS Global Asset Management ❑ Description: General Commodity Blend ❑ Geography: Global ❑ Morningstar Rating: NR ❑ Marco Polo XTF Rating: NR ❑ Yield: NM ❑ Expense Ratio: 0.65% (Benchmark: 0.75%)

Stated Purpose

The investment seeks to track the price and performance yield, before fees and expenses, of the UBS Bloomberg CMCI Food Total Return Index. The fund is designed to be representative of the entire liquid forward curve of each commodity in the index. The index measures the collateralized returns from a diversified basket of agriculture and livestock futures contracts. It is comprised of the eleven agriculture futures contracts and two livestock futures contracts included in the CMCI with three target maturities for each individual commodity.

Our Take

Feeling hungry? It was hard to resist this fund just based on the ticker symbol, FUD.

Upon a closer look, the UBS ETRACS UBS Bloomberg CMCI Food Trust ETN is really a whole meal. While it is heavy on the softs—sugar, soybeans, corn, and wheat top the list and make up almost 70 percent of the index—it goes beyond these "soft" portions to include meat (live cattle, lean hogs), beverages (coffee and cocoa), and a couple of soybean products for good measure (dessert?).

This mix makes the fund a good play on the eleven most common and highly demanded foodstuffs. It's a solid play on both long-term and shorter-term food supply and demand dynamics.

Why Should I Care?

As a play on longer-term food shortages and increased demand from developing nations, this fund makes sense for a foundation portfolio. As a play on short-term supply disruptions and demand shifts, this fund also works in a rotational portfolio.

Upside

- Strong recent performance
- Full representation of foodstuffs, not just softs
- Not *too* diversified, most holdings positively correlate

Downside

- A bit small, a bit new
- High tracking error
- ETN credit risk

Just the Facts

INCEPTION DATE: **April 1, 2008**

TOTAL ASSETS: **$43.8 million**

AVERAGE DAILY VOLUME: **7,500**

TOTAL HOLDINGS: **11**

PERCENT NORTH AMERICA HOLDINGS: **NM**

TOP 10 HOLDINGS PERCENTAGE (CONCENTRATION): **100%**

PORTFOLIO TURNOVER: **NM**   BENCHMARK: **NM**

BETA COEFFICIENT: **1.05**

R-SQUARED (1 YEAR): **56.66%**

1-YEAR RETURN: **49.5%**   BENCHMARK: **38.15%**

3-YEAR RETURN: **-0.76**   BENCHMARK: **-8.80%**

TRACKING ERROR (PRICE VS. NAV)   1 YEAR: **17.05%**   ASSET CLASS MEDIAN: **20.35%**

$10,000 Invested at inception	2006	2007	2008	2009	2010	2011
	$—	$—	$7,555	$8,486	$11,309	$10,981

What's Under the Hood

Symbol	Name	Percentage of fund
FSB	Sugar	24.47%
S	Soybean	18.53%
C	Corn	15.69%
W	Wheat	10.27%
LC	Live Cattle	7.36%
BO	Soybean Oil	7.00%
LH	Lean Hogs	5.09%
SM	Soybean Meal	4.72%
KC	Coffee 'C'	3.97%
CC	Cocoa	2.90%

UBS AG
Bahnhofstr. 45
P.O. Box CH-8098
Zurich, Switzerland
(877) 387-2275
Website: *www.ubs.com/etracs*

100 BEST STRATEGY: **FOUNDATION/ROTATIONAL**

100 BEST CATEGORY: **COMMODITY—SPECIALIZED**

PowerShares DB Energy Fund ETF

Ticker Symbol: DBE ❑ Issuer: Invesco ❑ Description: Energy Futures ETF ❑ Geography: Global ❑ Morningstar Rating: NR ❑ Marco Polo XTF Rating: 8.7 ❑ Yield: NM ❑ Expense Ratio: 0.75% (Benchmark: 0.75%)

Stated Purpose

The investment seeks to track the price and yield performance, before fees and expenses, of the Deutsche Bank Liquid Commodity Index Optimum Yield Energy Excess Return. The index is a rules-based index composed of futures contracts on some of the most heavily traded energy commodities in the world—Light Sweet Crude Oil (WTI), Heating Oil, Brent Crude Oil, RBOB gasoline, and Natural Gas. The index is intended to reflect the performance of the energy sector.

Our Take

If you think about it, with increasing demand and decreasing supply and absolutely no more of it being made anywhere, fossil-fuel energy products are the place you'd want to be long term. In fact, what more could be better than storing a few thousand barrels of oil, refined gasoline, heating oil, and natural gas in your backyard (aside from the fire risk) for your long-term energy and financial security?

There are two problems, of course. One is the obvious difficulty in storing energy products for that next energy crisis. The other is in knowing when that crisis will happen. So if you want to make a fairly pure bet on energy, and especially if you aren't sure that oil alone is the place to be, that refined products will gain value because of supply chain problems, and/or natural gas will become more scarce and more sought after, then the PowerShares DB Energy Fund ETF might be the place to be.

Now, this fund could suffer from some of the negatives of other ETFs buying futures contracts outright, namely, the so-called "contango" effect where current month "forward" contracts are purchased each month, and each month have a time premium that dissipates during that month. PowerShares and the underlying Deutsche Bank Liquid Commodity Index—Optimum Yield

Energy Excess Return index have a highly engineered solution to that problem (and they'd better, with a long name like that!). Going into the details would be like knowing every ingredient in your sausage, but it starts with not investing in the current month's expiration, but rather in an assortment of expirations to take advantage of longer-term price differentials and "backwardization," where a longer contract might actually sell for less than today's contract because the market expects a current price run-up to correct itself.

Why Should I Care?

All that aside, if you want a fund focused on fossil-fuel energy, and you don't really care or know enough about what kind of energy will be most sought after in the short or long term, this fund might work for you.

Upside
- Focused on energy . . . yet not locked into one form of energy
- Don't have to deal with vagaries of corporate management
- Actually an ETF (you own something) with contango strategy

Downside
- Higher costs than comparable stock fund—XLE, for example
- Poorer performance than XLE
- Financial engineering not easy to understand, may bite

Just the Facts

INCEPTION DATE: **January 5, 2007**

TOTAL ASSETS: **$200 million**

AVERAGE DAILY VOLUME: **164,900**

TOTAL HOLDINGS: **4**

PERCENT NORTH AMERICA HOLDINGS: **NM**

TOP 10 HOLDINGS PERCENTAGE (CONCENTRATION): **100%**

PORTFOLIO TURNOVER: **NM**   BENCHMARK: **NM**

BETA COEFFICIENT: **1.00**

R-SQUARED (1 YEAR): **66.07%**

1-YEAR RETURN: **28.49%**   BENCHMARK: **38.15%**

3-YEAR RETURN: **-17.49%**   BENCHMARK: **-8.80%**

TRACKING ERROR (PRICE VS. NAV)   1 YEAR: **11.46%**   ASSET CLASS MEDIAN: **20.35%**

$10,000 Invested at inception	2006	2007	2008	2009	2010	2011
	$—	$14,418	$8,741	$10,910	$11,283	$12,525

What's Under the Hood

Symbol	Name	Percentage of fund
HO	Heating Oil	23.59%
CO	Brent Crude Oil	23.40%
XB	Gasoline RBOB	23.31%
CL	Sweet Light Crude Oil (WTI)	21.45%
NG	Natural Gas	8.25%

Invesco PowerShares Capital Management LLC
301 West Roosevelt Road
Wheaton, IL 60187
(800) 803-0903
Website: *www.invescopowershares.com*

PowerShares DB Oil Fund ETF

Ticker Symbol: DBO ▫ Issuer: Invesco ▫ Description: Oil Futures ETF ▫ Geography: Global ▫ Morningstar Rating: NR ▫ Marco Polo XTF Rating: 8.4 ▫ Yield: NM ▫ Expense Ratio: 0.75% (Benchmark: 0.75%)

Stated Purpose

The investment seeks to track the price and yield performance, before fees and expenses, of the Deutsche Bank Liquid Commodity Index—Optimum Yield Oil Excess Return. The index is a rules-based index composed of futures contracts on Light Sweet Crude Oil (WTI) and is intended to reflect the performance of crude oil.

Our Take

You're pretty sure the world is going to run out of fossil-fuel energy resources someday. You're just not sure when. Demand is going up, supply is going down. You want to invest in an energy-focused commodity fund. You might look at this fund's close sibling—the PowerShares DB Energy Fund ETF (DBE).

But wait. You know they're drilling for natural gas like crazy. You know that gasoline demand goes up and down like a yo-yo, and many uncontrollable factors play into refining output, transport, and so forth. You know that demand for heating oil and a lot of other energy products is seasonal.

You just want to stick to the black stuff. The most useful, the shortest in supply, and the most geopolitically tense of all the energy resources—just plain oil. Black gold. Texas tea. The stuff from which just about everything else is made.

Structured very similar to the DBE fund, the PowerShares DB Oil Fund, as the name implies, is just about oil. It invests in the futures contract of the West Texas Intermediate Sweet Light Crude—a bellwether of the industry, albeit less of one recently as the North Sea's Brent product has come into favor.

Of course, it looks a little strange to have a fund with just a single investment. The truth is that this fund keeps a lot of financial professionals busy sharpening the mix of terms and entry and exit of the futures contracts that underlie the fund. As mentioned in the DBE write-up, DBO employs a specialized strategy to manage "contango" —the regular diminishment of fund value due to disappearing time premiums. We're not totally sold on the methodology, but it seemed to give better returns than some of the energy commodity alternatives, and has come back well from the 2008–09 energy lows.

Why Should I Care?

If you want to buy oil—pure oil—but you're not sure when it will get expensive, and you don't trust "big oil" companies and their management, this fund could be for your foundation portfolio or for your rotational portfolio for short-term anomalies in energy prices.

Upside

- Very focused
- Pure play, not dependent on oil companies
- Real ETF, with protections against contango

Downside

- High expenses for one-product portfolio
- Stock funds are cheaper and pay dividends
- Returns not that great—do contango protections work?

Just the Facts

INCEPTION DATE: **January 5, 2007**

TOTAL ASSETS: **$595.3 million**

AVERAGE DAILY VOLUME: **549,100**

TOTAL HOLDINGS: **1**

PERCENT NORTH AMERICA HOLDINGS: **NM**

TOP 10 HOLDINGS PERCENTAGE (CONCENTRATION): **100%**

PORTFOLIO TURNOVER: **NM**   BENCHMARK: **NM**

BETA COEFFICIENT: **1.10**

R-SQUARED (1 YEAR): **70.60%**

1-YEAR RETURN: **20.92%**   BENCHMARK: **38.15%**

3-YEAR RETURN: **-18.05%**   BENCHMARK: **-8.80%**

TRACKING ERROR (PRICE VS. NAV)   1 YEAR: **11.15%**   ASSET CLASS MEDIAN: **20.35%**

$10,000 Invested at inception	2006	2007	2008	2009	2010	2011
	$—	$14,666	$8,658	$11,730	$12,204	$12,323

What's Under the Hood

Symbol	Name	Percentage of fund
CL	Sweet Light Crude Oil (WTI)	100%

Invesco PowerShares Capital Management LLC
301 West Roosevelt Road
Wheaton, IL 60187
(800) 803-0903
Website: *www.invescopowershares.com*

100 BEST STRATEGY: **FOUNDATION/ROTATIONAL**

100 BEST CATEGORY: **COMMODITY—SPECIALIZED**

iShares Comex Gold Trust

Ticker Symbol: IAU ❑ Issuer: BlackRock/iShares ❑ Description: Gold Physical Commodity ETF ❑ Geography: Global ❑ Morningstar Rating: NR ❑ Marco Polo XTF Rating: 9.8 ❑ Yield: NM ❑ Expense Ratio: 0.25% (Benchmark: 0.75%)

Stated Purpose

The investment seeks to replicate, net of expenses, the day-to-day movement of the price of gold bullion. The trust is not an investment company registered under the Investment Company Act of 1940 or a commodity pool for purposes of the Commodity Exchange Act. It receives gold deposited with it in exchange for the creation of baskets of iShares, sells gold as necessary to cover the trust's liabilities, and delivers gold in exchange for baskets of iShares surrendered to it for redemption.

Our Take

It's really pretty simple. You buy shares of the iShares Comex Gold

Trust, and it buys real, physical gold and holds it for you. You sell shares, it sells gold, and gives you the current price in cash. Well, almost, anyway. They may delay the purchase somewhat until they get enough people buying shares to buy the gold, etc. In iShares's words: "The shares are backed by gold, identified on the custodian's books as property of the Trust and held by the custodian in vaults in the vicinity of New York, Toronto, London and other locations."

Upshot: This is among the purest and simplest of ways to own gold without actually owning physical gold in your own physical safe. The price movements correlate quite closely with gold, and as you can see from the low beta and R-squared, they correlate with little else, which is what you want if you're a gold investor.

There's a small catch in the "stated purpose" statement: The fund is technically and legally a type of trust, not an investment company. What that means is that, given current tax law, there will be a "mark to market" each year making you liable (or the beneficiary of) capital gains tax (or a write-off) each year according to price changes, whether or not you sell.

We gave IAU a slight edge over its much larger competitor, the SPDR Gold Trust (GLD), because of lower expenses (0.25 percent vs. 0.40 percent). Of course, buying and selling this fund is based strictly on where you think the price of gold is going.

Why Should I Care?
The iShares Comex Gold Trust is a good way to put direct gold exposure into a foundation or rotational portfolio.

Upside
- Closely tracks price of gold without cost and headaches of direct ownership
- Low expense ratio
- Large and liquid

Downside
- Is gold a bubble?
- High tracking error—are we efficient?
- "Mark to market" tax implications for taxable accounts

Just the Facts

INCEPTION DATE: **January 21, 2005**

TOTAL ASSETS: **$7.0 billion**

AVERAGE DAILY VOLUME: **6.2 million**

TOTAL HOLDINGS: **1**

PERCENT NORTH AMERICA HOLDINGS: **NM**

TOP 10 HOLDINGS PERCENTAGE (CONCENTRATION): **100%**

PORTFOLIO TURNOVER: **NM**   BENCHMARK: **NM**

BETA COEFFICIENT: **0.09**

R-SQUARED (1 YEAR): **1.09%**

1-YEAR RETURN: **20.59%**   BENCHMARK: **38.15%**

3-YEAR RETURN: **17.18%**   BENCHMARK: **-8.80%**

TRACKING ERROR (PRICE VS. NAV)   1 YEAR: **20.60%**   ASSET CLASS MEDIAN: **20.35%**

$10,000 Invested at inception	2006	2007	2008	2009	2010	2011
	$13,167	$14,924	$9,308	$13,111	$17,078	$18,879

What's Under the Hood

Symbol	Name	Percentage of fund
GOLDS	Gold	100%

BlackRock iShares
525 Washington Boulevard, Suite 1405
Jersey City, NJ 07310
(800) 474-2737
Website: *www.ishares.com*

100 BEST STRATEGY: **FOUNDATION/ROTATIONAL**

100 BEST CATEGORY: **COMMODITY—SPECIALIZED**

ETFS Physical Precious Metal Basket Shares ETF

Ticker Symbol: GLTR ❏ Issuer: ETF Securities ❏ Description: Precious Metal Physical Commodity ETF ❏ Geography: Global ❏ Morningstar Rating: NR ❏ Marco Polo XTF Rating: NR ❏ Yield: NM ❏ Expense Ratio: 0.60% (Benchmark: 0.75%)

Stated Purpose

The investment seeks to replicate, net of expenses, the performance of the prices of physical gold, silver, platinum, and palladium.

Our Take

You're not sure about the United States or the world economy. You're not sure about the long-term value and worth of the world's paper currencies, in particular your own, the once-almighty U.S. dollar. You would like to store at least some of

your wealth in precious metals. But you're not a pure-and-simple gold bug and feel that the yellow metal might just be a bit overbought by the world's other safe-haven seekers. You want to diversify just a bit into other precious metals—silver, platinum, palladium—but you, like most gold bugs, don't want the headaches, costs, and risks of physical storage.

That's where the ETFS Physical Precious Metal Basket Shares ETF comes in.

As the name states almost directly, GLTR sells you shares and takes your money and buys an allocation of physical gold, silver, platinum, and palladium, and in this case, puts it in a vault in either London or Zurich. One of the things we like about ETFs is transparency, and this one is about as transparent as you can get. You can easily download an Excel spreadsheet showing what and where all of the physical metal is at *www.etfsecurities.com/ us/securities/etfs_physical_exposure .asp-bars*. (By the way, the latest allocation is 44.4 percent gold, 44 percent silver, 7.1 percent platinum, and 4.5 percent palladium.)

The fund goes a step further to assure you of its security, giving insight into its own audit process: "Vault inspections are required by the Sponsor to ensure all metal held on behalf of the Trusts can be accounted for. The inspections are undertaken by an independent third party called Inspectorate International, a world leader in independent physical audits and inspections. The inspections are carried out on behalf of the Trustees and, as stipulated in the prospectuses, are required twice per year."

Wi[...] what [...] is h[...] update [...] ative newness [...] manager. We shou[...] as a grantor trust, there [...] implications each year for ta[...] accounts as the value of the portfolio is "marked to market." But it's a good bet for those wanting to get into precious metals without maintaining a bank vault of their own.

Why Should I Care?

This fund makes sense as a way to hedge against currency inflation in a relatively more diverse way without the downsides of physical precious metal ownership.

Upside

- Some diversification, not just gold
- Physical ownership, not futures contracts
- Transparency

Downside

- High expenses compared to pure gold IAU
- New and untested
- Tax implications for taxable accounts

e Facts

ON DATE: **October 22, 2010**

L ASSETS: **$232.1 million**

VERAGE DAILY VOLUME: **51,600**

TOTAL HOLDINGS: **4**

PERCENT NORTH AMERICA HOLDINGS: **NM**

TOP 10 HOLDINGS PERCENTAGE (CONCENTRATION): **100%**

PORTFOLIO TURNOVER: **NM**   BENCHMARK: **NM**

BETA COEFFICIENT: **NA**

R-SQUARED (1 YEAR): **NA**

1-YEAR RETURN: **NA**   BENCHMARK: **38.15%**

3-YEAR RETURN: **NA**   BENCHMARK: **-8.80%**

TRACKING ERROR (PRICE VS. NAV)   1 YEAR: **NA**   ASSET CLASS MEDIAN: **20.35%**

$10,000 Invested at inception	2006	2007	2008	2009	2010	2011
	$—	$—	$—	$—	$11,315	$12,243

What's Under the Hood

Symbol	Name	Percentage of fund
GOLDS	Gold	44.36%
SILV	Silver	44.02%
PLAT	Platinum	7.14%
PALL	Palladium	4.47%

ETF Securities USA LLC
48 Wall Street, 11th Floor
New York, NY 10005
(212) 918 4954
Website: *www.etfsecurities.com*

MCLX Biofuels ETN

Ticker Symbol: FUE ❑ Issuer: ELEMENTS/Swedish Export Credit Corporation ❑ Description: Specialized Energy ETN ❑ Geography: Global ❑ Morningstar Rating: NR ❑ Marco Polo XTF Rating: NR ❑ Yield: NM ❑ Expense Ratio: 0.60% (Benchmark: 0.75%)

Stated Purpose

The investment seeks to replicate, net of expenses, the MLCX Biofuels Total Return Index. The index is designed to reflect the performance of a fully collateralized investment in the seven exchange-traded futures contracts on seven physical commodities: barley, canola, corn, rapeseed, soybeans, soybean oil, and sugar.

Our Take

Okay, it sounds kind of groovy—biofuels. But we're not really talking about used French fry oil or switchgrass or anything like that. We're simply talking about a basket of already traded and fairly common commodities that just happen to be feedstock for biofuels. They also happen to be commodities that tend to get in short supply when oil shortages and price escalations arise. So why not hedge yourself against the oil market, take a position in some important foodstuffs, and yes, be in the right place when we all finally do the right thing for the planet?

That's the idea behind the MCLX Biofuels ETN. The underlying index is designed to track seven physical commodities (it only tracked six at the time we researched it). Those who invested in this fund in 2010, whether it was to "do good" or not, did very well, because the underlying commodities, notably corn, rose substantially through the year due to factors largely outside the biofuel industry. (Rising oil prices didn't hurt, though.) The fund gained almost 60 percent last year.

Why Should I Care?

This investment makes sense for foundation and rotational portfolios as a hedge against energy prices and, in the long term, as a bet that biofuels will become mainstream. Think of it as buying energy without buying oil and gas.

Upside

• Hedge against oil prices
• Focused on a theme
• Environmentally positive

Downside

• Vulnerable to oil price swings
• Small and somewhat illiquid
• ETN credit risk

Just the Facts

INCEPTION DATE: **February 5, 2008**

TOTAL ASSETS: **$9.9 million**

AVERAGE DAILY VOLUME: **14,600**

TOTAL HOLDINGS: **6**

PERCENT NORTH AMERICA HOLDINGS: **NM**

TOP 10 HOLDINGS PERCENTAGE (CONCENTRATION): **100%**

PORTFOLIO TURNOVER: **NM**   BENCHMARK: **NM**

BETA COEFFICIENT: **0.95**

R-SQUARED (1 YEAR): **46.46%**

1-YEAR RETURN: **59.52%**   BENCHMARK: **38.15%**

3-YEAR RETURN: **-0.93%**   BENCHMARK: **-8.80%**

TRACKING ERROR (PRICE VS. NAV)   1 YYEAR: **22.10%**   ASSET CLASS MEDIAN: **20.35%**

$10,000 Invested at inception	2006	2007	2008	2009	2010	2011
	$—	$—	$6,148	$7,453	$4,855	$9,835

What's Under the Hood

Symbol	Name	Percentage of fund
S	Soybean	32.73%
C	Corn	21.06%
BO	Soybean Oil	19.45%
FSB	Sugar	15.71%
RS	Canola	7.21%
WA	Barley	3.84%

ELEMENTS
Swedish Export Credit Corporation
Vasta Tradgardsgatan 11B
10327 Stockholm, Sweden
(877) 386-2384
Website: *www.sek.se/en/*

100 BEST STRATEGY: **FOUNDATION/ROTATIONAL**

100 BEST CATEGORY: **COMMODITY—SPECIALIZED**

Elements Rogers International Commodity Index Metals Total Return ETN

Ticker Symbol: RJZ ▫ Issuer: Swedish Export Credit Corporation ▫ Description: Specific Commodity Futures Basket ETN ▫ Geography: Global ▫ Morningstar Rating: NR ▪ Marco Polo XTF Rating: NR ▫ Yield: NM ▫ Expense Ratio: 0.75% (Benchmark: 0.75%)

Stated Purpose

The investment seeks to replicate, net of expenses, the Rogers International Commodity Index—Metals Total Return index. The index represents the value of a basket of ten metals commodity futures contracts.

Our Take

Let's say you've made up your mind that, at least for part of your portfolio, metals are where you want to be. Industrial metals are the cornerstone of industry, and precious metals are the cornerstone of our financial system, especially in an environment of depreciating paper currency. Metals are strategic in many ways, and demand tends to boom when new economies come on line, as is what's happening with China right now.

Only thing is, you're just not sure which metals will emerge from the pack. They all have their own uses, and they all have their own supply and demand profile.

That's where the Elements Rogers International Commodity Index Metals Total Return ETN weighs in.

The index is production weighted; that is, the commodities with the greatest dollar production amounts float to the top as a nod to the idea of following most closely what is in greatest demand—in this case, copper and aluminum. The resulting mix is 47 percent industrial metals, 34 percent precious metals, and 19 percent uncategorized.

Why Should I Care?

This portfolio would be appropriate for investors looking for a broad inflation hedge in a foundation or sometimes a rotational portfolio.

Upside

- Diversified, but all in metals
- Fairly safe in down markets
- Exposure—but not too much exposure—to precious metals

Downside

- Metals always vulnerable to supply increases—mining, reclamation
- Watch out for high premium to NAV
- ETN credit risk

Just the Facts

INCEPTION DATE: **October 17, 2007**

TOTAL ASSETS: **$81.2 million**

AVERAGE DAILY VOLUME: **69,300**

TOTAL HOLDINGS: **10**

PERCENT NORTH AMERICA HOLDINGS: **NM**

TOP 10 HOLDINGS PERCENTAGE (CONCENTRATION): **100%**

PORTFOLIO TURNOVER: **NM**   BENCHMARK: **NM**

BETA COEFFICIENT: **0.88**

R-SQUARED (1 YEAR): **70.28%**

1-YEAR RETURN: **36.26%**   BENCHMARK: **38.15%**

3-YEAR RETURN: **5.75%**   BENCHMARK: **-9.8%**

TRACKING ERROR (PRICE VS. NAV)   1 YEAR: **8.18%**   ASSET CLASS MEDIAN: **20.35%**

$10,000 Invested at inception	2006	2007	2008	2009	2010	2011
	$—	$9,244	$5,697	$9,819	$12,108	$12,286

What's Under the Hood

Symbol	Name	Percentage of fund
HG	Copper Future	18.96%
LA	Aluminum	18.96%
GC	Gold 100 Oz.	14.22%
LX	Zinc	9.48%
LL	Lead	9.48%
SI	Silver	9.48%
PL	Platinum	8.53%
LN	Nickel	4.74%
LT	Tin	4.74%
PA	Palladium	1.42%

ELEMENTS

Swedish Export Credit Corporation

Vasta Tradgardsgatan 11B

10327 Stockholm, Sweden

(877) 386-2384

Website: *www.sek.se/en/*

iPath Dow Jones UBS Softs Subindex Total Return ETN

Ticker Symbol: JJS ▫ Issuer: iPATH/Barclays ▫ Description: Specific Commodity Futures Basket ETN ▫ Geography: Global ▫ Morningstar Rating: NR ▫ Marco Polo XTF Rating: NR ▫ Yield: NM ▫ Expense Ratio: 0.75% (Benchmark: 0.75%)

Stated Purpose

The investment seeks to replicate, net of expenses, the Dow Jones-UBS Softs Total Return Sub-Index. The index is intended to reflect the returns that are potentially available through an unleveraged investment in the futures contracts as well as the rate of interest that could be earned on cash collateral invested in specified Treasury Bills. It consists of three commodity futures contracts: coffee, cotton, and sugar.

Our Take

Coffee, sugar, milk? Your morning cup of coffee? Not quite—substitute cotton for milk, and you've arrived at the iPath Dow Jones UBS Softs Subindex Total Return ETN.

Now aside from coffee, this group of three "soft" commodities may not really seem that interesting. Certainly, it's not as sexy as gold, oil, gasoline, or Japanese yen futures, for sure, but you know what? This fund was one of the top returners on our list for the past twelve-month period, with a whopping 75.75 percent return. Where were you when this

was going on? Hope you didn't tie up all your loose change in Apple stock or some such modest performer. . . .

The portfolio mix is straightforward. Cotton and sugar just happen to have gone through some pretty surprising gains this year, anchored by foreign demand and a persistent decrease in agricultural acreage devoted to them, particularly sugar (a good bit of Hawaii has turned from cane fields to resort hotels and macadamia nut plantations, for example). And coffee hasn't been too bad either—people continue to drink more and more of it, especially in Asia and other parts of the world where its prominence is a recent phenomenon.

If you expect more of the same in the coming years, this simple, easy-to-follow investment just might be your cup of tea.

Why Should I Care?

The "softs" ETN makes sense for foundational portfolios looking to capitalize on long-term supply and demand imbalances in these three staple commodities.

Upside

- A big awakening last year
- Emerging economy demand on top of stable base
- Big companies and countries don't control the market (unlike oil)

Downside

- Current commodity prices a bit frothy?
- Not diverse enough—just three commodities?
- ETN credit risk

Just the Facts

INCEPTION DATE: **June 24, 2008**

TOTAL ASSETS: **$58.2 million**

AVERAGE DAILY VOLUME: **24,000**

TOTAL HOLDINGS: **3**

PERCENT NORTH AMERICA HOLDINGS: **NM**

TOP 10 HOLDINGS PERCENTAGE (CONCENTRATION): **100%**

PORTFOLIO TURNOVER: **NM**   BENCHMARK: **NM**

BETA COEFFICIENT: **1.33**

R-SQUARED (1 YEAR): **49.76%**

1-YEAR RETURN: **75.75%**   BENCHMARK: **38.15%**

3-YEAR RETURN: **NA**   BENCHMARK: **-9.8%**

TRACKING ERROR (PRICE VS. NAV)   1 YEAR: **27.31%**   ASSET CLASS MEDIAN: **20.35%**

$10,000 Invested at inception	2006	2007	2008	2009	2010	2011
	$—	$—	$6,995	$10,041	$16,031	$16,041

What's Under the Hood

Symbol	Name	Percentage of fund
FSB	Sugar	35.13%
CT	Cotton No. 2	33.41%
KC	Coffee 'C'	31.46%

iPATH/Barclays
1 Churchill Place
London E14 5HP, England
(877) 764-7284
Website: *www.ipathetn.com*

Strategy/Sector

Now we get to thirty funds chosen to offer you exposure to identifiable (and we think, superior) investing strategies or to specific industries we think you should consider being exposed to. Examples of the former include the Powershares Buyback Achievers Portfolio, targeting companies with strong share buyback programs; and the latter, the Market Vectors Global Alternative Energy Fund, giving you exposure to an industry otherwise difficult to invest in. These funds have expenses ranging from 0.19 percent to 0.75 percent for the more esoteric and more international members of the group.

100 BEST STRATEGY: **FOUNDATION/ROTATIONAL**

100 BEST CATEGORY: **STRATEGY/SECTOR**

Market Vectors Agribusiness ETF

Ticker Symbol: MOO ❑ Issuer: Van Eck Associates ❑ Description: Specific Industry Equity Blend ❑ Geography: Global ❑ Morningstar Rating: 3 stars ❑ Marco Polo XTF Rating: 7.4 ❑ Yield: 0.59% ❑ Expense Ratio: 0.50% (Benchmark: 0.60%)

Stated Purpose

The investment seeks to replicate as closely as possible, before fees and expenses, the price and yield performance of the DAXglobal Agribusiness Index. The fund normally invests at least 80 percent of total assets in equity securities of U.S. and foreign companies primarily engaged in the business of agriculture, which derive at least 50 percent of their total revenues from agribusiness. Such companies may include small- and medium-capitalization companies. It is nondiversified.

Our Take

It would be easy to guess that we picked this fund simply for its clever

ticker symbol, but really there's much more to it than that. We think that in the long term agriculture is an excellent place for investors to be.

Why?

Because the world population will never stop eating. Moreover, we expect that food demand, and particularly demand for a broader and more complete Western-style assortment of foodstuffs will rise dramatically with the rise of the middle class, particularly in China and to some extent in other developing economies. This will, of course, not only maintain growth in food demand at normal population growth rates but should increase the consumption of major foodstuffs.

What we like about MOO is that it doesn't so much own companies that *produce* food; it owns companies that produce the materials and equipment to produce food—picks and shovels for gold miners, if you will. Monsanto, Potash Corp. of Saskatchewan, and Deere are good examples right at the top of the list. It also invests in companies that process and distribute food and foodstuffs, such as Archer Daniels Midland, Bunge, and ICI. In short, it is a nice blend of firms and sub-industries within the food theme.

The fund has done quite well in the past year and has sound fundamentals.

Why Should I Care?

This fund would be well placed as a long-term holding in a foundation portfolio but can also work for those wanting to play the agricultural commodity cycle, which has seen sharp ups and downs over the past three years.

Upside

- Well-balanced, strategic portfolio
- Right number of holdings, diverse but not overdiversified
- Large and liquid

Downside

- Vulnerable to commodity cycle downturns
- Could yield be higher and expenses lower?
- High energy prices can hurt these companies

Just the Facts

INCEPTION DATE: **August 31, 2007**

TOTAL ASSETS: **$5.3 billion**

AVERAGE DAILY VOLUME: **2.3 million**

TOTAL HOLDINGS: **46**

PERCENT NORTH AMERICA HOLDINGS: **52.3%**

TOP 10 HOLDINGS PERCENTAGE (CONCENTRATION): **58.1%**

PORTFOLIO TURNOVER: **20.0%**   BENCHMARK: **20.0%**

BETA COEFFICIENT: **0.88**

R-SQUARED (1 YEAR): **42.38%**

1-YEAR RETURN: **47.76%**   BENCHMARK: **30.69%**

3-YEAR RETURN: **-3.90%**   BENCHMARK: **3.34%**

TRACKING ERROR (PRICE VS. NAV)   1 YEAR: **15.55%**   ASSET CLASS MEDIAN: **10.41%**

$10,000 Invested at inception	2006	2007	2008	2009	2010	2011
	$—	$13,871	$6,848	$10,896	$13,399	$13,437

What's Under the Hood

Symbol	Name	Percentage of fund
POT	Potash Corp. of Saskatchewan Inc.	8.18%
MON	Monsanto Co.	7.78%
F34:SG	Wilmar International Ltd.	6.69%
DE	Deere & Co.	6.58%
SYNN	Syngenta AG	6.02%
BRFS	BRF Brasil Foods SA	5.01%
ADM	Archer Daniels Midland Co.	4.94%
MOS	Mosaic Co.	4.52%
YAR:NO	Yara International ASA	4.09%
AGU	Agrium Inc.	4.05%
6326:JP	Kubota Corp.	3.38%
IOICORP:MY	IOI Corporation Bhd	3.27%
CF	CF Industries Holdings Inc.	3.26%
BG	Bunge Ltd.	2.98%
CNH	CNH Global NV	2.67%
KLK:MY	Kuala Lumpur Kepong Bhd	2.30%
SQM	Sociedad Quimica y Minera de Chile SA	2.27%
E5H:SG	Golden Agri Resources Ltd.	2.17%
TSN	Tyson Foods Inc.	1.60%
TATE:GB	Tate and Lyle PLC	1.41%

Van Eck Global
335 Madison Avenue, 19th Floor
New York, NY 10017
(212) 293-2000
Website: *www.vaneck.com*

iShares MSCI Global Energy Sector Index Fund

Ticker Symbol: IXC ◻ Issuer: BlackRock/iShares ◻ Description: International Equity Sector Blend
◻ Geography: Global ◻ Morningstar Rating: 4 stars ◻ Marco Polo XTF Rating: 6.8 ◻ Yield: 1.91%
◻ Expense Ratio: 0.48% (Benchmark: 0.60%)

Stated Purpose

The investment seeks to replicate, net of expenses, the S&P Global Energy Sector Index. The fund invests at least 90 percent of its assets in securities of the index and in depositary receipts representing in the index. The index includes oil equipment and services, oil exploration and production, oil refinery, oil storage and transportation, and coal and uranium mining companies. The fund is nondiversified.

Our Take

After years of energy shortages and the spectacle of shrinking energy supplies hanging over your head, you may justifiably feel an urge to buy into this critical, strategic sector. You're not sure what energy company to buy, and you're not even sure what part of the energy industry you want to be in—oil exploration and production (E&P), refining and marketing, drilling and oil field service equipment, or on some non-oil extractive energy industry such as coal or uranium. But you still want to have a stake in this game.

Further, you would like that play to be international. International is

where the market growth is on the demand side—China, India, and other emerging countries. And further still, international seems to be where the oil is these days—when's the last time you heard about a big oil strike in the good old U.S. of A.? Natural gas, maybe, but really, the United States is well past its energy production prime.

The iShares MSCI Global Energy Sector fund is right in the sweet spot of the idea that energy is strategic, and international is where the supply and demand dynamics really occur. The fund emphasizes production and distribution and is centered on large-cap multinational names. It is about 86 percent oil and gas, 12 percent equipment and supplies, and the rest "other." The fund tracks its index well for an international fund and has done quite well over time, although it does tend to rise and fall with energy prices.

Why Should I Care?

This fund makes sense to give foundation portfolios a long-term energy component; it also works as a rotational play when energy markets and prices are strengthening.

Upside
- Adds energy and international component to portfolio
- Strong recent returns
- Large, liquid, and experienced

Downside
- Vulnerable to energy price cycles
- May be vulnerable to global political turmoil
- Yield, while okay, could be better?

Just the Facts

INCEPTION DATE: **November 12, 2001**

TOTAL ASSETS: **$1.3 billion**

AVERAGE DAILY VOLUME: **234,600**

TOTAL HOLDINGS: **86**

PERCENT NORTH AMERICA HOLDINGS: **65.9%**

TOP 10 HOLDINGS PERCENTAGE (CONCENTRATION): **52.21%**

PORTFOLIO TURNOVER: **5.0%**   BENCHMARK: **20.0%**

BETA COEFFICIENT: **1.20**

R-SQUARED (1 YEAR): **89.63%**

1-YEAR RETURN: **45.34%**   BENCHMARK: **30.69%**

3-YEAR RETURN: **-4.21%**   BENCHMARK: **3.34%**

TRACKING ERROR (PRICE VS. NAV)   1 YEAR: **7.52%**   ASSET CLASS MEDIAN: **10.41%**

$10,000 Invested at inception	2006	2007	2008	2009	2010	2011
	$25,456	$33,192	$20,781	$20,849	$29,149	$31,649

What's Under the Hood

Symbol	Name	Percentage of fund
XOM	Exxon Mobil Corp.	13.59%
CVX	Chevron Corp.	7.22%
BP_:GB	BP Plc	4.94%
RDSA:GB	Royal Dutch Shell Plc	4.52%

Symbol	Name	Percentage of fund
FP:FR	Total SA	4.44%
SLB	Schlumberger NV	4.25%
COP	ConocoPhillips	3.52%
RDSB:GB	Royal Dutch Shell Plc	3.47%
BG_:GB	BG Group Plc	2.79%
OXY	Occidental Petroleum Corp.	2.77%
PBR/A	Petroleo Brasileiro SA Petrobras	2.26%
ENI:IT	Eni SpA	2.13%
SU:CA	Suncor Energy Inc.	2.11%
HAL	Halliburton Co.	1.75%
APA	Apache Corp.	1.63%
CNQ:CA	Canadian Natural Resources Ltd.	1.54%
APC	Anadarko Petroleum Corp.	1.43%
883:HK	CNOOC Ltd.	1.25%
NOV	National Oilwell Varco Inc.	1.19%
BHI	Baker Hughes Inc.	1.17%

BlackRock/iShares
525 Washington Boulevard, Suite 1405
Jersey City, NJ 07310
(800) 474-2737
Website: *www.ishares.com*

100 BEST STRATEGY: **FOUNDATION**

100 BEST CATEGORY: **STRATEGY/SECTOR**

PowerShares S&P 500 High Quality Portfolio

Ticker Symbol: PIV ▫ Issuer: Invesco ▫ Description: Equity Index Strategic Selection ▫ Geography: U.S. ▫ Morningstar Rating: 1 star ▫ Marco Polo XTF Rating: 8.5 ▫ Yield: 1.39% ▫ Expense Ratio: 0.50% (Benchmark: 0.60%)

Stated Purpose

The investment seeks to replicate, net of expenses, the S&P 500 High Quality Rankings Index. The fund normally invests at least 90 percent of its total assets in common stocks that comprise the index. The index is composed of stocks identified by S&P Quality Ranking as high quality stocks. The fund is nondiversified.

Our Take

Anyone who has read and subscribes to the basic premises of our *100 Best Stocks You Can Buy* will like the PowerShares S&P 500 High Quality Portfolio. Why? It's simple—this fund contains a large number of the same names!

Now, before you jump to the conclusion that S&P simply took our book and created this index, the venerable ratings firm does have its own secret formula for determining "High Quality." They don't tell us much about it though, except that it contains "stocks with Quality Rankings of A- and above. The Standard & Poor's Quality Rankings System attempts to measure the growth and stability of earnings and the dividends record within a single rank, and has been calculated on common stocks since 1956."

Okay, the formula has been around for a while, and from the results, we suspect they're looking at a lot of the same things we're looking at, except no mention is made of the intangibles and company "story" we seek as a leading indicator of *future* financial performance. Regardless, nineteen of their top twenty-four stocks are also on our *100 Best Stocks* list, and thirty-six of their top forty-eight—that tracks pretty closely.

How could we possibly like any other fund better? We are a bit concerned about the yield of around

1.4 percent; our list is closer to 2.2 percent, and we wonder why their twelve-month performance was only 2 percent higher than the S&P benchmark, while ours was 7 percent higher. It could be a timing thing, as our measurement periods were different. Or, it could be that the fifty or sixty stocks out of their 132 that were not on the *100 Best* list were not so high quality. Or, it could be their "equal weighting" approach, where they don't ride their winners long enough. Regardless, for those looking for *100 Best Stocks* results with the simplicity of buying a single fund should look at this one, as well as First Trust Value Line ETF (FVI).

Why Should I Care?

This portfolio is a good way to capture a broad selection of "select or better" stocks, matching well with our current *100 Best Stocks You Can Buy* list. It fits best in a foundation portfolio.

Upside

- Tracks *100 Best Stocks* list
- S&P "high-quality" stocks have done well over time
- Safety: right amount of diversification

Downside

- "High quality" index basis not clear
- Could yield more?
- Could perform better? Equal weighting a hindrance?

Just the Facts

INCEPTION DATE: **December 6, 2005**

TOTAL ASSETS: **$120.4 million**

AVERAGE DAILY VOLUME: **51,900**

TOTAL HOLDINGS: **132**

PERCENT NORTH AMERICA HOLDINGS: **100%**

TOP 10 HOLDINGS PERCENTAGE (CONCENTRATION): **12.62%**

PORTFOLIO TURNOVER: **64.0%**   BENCHMARK: **20.0%**

BETA COEFFICIENT: **0.85**

R-SQUARED (1 YEAR): **93.76%**

1-YEAR RETURN: **32.91%**   BENCHMARK: **30.69%**

3-YEAR RETURN: **-4.72%**   BENCHMARK: **3.34%**

TRACKING ERROR (PRICE VS. NAV)   1 YEAR: **3.42%**   ASSET CLASS MEDIAN: **10.41%**

$10,000 Invested at inception	2006	2007	2008	2009	2010	2011
	$10,466	$12,182	$6,597	$7,320	$8,889	$9,619

What's Under the Hood

Symbol	Name	Percentage of fund
IBM	International Business Machines Corp.	1.33%
K	Kellogg Co.	1.31%
TGT	Target Corp.	1.30%
TJX	TJX Companies Inc.	1.30%
GIS	General Mills Inc.	1.30%
KO	Coca Cola Co.	1.28%
MKC	McCormick & Co Inc.	1.28%
FDO	Family Dollar Stores Inc.	1.26%
WMT	Wal-Mart Stores Inc.	1.26%
SYY	Sysco Corp.	1.26%
XOM	Exxon Mobil Corp.	1.25%
OMC	Omnicom Group Inc.	1.25%
HRL	Hormel Foods Corp.	1.25%
CL	Colgate Palmolive Co.	1.24%
NKE	Nike Inc.	1.24%
JNJ	Johnson & Johnson	1.24%

Symbol	Name	Percentage of fund
CVS	CVS Caremark Corp.	1.23%
UNH	Unitedhealth Group Inc.	1.23%
PG	Procter & Gamble Co.	1.22%
ROST	Ross Stores Inc.	1.22%

Invesco PowerShares Capital Management LLC
301 West Roosevelt Road
Wheaton, IL 60187
(800) 803-0903
Website: *www.invescopowershares.com*

PowerShares Morningstar Stock Investor Core Portfolio

Ticker Symbol: PYH ❑ Issuer: Invesco ❑ Description: Equity Large Cap Enhanced Index Selection ❑ Geography: U.S. ❑ Morningstar Rating: 1 star ❑ Marco Polo XTF Rating: 5.2 ❑ Yield: 1.37% ❑ Expense Ratio: 0.52% (Benchmark: 0.60%)

Stated Purpose

The investment seeks to replicate, net of expenses, the Morningstar StockInvestor Core Index. The fund invests at least 90 percent of its assets in common stocks that comprise the index. The index is comprised of approximately 50 stocks that have market capitalizations in excess of $100 million and have underlying businesses with a Morningstar Economic Moat Rating of narrow or wide and a Morningstar rating for stocks of at least 4 stars. The fund is nondiversified.

Our Take

Here's an idea we really like, and those of you who have read and follow our *100 Best Stocks You Can Buy* and other books in our series will see why. Morningstar, the index provider, describes their "StockInvestor" index as one that "invests in companies with established competitive advantages and generous free cash flows, trading at discounts to their intrinsic values." In short—companies with a "moat" and a 4-star Morningstar rating.

You could have taken these words right out of our *100 Best*

Stocks selection mantra. We look for so-called "moats" (competitive advantages and barriers to entry that protect a business, its brand, and ultimately, its pricing and profitability), cash flow, and price relative to value, among other things. We also look for dividends and price stability, which are not in abundance here—this portfolio has a more growth-oriented track. The index—and this fund—contain some of the more interesting, and frankly, more enlightened picks from our *100 Best Stocks* and *100 Best Aggressive Stocks* lists—Discover Financial Services, CarMax, Paychex, and others further down the list.

These companies, for the most part, are solid long-term performers. As Morningstar describes: "Given our focus on wide-moat companies, StockInvestor's model portfolios are poised to thrive in any economic climate. And thrive they have. For eight years, our picks have greatly outperformed the S&P 500."

Outperform it has, with a ten-year gain of approximately 103 percent compared to the S&P 500's 34 percent gain.

So we like the basis, and we like the individual stock selections, but wonder—why the underperformance in the last year and three-year time spans? We're not sure. Frankly, we're a bit surprised and think this fund could be a good value going forward.

Why Should I Care?

The PowerShares Morningstar Stock Investor Core Portfolio makes sense as a slightly more aggressive, growth-oriented component of a foundation portfolio.

Upside

- Interesting stock picks, congruent with our more aggressive *100 Best* picks
- Decent yield considering forty-six holdings, yet diverse enough
- Dynamic companies, won't be boring

Downside

- Recent underperformance
- High portfolio turnover
- Morningstar 1-star rating—for their own index!

Just the Facts

INCEPTION DATE: **December 1, 2006**

TOTAL ASSETS: **$16.9 million**

AVERAGE DAILY VOLUME: **2,800**

TOTAL HOLDINGS: **46**

PERCENT NORTH AMERICA HOLDINGS: **96.1%**

TOP 10 HOLDINGS PERCENTAGE (CONCENTRATION): **37.53%**

PORTFOLIO TURNOVER: **91.0%**   BENCHMARK: **20.0%**

BETA COEFFICIENT: **0.94**

R-SQUARED (1 YEAR): **88.30%**

1-YEAR RETURN: **21.30%**   BENCHMARK: **30.69%**

3-YEAR RETURN: **-8.64%**   BENCHMARK: **3.34%**

TRACKING ERROR (PRICE VS. NAV)   1 YEAR: **6.25%**   ASSET CLASS MEDIAN: **10.41%**

$10,000 Invested at inception	2006	2007	2008	2009	2010	2011
	$10,000	$11,453	$6,474	$7,147	$7,865	$8,349

What's Under the Hood

Symbol	Name	Percentage of fund
JOE	St Joe Co.	5.11%
EXC	Exelon Corp.	4.48%
CMP	Compass Minerals International Inc.	4.33%
ABT	Abbott Laboratories	4.08%
BRK/B	Berkshire Hathaway Inc.	3.57%
DFS	Discover Financial Services	3.52%
XOM	Exxon Mobil Corp.	3.20%
NVS	Novartis AG	3.11%
KMX	Carmax Inc.	3.08%
EBAY	eBay Inc.	2.97%
LOW	Lowes Companies Inc.	2.97%
GOOG	Google Inc.	2.83%
PAYX	Paychex Inc.	2.72%
APOL	Apollo Group Inc.	2.72%
PFE	Pfizer Inc.	2.49%
MA	Mastercard Inc.	2.49%
ADP	Automatic Data Processing Inc.	2.48%
CLD	Cloud Peak Energy Inc.	2.45%
ADSK	Autodesk Inc.	2.37%
JNJ	Johnson & Johnson	2.31%

Invesco PowerShares Capital Management LLC
301 West Roosevelt Road
Wheaton, IL 60187
(800) 803-0903
Website: *www.invescopowershares.com*

PowerShares S&P 500 Buy/Write Portfolio

Ticker Symbol: PBP ◻ Issuer: Invesco ◻ Description: Equity Large Cap Enhanced Strategy Fund ◻ Geography: U.S. ◻ Morningstar Rating: 3 stars ◻ Marco Polo XTF Rating: 2.9 ◻ Yield: 1.4%/7.73% ◻ Expense Ratio: 0.75% (Benchmark: 0.60%)

Stated Purpose

The investment seeks results that correspond generally to the price and yield performance, before fees and expenses, of the CBOE S&P 500 Buy/Write Index. The fund normally invests at least 80 percent of total assets in common stocks of the 500 companies included in the S&P 500 index and writes (sells) call options thereon. It writes (sells) one month call options on the S&P 500 Index, in order to generate income on its portfolio holdings each calendar month. The options generally are the prevailing price of the S&P 500 Index, and are expired in the next calendar month. The fund is nondiversified.

Our Take

The PowerShares S&P 500 Buy/Write Portfolio would appear on first glance to be a run-of-the mill, equity-weighted S&P 500 index tracking fund, say, like the SPDR S&P 500 ETF (SPY). But wait—there's something else. What's that "buy/write" thing? What's the "enhanced strategy" we mention in the Description?

This fund is based on, and in fact, includes, all S&P 500 stocks. But the "strategy enhancement" involves the *selling* of "covered call" options on the portfolio. Call options are the right to buy a particular stock (say, Microsoft) at a particular price (the "strike" price) on or before a particular date (the expiration date). An investor wanting to make a bet that Microsoft exceeds $25 by June 2012 would buy a June 25 call and pay a "premium" (like an insurance premium) for that right. If they paid a premium of $0.50 when the stock was selling for $24, and the stock rose to $26 at expiration, the option would be worth $1 and they would double their money.

But this fund isn't about *buying* options. It's about *selling* them to investors like the one just described. Selling them is also called writing them, hence the name of the fund. The fund buys the stock, and then writes call options. Why? To collect the premiums and pay those premiums back to investors in the form of a short-term capital gains distribution. Investors are effectively willing to give up a long-term gain on the stock to capture short-term income by selling options.

Okay, enough about options; to gain a better understanding of them, you can research in specialized books or at a number of investing sites. The point is made clear by the distribution yield, that is, the 7.73 percent this fund paid last year in distributions including the 1.4 percent dividend yield on the base stocks. The options generated enough yield to pay a very nice return.

Of course, the downside with this strategy is not only longer-term gains forgone in favor of current option income but also continued exposure to the downside of the market. But such a specialty fund is a good way to generate healthy income in a steady or slightly falling or rising market.

Why Should I Care?
This fund makes sense to spice up returns for an income-oriented portion of a foundation portfolio.

Upside
- High current yield
- Diversification
- Does well in a "sideways" or slightly down market

Downside
- Still exposed to market downside
- Does poorly in a sharply up or sharply down market
- High expense ratio

Just the Facts
INCEPTION DATE: **December 20, 2007**

TOTAL ASSETS: **$113.1 million**

AVERAGE DAILY VOLUME: **31,200**

TOTAL HOLDINGS: **500**

PERCENT NORTH AMERICA HOLDINGS: **98.8%**

TOP 10 HOLDINGS PERCENTAGE (CONCENTRATION): **19.64%**

PORTFOLIO TURNOVER: **61.0%**   BENCHMARK: **20.0%**

BETA COEFFICIENT: **0.47**

R-SQUARED (1 YEAR): **67.89%**

1-YEAR RETURN: **18.49%**   BENCHMARK: **30.69%**

3-YEAR RETURN: **0.0%**   BENCHMARK: **3.34%**

TRACKING ERROR (PRICE VS. NAV)   1 YEAR: **8.51%**   ASSET CLASS MEDIAN: **10.41%**

$10,000 Invested at inception	2006	2007	2008	2009	2010	2011
	$—	$10,000	$7,028	$8,788	$9,193	$9,373

What's Under the Hood

Symbol	Name	Percentage of fund
XOM	Exxon Mobil Corp.	3.38%
AAPL	Apple Inc.	3.09%
IBM	International Business Machines Corp.	1.89%
CVX	Chevron Corp.	1.80%
MSFT	Microsoft Corp.	1.75%
GE	General Electric Co.	1.63%
JNJ	Johnson & Johnson	1.53%
T	AT&T Inc.	1.49%
PG	Procter & Gamble Co.	1.47%
JPM	JPMorgan Chase and Co.	1.38%
KO	Coca Cola Co.	1.34%
GOOG	Google Inc.	1.32%
PFE	Pfizer Inc.	1.31%
WFC	Wells Fargo & Co.	1.27%
BRK/B	Berkshire Hathaway Inc.	1.10%
PM	Philip Morris International Inc.	1.09%
SLB	Schlumberger NV	1.05%
INTC	Intel Corp.	1.02%
ORCL	Oracle Corp.	1.02%
C	Citigroup Inc.	0.96%

Invesco PowerShares Capital Management LLC
301 West Roosevelt Road
Wheaton, IL 60187
(800) 803-0903
Website: *www.invescopowershares.com*

100 BEST STRATEGY: **FOUNDATION/ROTATIONAL**

100 BEST CATEGORY: **STRATEGY/SECTOR**

First Trust Value Line 100 ETF

Ticker Symbol: FVL ◻ Issuer: First Trust Advisors ◻ Description: Equity Specialty Index Blend ◻ Geography: U.S. ◻ Morningstar Rating: 1 star ◻ Marco Polo XTF Rating: 5.9 ◻ Yield: 0.11% ◻ Expense Ratio: 0.70% (Benchmark: 0.60%)

Stated Purpose

The investment seeks results that correspond generally to the price and yield (before the fund's fees and expenses) of an equity index called the Value Line 100 Index. The fund invests at least 90 percent of total assets in common stocks that comprise the index. The index is an equal-dollar weighted index that is designed to objectively identify and select 100 stocks from the universe of stocks to which Value Line assigns a number-one ranking in the Value Line Timeliness Ranking System.

Our Take

Like the two of us, those of you individual investors who have read and used the Value Line Investment Survey over the years have come to know, use, and appreciate their "timeliness" ranks as a valued investing tool. Typically, Value Line looks at industries and subindustries for what's in favor and what is not. In its own words, the publication "measures probable relative price performance of the approximately 1,700 stocks during the next six to twelve months on an easy-to-understand scale from 1 (Highest) to 5 (Lowest)." The "1" stocks are the 100 that are expected to perform best out of their 1,700-stock universe.

The scale has proven valuable over time. Value Line publishes some amazing statistics on its performance record. For instance, from 1965 through 2011, Timeliness Rank 1 stocks gained 39,478 percent through the years, or a 13.8 percent compounded annual rate of return. That compares to 5,366 percent and 9.0 percent respectively for Rank 2,338 percent and 3.2 percent for Rank 3, -52 percent and -1.6 percent for Rank 4, and -99 percent and -8.9 percent for Rank 5.

So a fund of Timeliness Rank 1 stocks is pretty compelling, and that's the rationale for this fund.

With that in mind, the recent performance has been so-so. We think that's a combination of the high expense ratio and the equal weighting, which brings higher turnover and reduces weighting on winners perhaps too soon. We also think that the recent volatility and economic shifts make for tough sledding for this kind of index, as what is "timely" can change fast. All that said, the basic investing idea is compelling and should do well over the longer term.

Why Should I Care?

We like this portfolio for more aggressive portions of foundation portfolios, or possibly for some rotation as the emphasis shifts to riskier and more aggressive growth stocks.

Upside
- Compelling index basis
- Good long-term track record
- Right amount of diversification

Downside
- Equal weighting may diminish performance (but also reduces risk)
- More volatile than most
- Relatively high expense ratio

Just the Facts

INCEPTION DATE: **June 12, 2003**

TOTAL ASSETS: **$76.2 million**

AVERAGE DAILY VOLUME: **105,500**

TOTAL HOLDINGS: **100**

PERCENT NORTH AMERICA HOLDINGS: **93.2%**

TOP 10 HOLDINGS PERCENTAGE (CONCENTRATION): **11.48%**

PORTFOLIO TURNOVER: **266.0%**   BENCHMARK: **20.0%**

BETA COEFFICIENT: **1.25**

R-SQUARED (1 YEAR): **86.26%**

1-YEAR RETURN: **38.03%**   BENCHMARK: **30.69%**

3-YEAR RETURN: **-4.46%**   BENCHMARK: **3.34%**

TRACKING ERROR (PRICE VS. NAV)   1 YEAR: **8.14%**   ASSET CLASS MEDIAN: **10.41%**

$10,000 Invested at inception	2006	2007	2008	2009	2010	2011
	$15,920	$19,096	$9,872	$11,131	$14,415	$15,232

What's Under the Hood

Symbol	Name	Percentage of fund
AVD	American Vanguard Corp.	1.22%
OXM	Oxford Industries Inc.	1.20%
GCO	Genesco Inc.	1.14%
HUN	Huntsman Corp.	1.12%
MTRN	Materion Corp.	1.12%
CF	CF Industries Holdings Inc.	1.12%
TGI	Triumph Group Inc.	1.12%
DPZ	Domino's Pizza Inc.	1.11%
AXL	American Axle and Manufacturing Holdings Inc.	1.11%
FCX	Freeport Mcmoran Copper and Gold Inc.	1.11%
RES	RPC Inc.	1.10%
IBM	International Business Machines Corp.	1.10%
DDS	Dillard's Inc.	1.09%
ADS	Alliance Data Systems Corp.	1.09%
DSW	DSW Inc.	1.09%
SJR	Shaw Communications Inc.	1.08%
CLF	Cliffs Natural Resources Inc.	1.08%
ARLP	Alliance Resource Partners LP	1.08%
IP	International Paper Co.	1.08%
SHS	Sauer Danfoss Inc.	1.08%

First Trust Portfolios L.P.
120 E. Liberty Drive, Suite 400
Wheaton, IL 60187
(800) 621-1675
Website: *www.ftportfolios.com*

100 BEST STRATEGY: **FOUNDATION**

100 BEST CATEGORY: **STRATEGY/SECTOR**

First Trust Value Line Equity Allocation ETF

Ticker Symbol: FVI ▫ Issuer: First Trust Advisors ▫ Description: Equity Specialty Index Blend ▫ Geography: U.S. ▫ Morningstar Rating: 3 stars ▫ Marco Polo XTF Rating: 4.2 ▫ Yield: 1.06% ▫ Expense Ratio: 0.70% (Benchmark: 0.60%)

Stated Purpose

The investment seeks results that correspond generally to the price and yield (before the fund's fees and expenses) of an equity index called the Value Line Equity Allocation Index. The fund invests at least 90 percent of assets in common stocks that comprise the index. The index is designed to objectively identify and select those stocks from the Value Line 1700 universe of stocks across market capitalizations and investment styles for growth and value that appear to have the greatest potential for capital appreciation.

Our Take

This fund is based on a relatively complex formulation of ratings taken from the Value Line Investment Survey universe of 1,700 stocks, which is designed to make up 95 percent of all the U.S total market capitalization.

Value Line rates each stock: 1 through 5 (1 is best, 5 is worst) for timeliness, safety, and technical (that is, stock price behavior). The Equity Allocation Index is derived by taking stocks with either a 1 or 2

rating in each of the three categories, then by selecting "those stocks that appear to have the greatest potential for capital appreciation" based on several factors, including price to cash flow, price to book value, return on assets, and recent price performance. Stocks are chosen from six style classifications based on growth and value for large-, medium-, and small-cap stocks, thus providing a balanced blend of styles. The index chooses the twenty-five top stocks from each of the six style "boxes," and they become part of the index. The index is weighted equally.

The result is a list mixing large and familiar names with smaller, less familiar, or unheard-of entries. It's an interesting mix, and we wish, like the First Trust Value Line 100 ETF (FVL), that they had avoided the equal weighting because it may have affected performance.

Why Should I Care?

This is a well-diversified portfolio with compelling selection criteria, and probably makes sense as a long-term foundation holding.

Upside

- Compelling index base
- Diversified but not too diversified
- Blends familiar names with new ones

Downside

- Lackluster performance
- High portfolio turnover
- Relatively high cost

Just the Facts

INCEPTION DATE: **December 5, 2006**

TOTAL ASSETS: **$7.22 million**

AVERAGE DAILY VOLUME: **5,500**

TOTAL HOLDINGS: **151**

PERCENT NORTH AMERICA HOLDINGS: **88.8%**

TOP 10 HOLDINGS PERCENTAGE (CONCENTRATION): **14.12%**

PORTFOLIO TURNOVER: **205.0%**   BENCHMARK: **20.0%**

BETA COEFFICIENT: **0.95**

R-SQUARED (1 YEAR): **96.14%**

1-YEAR RETURN: **24.24%**   BENCHMARK: **30.69%**

3-YEAR RETURN: **-5.04%**   BENCHMARK: **3.34%**

TRACKING ERROR (PRICE VS. NAV)   1 YEAR: **4.84%**   ASSET CLASS MEDIAN: **10.41%**

$10,000 Invested at inception	2006	2007	2008	2009	2010	2011
	$10,000	$10,465	$6,755	$9,063	$10,862	$11,099

What's Under the Hood

Symbol	Name	Percentage of fund
AET	Aetna Inc.	1.53%
ACN	Accenture Public Ltd. Co.	1.45%
IBM	International Business Machines Corp.	1.44%
CHK	Chesapeake Energy Corp.	1.44%
EL	Estee Lauder Cos. Inc.	1.43%
LLY	Eli Lilly And Co.	1.43%
MRO	Marathon Oil Corp.	1.42%

Symbol	Name	Percentage of fund
GILD	Gilead Sciences Inc.	1.42%
TJX	TJX Companies Inc.	1.40%
TEL	TE Connectivity Ltd.	1.37%
MAT	Mattel Inc.	1.34%
CLF	Cliffs Natural Resources Inc.	1.33%
COP	ConocoPhillips	1.30%
BCR	C R Bard Inc.	1.30%
MSFT	Microsoft Corp.	1.29%
STJ	St Jude Medical Inc.	1.28%
ALTR	Altera Corp.	1.27%
TWX	Time Warner Inc.	1.24%
XOM	Exxon Mobil Corp.	1.24%
TYC	Tyco International Ltd.	1.23%

First Trust Portfolios L.P.
120 E. Liberty Drive, Suite 400
Wheaton, IL 60187
(800) 621-1675
Website: *www.ftportfolios.com*

100 BEST STRATEGY: **FOUNDATION**

100 BEST CATEGORY: **STRATEGY/SECTOR**

PowerShares Buyback Achievers

Ticker Symbol: PKW ▫ Issuer: Invesco ▫ Description: Equity Enhanced Strategy Blend ▫ Geography: U.S. ▫ Morningstar Rating: 5 stars ▫ Marco Polo XTF Rating: 3.7 ▫ Yield: 0.60% ▫ Expense Ratio: 0.70% (Benchmark: 0.60%)

Stated Purpose

The investment seeks results that correspond generally to the price and yield (before the fund's fees and expenses) of an equity index called the Mergent Buyback Achievers Index. The fund normally invests at least 90 percent of total assets in common stocks that comprise the Buyback Achievers Index.

Our Take

Over time, whether or not a company thinks its own shares are a good value is one of the better indicators of stock performance. The reasons are pretty simple: the company and its managers, after all, should have the best idea of what the company is really worth today and in the future. If a stock is selling cheap, so the model goes, a company focused on shareholder value may well want to buy back and retire shares to improve the earnings and thus the value of the shareholders' shares.

So companies that buy back stock, in theory, anyway, view their stock as cheap and are oriented to delivering shareholder value—both being compelling arguments in favor of buying shares in such a company. But companies buy back shares for other reasons too, like to fund stock purchase and stock incentive plans for employees. Companies may also buy back shares when they have cash on hand they simply don't know what to do with.

The latter two reasons send a less-favorable signal to investors. But we feel that for the most part, companies that persistently buy back shares and particularly those that reduce share counts over time by doing so are good values.

The PowerShares Buyback Achievers portfolio capitalizes on companies with a strong long-term buyback performance and has done well as the markets have recovered from the 2008 dip, although not so well since the 2006 fund inception. The record amounts of cash held by corporations today and the August 2011 market jitters suggest that these "achievers" will have plenty of ammo to keep buying shares, and we think this gives a built-in platform for future success. We also like the resulting portfolio of stocks on its own merits.

Why Should I Care?

This fund makes sense as a long-term value holding for a foundation portfolio.

Upside

- Compelling rationale
- Strong recovery from 2008 dip
- Cash rich companies may step up buybacks

Downside

- Different reasons for buybacks
- Overall return since 2006 not that strong
- High expense ratio

Just the Facts

INCEPTION DATE: **December 20, 2006**

TOTAL ASSETS: **$43 million**

AVERAGE DAILY VOLUME: **18,000**

TOTAL HOLDINGS: **143**

PERCENT NORTH AMERICA HOLDINGS: **97.4%**

TOP 10 HOLDINGS PERCENTAGE (CONCENTRATION): **40.12%**

PORTFOLIO TURNOVER: **26.0%**   BENCHMARK: **20.0%**

BETA COEFFICIENT: **0.87**

R-SQUARED (1 YEAR): **85.99%**

1-YEAR RETURN: **36.46%**   BENCHMARK: **30.69%**

3-YEAR RETURN: **9.94%**   BENCHMARK: **3.34%**

TRACKING ERROR (PRICE VS. NAV)   1 YEAR: **4.94%**   ASSET CLASS MEDIAN: **10.41%**

$10,000 Invested at inception	2006	2007	2008	2009	2010	2011
	$10,000	$9,835	$6,529	$10,110	$11,220	$10,894

What's Under the Hood

Symbol	Name	Percentage of fund
IBM	International Business Machines Corp.	5.56%
WMT	Wal-Mart Stores Inc.	5.04%
UNH	UnitedHealth Group Inc.	4.50%
HPQ	Hewlett Packard Co.	4.46%
AMGN	Amgen Inc.	4.17%
BMY	Bristol Myers Squibb Co.	4.07%
DTV	DirecTV	3.35%
TWX	Time Warner Inc.	3.21%
WAG	Walgreen Co.	3.01%
TGT	Target Corp.	2.97%
TXN	Texas Instruments Inc.	2.92%
GILD	Gilead Sciences Inc.	2.80%
LOW	Lowes Companies Inc.	2.38%
LMT	Lockheed Martin Corp.	2.20%
BIIB	Biogen Idec Inc.	2.11%
MHS	Medco Health Solutions Inc.	2.10%
WLP	Wellpoint Inc.	2.03%
TRV	Travelers Companies Inc.	1.95%
TJX	TJX Companies Inc.	1.81%
MCK	McKesson Corp.	1.73%

Invesco PowerShares Capital Management LLC
301 West Roosevelt Road
Wheaton, IL 60187
(800) 803-0903
Website: *www.invescopowershares.com*

100 BEST STRATEGY: **FOUNDATION**

100 BEST CATEGORY: **STRATEGY/SECTOR**

PowerShares Preferred Portfolio

Ticker Symbol: PGX ❑ Issuer: Invesco ❑ Description: Preferred Equity Blend ❑ Geography: Global ❑ Morningstar Rating: NR ❑ Marco Polo XTF Rating: 9.0 ❑ Yield: 6.68% ❑ Expense Ratio: 0.50% (Benchmark: 0.48%)

Stated Purpose

The investment seeks results that correspond generally to the price and yield (before the fund's fees and expenses) of an index called the BofA Merrill Lynch Core Fixed Rate Preferred Securities Index (the "Underlying Index"). The fund normally invests at least 80 percent of total assets in fixed rate U.S. dollar-denominated preferred securities. It normally invests at least 90 percent of total assets in the securities that comprise the ML Preferred index.

Our Take

Preferred stock is one of those dark corners of the investing world. For a corporation, a preferred stock is like a bond that never matures, or at least, doesn't have a specified maturity date. The company gets your capital to use for its purposes and pays you a decent return, and you have priority over common stockholders (but less than bondholders) in case of bankruptcy. Since there is no maturity date, the returns are often pretty attractive. But you don't get to participate in earnings

growth or any dividend growth that may occur; that "bennie" is reserved for common stockholders.

So why would you buy a preferred stock? Very simple—to get a good yield, and so it is with the PowerShares Preferred Portfolio. The yield of almost 6.7 percent is attractive in today's low interest rate environment.

The main risk, of course, is that interest rates rise, making these investments relatively less attractive as other higher-rate investments are available. What happens? The stock price goes down to effectively adjust the yield rate to market rates (this is called "interest rate risk"). Since there is no specified maturity, where you're more or less guaranteed to get your full principal back (like bonds), this risk is greater. But it's hard to get such a yield these days on a diverse portfolio.

Why Should I Care?

The PowerShares Preferred Portfolio makes sense for the income-generating portion of a foundation portfolio.

Upside
- High yield
- Safe from market risk, downturns (beta = 0.02)
- Right amount of diversification

Downside
- Vulnerable to interest rate hikes
- A lot of financial stocks
- Boring, will miss out on company successes

Just the Facts

INCEPTION DATE: **January 31, 2008**

TOTAL ASSETS: **$1.4 billion**

AVERAGE DAILY VOLUME: **411,000**

TOTAL HOLDINGS: **81**

PERCENT NORTH AMERICA HOLDINGS: **75.3%**

TOP 10 HOLDINGS PERCENTAGE (CONCENTRATION): **40.79%**

PORTFOLIO TURNOVER: **12.0%**   BENCHMARK: **20.0%**

BETA COEFFICIENT: **0.02**

R-SQUARED (1 YEAR): **0.56%**

1-YEAR RETURN: **13.3%**   BENCHMARK: **30.69%**

3-YEAR RETURN: **2.26%**   BENCHMARK: **3.34%**

TRACKING ERROR (PRICE VS. NAV)   1 YEAR: **14.16%**   ASSET CLASS MEDIAN: **10.41%**

$10,000 Invested at inception	2006	2007	2008	2009	2010	2011
	$—	$—	$6,647	$7,933	$8,902	$9,323

What's Under the Hood

Symbol	Name	Percentage of fund
WFC.PJ	Wells Fargo & Co.	5.41%
C.PN	Citigroup Capital XIII	4.71%
BCS.PD	Barclays Bank Plc	4.55%
C.PJ	Citigroup Capital XII	4.15%
JPM.PI	J P Morgan Chase & Co.	3.94%
MSZ	Morgan Stanley Capital Trust VII	3.74%

Symbol	Name	Percentage of fund
HCS.PB	HSBC Holdings Plc	3.66%
BML.PQ	Bank of America Corp.	3.66%
BAC.PH	Bank of America Corp.	3.44%
HCS	HSBC Holdings Plc	3.34%
GEC	General Electric Capital	6.10%
DKT	Deutsche Bank Contingent Capital Trust V	2.71%
USB.PJ	USB Capital XI	2.63%
WB.PB	Wachovia Capital Trust IV	2.50%
PSA.PQ	Public Storage	2.50%
JPM.PJ	J P Morgan Chase Capital X	2.46%
CFC.PB	Countrywide Capital V	2.37%
AEH	AEGON NV	2.22%
DTT	Deutsche Bank Capital Funding Trust IX	1.91%
CCW	Comcast 7.00% Notes	1.66%

Invesco PowerShares Capital Management LLC
301 West Roosevelt Road
Wheaton, IL 60187
(800) 803-0903
Website: *www.invescopowershares.com*

100 BEST STRATEGY: **FOUNDATION/ROTATIONAL**

100 BEST CATEGORY: **STRATEGY/SECTOR**

Guggenheim Insider Sentiment ETF

Ticker Symbol: NFO ◻ Issuer: Guggenheim Funds Distributors, Inc. ◻ Description: Equity Enhanced Strategy Blend ◻ Geography: U.S. ◻ Morningstar Rating: 5 stars ◻ Marco Polo XTF Rating: 7.6 ◻ Yield: 0.55% ◻ Expense Ratio: 0.60% (Benchmark: 0.60%)

Stated Purpose

The investment seeks results that correspond generally to the performance, before the fund's fees and expenses, of an equity index called the Sabrient Insider Sentiment Index. The fund invests at least 90 percent of total assets in common stocks, ADRs, and MLPs (Master Limited Partnerships) that comprise the index and depositary receipts representing common stocks included in the index. It generally invests in all of the securities comprising the index in proportion to their weightings in the index. The index is comprised of approximately

100 securities selected, based on investment and other criteria, from a broad universe of U.S.-traded securities, including MLPs and ADRs.

Our Take

If a company's top managers are buying its stock, wouldn't you want to also? After all, they should know the most about the business, its products, and its customers, right? They should know how well the company is doing today and have a pretty good idea how it will do in the future based on things we individual investors haven't a clue about.

Put differently—wouldn't we all like to be "insiders," knowing more about the company's business and prospects than the average schmo? Well, we can't be. Even if our best friends are insiders, we can't trade on information they provide about their companies. That's illegal. Rats. What do we do? We can watch the SEC filings to see what insiders are legally doing with their own company's shares. If they're buying, that's

a compelling reason to buy. That's insider information enough.

And so why not create an index and a fund that does nothing but buy companies that are being bought by their insiders? That's what the Guggenheim Insider Sentiment ETF is all about, and its track record speaks for itself.

Why Should I Care?

This fund makes sense to capture longer-term growth prospects in a cornerstone portfolio and might also make sense as a rotational holding during periods of market turbulence when insiders are more likely to buy.

Upside

- Very compelling strategy
- Interesting portfolio; some names you wouldn't think of
- Solid performance

Downside

- Insiders don't *always* know what they're doing
- A bit expensive
- Equal weighting may dilute returns

Just the Facts

INCEPTION DATE: **September 21, 2006**

TOTAL ASSETS: **$176.7 million**

AVERAGE DAILY VOLUME: **79,800**

TOTAL HOLDINGS: **101**

PERCENT NORTH AMERICA HOLDINGS: **94.3%**

TOP 10 HOLDINGS PERCENTAGE (CONCENTRATION): **11.50%**

PORTFOLIO TURNOVER: **65.0%**   BENCHMARK: **20.0%**

BETA COEFFICIENT: **1.11**

R-SQUARED (1 YEAR): **92.0%**

1-YEAR RETURN: **43.09%**   BENCHMARK: **30.69%**

3-YEAR RETURN: **13.46%**   BENCHMARK: **3.34%**

TRACKING ERROR (PRICE VS. NAV)   1 YEAR: **5.16%**   ASSET CLASS MEDIAN: **10.41%**

$10,000 Invested at inception	2006	2007	2008	2009	2010	2011
	$10,802	$11,756	$7,370	$10,891	$13,766	$15,241

What's Under the Hood

Symbol	Name	Percentage of fund
HFC	HollyFrontier Corp.	1.29%
VFC	VF Corp.	1.25%
SCL	Stepan Co.	1.21%
FOSL	Fossil Inc.	1.20%
WFM	Whole Foods Market Inc.	1.20%
MKTX	Marketaxess Holdings Inc.	1.18%
SCSS	Select Comfort Corp.	1.17%
LAD	Lithia Motors Inc.	1.16%
KEG	Key Energy Services Inc.	1.15%
BPFH	Boston Private Financial Hldg Inc.	1.13%
AXL	American Axle and Manufacturing Holdings Inc.	1.13%
WTI	W&T Offshore Inc.	1.12%
KRO	KRONOS Worldwide Inc.	1.12%
ALJ	Alon USA Energy Inc.	1.11%
TSO	Tesoro Corp.	1.11%
DDS	Dillard's Inc.	1.09%
EE	El Paso Electric Co.	1.08%
COH	Coach Inc.	1.08%
ANF	Abercrombie & Fitch Co.	1.08%
HUN	Huntsman Corp.	1.08%

Guggenheim Funds Distributors, Inc.
2455 Corporate West Drive
Lisle, IL 60532
(888) 949-3837
Website: *www.guggenheimfunds.com*

Guggenheim Defensive Equity ETF

Ticker Symbol: DEF ◻ Issuer: Guggenheim Funds Distributors, Inc. ◻ Description: Equity Enhanced Strategy Blend ◻ Geography: U.S. ◻ Morningstar Rating: 5 stars ◻ Marco Polo XTF Rating: 6.0 ◻ Yield: 1.45% ◻ Expense Ratio: 0.60% (Benchmark: 0.60%)

Stated Purpose

The investment seeks results that correspond generally to the performance, before the fund's fees and expenses, of an equity index called the Sabrient Defensive Equity Index. The fund invests at least 90 percent of total assets in common stock, ADRs, and MLPs (Master Limited Partnerships) that comprise the index and depositary receipts representing common stocks included in the index. The index is comprised of approximately 100 securities selected, based on investment and other criteria, from a broad universe of U.S.-traded securities.

Our Take

The Guggenheim website for the underlying Sabrient Defensive Equity describes the mechanics and rationale of this index and stock selection pretty well, if with a bit too much jargon: "These companies selected have potentially superior risk-return profiles during periods of stock market weakness, but still offer the potential for gains during periods of market strength. The universe of companies includes approximately

1,000 listed companies, generally with market capitalizations in excess of $1 billion."

It goes on to clarify: "The Index does not take the traditional approach to defensive portfolios by focusing solely upon low-beta, noncyclical, 'steady-Eddy' stocks. Instead, using a rules-based quantitative approach, the Index selects stocks that reflect qualities such as a strong balance sheet, dividend payments, conservative accounting practices, and a recent history of out-performance during weak market days."

This does sound like a pretty good way to select stocks, doesn't it? Indeed, the fund outperformed the S&P 500 benchmark during the down cycle 2008–2010, and almost kept up with it during the relative boom times of 2010–2011. Indeed, that's something most defensive portfolios don't do. Most do better during downturns but significantly underperform during upturns.

So while the performance stats aren't stellar, at least in theory you should be able to get through the night without losing too much sleep about forgone potential gains. That said, we might lose a little sleep over the top-holding, Chipotle, which is trading today in the mid-$200 range. While it's an excellent company and an excellent performer, we'd hardly consider it "defensive." The rest of the portfolio does look more defensive, and the equal weighting is defense-oriented, but we agree, this fund does have some growth potential too.

Why Should I Care?

This portfolio can be used as a slightly safer core equity component of a foundation portfolio and in certain situations, in the rotational portfolio, although there are many funds that most would consider safer.

Upside
- Not *just* about reducing risk
- A lot of *100 Best* stocks
- Safety: right amount of diversification

Downside
- Not as defensive as the name implies
- Chipotle number one on list?
- Small and possibly illiquid

Just the Facts

INCEPTION DATE: **December 15, 2006**

TOTAL ASSETS: **$26.5 million**

AVERAGE DAILY VOLUME: **79,800**

TOTAL HOLDINGS: **101**

PERCENT NORTH AMERICA HOLDINGS: **91.6%**

TOP 10 HOLDINGS PERCENTAGE (CONCENTRATION): **11.26%**

PORTFOLIO TURNOVER: **33.0%**   BENCHMARK: **20.0%**

BETA COEFFICIENT: **0.55**

R-SQUARED (1 YEAR): **75.99%**

1-YEAR RETURN: **30.0%**   BENCHMARK: **30.69%**

3-YEAR RETURN: **6.4%**   BENCHMARK: **3.34%**

TRACKING ERROR (PRICE VS. NAV)   1 YEAR: **7.79%**   ASSET CLASS MEDIAN: **10.41%**

$10,000 Invested at inception	2006	2007	2008	2009	2010	2011
	$10,000	$10,466	$7,295	$8,291	$10,653	$10,531

What's Under the Hood

Symbol	Name	Percentage of fund
CMG	Chipotle Mexican Grill Inc.	1.26%
VFC	VF Corp.	1.19%
DLTR	Dollar Tree Inc.	1.17%
MCD	McDonald's Corp.	1.13%
FLO	Flowers Foods Inc.	1.12%
SJR	Shaw Communications Inc.	1.12%
WPZ	Williams Partners LP	1.11%
FE	Firstenergy Corp.	1.11%
ARLP	Alliance Resource Partners LP	1.09%
SYY	Sysco Corp.	1.09%
CNP	Centerpoint Energy Inc.	1.08%
CLX	Clorox Co.	1.08%
ERIE	Erie Indemnity Co.	1.08%
ERF	Enerplus Corp.	1.07%
DRI	Darden Restaurants Inc.	1.07%
KFT	Kraft Foods Inc.	1.06%
BCE	BCE Inc.	1.06%
NI	NiSource Inc.	1.06%
HNZ	H J Heinz Co.	1.06%
MMP	Magellan Midstream Partners LP	1.06%

Guggenheim Funds Distributors, Inc.
2455 Corporate West Drive
Lisle, IL 60532
(888) 949-3837
Website: *www.guggenheimfunds.com*

PowerShares Emerging Markets Infrastructure Portfolio

Ticker Symbol: PXR ❑ Issuer: Invesco ❑ Description: Equity Industry Specific Blend ❑ Geography: Global ❑ Morningstar Rating: NR ❑ Marco Polo XTF Rating: 1.7 ❑ Yield: 1.12% ❑ Expense Ratio: 0.75% (Benchmark: 0.60%)

Stated Purpose

The investment seeks to correspond (before fees and expenses) generally to the price and yield performance of S-Network Emerging Infrastructure Builders Index. The fund normally invests at least 90 percent of total assets in the securities and American Depositary Receipts (ADRs) and Global Depositary Receipts (GDRs) based on the securities that comprise the underlying index.

Our Take

We think that infrastructure in general is one of the most compelling broad investing themes for the next several years. Why? Because there is a pervasive global demand for infrastructure that, in our opinion, hasn't been matched for perhaps a century. That demand comes from two sources. First, there's the replacement of aging infrastructure in the developed world. Although roads, airports, and railways are part of this, most of the infrastructure we're talking about is of the type that you

don't see or think about—water pipes, sewer pipes, electrical transmission lines, and so forth. Much of this infrastructure hasn't been replaced since it was put in new as much as 130 years ago. Other funds on our *100 Best ETFs* list addressing this first need are the SPDR FTSE/Macquarie Global 100 Infrastructure ETF (GII) and the First Trust NASDAQ Clean Edge Smartgrid Infrastructure Index (GRID).

The second and more obvious infrastructure market is in the emerging countries: the Chinas and Indias of the world with booming economies and infrastructures struggling to keep up. We seek investments that capture the essence of both infrastructures, and we look for investments in companies that build or replace the infrastructure, not just operate it. This is where the PowerShares Emerging Markets Infrastructure Portfolio comes in.

The description of the underlying index by S-Net tells the rest: "S-Network Infrastructure Builders Indexes are designed to capture the collective performance of companies engaged in the construction, development and maintenance of infrastructure only and exclude companies that manage or operate infrastructure on an ongoing basis, such as public utilities. The indexes include companies engaged in the following sectors: a) Construction and Engineering, b) Construction Machinery, c) Construction Materials, d) Diversified Metals & Mining, f) Heavy Electrical Equipment, g) Industrial Machinery, and h) Steel."

There you have it. This index is further refined for emerging markets, mainly China, India, Taiwan, Russia, and others. As you can see from the performance data, this fund has done quite well since its late 2008 inception.

Why Should I Care?

This fund makes sense as a cornerstone long-term infrastructure play and as a play in emerging international markets, all rolled into one, primarily for a foundation portfolio.

Upside
- Attractive niche
- Good way to play emerging markets
- Strong performance

Downside
- Not global-recession-proof
- High expense ratio
- Might be expensive to buy now

Just the Facts

INCEPTION DATE: **October 16, 2008**

TOTAL ASSETS: **$234.6 million**

AVERAGE DAILY VOLUME: **30,900**

TOTAL HOLDINGS: **82**

PERCENT NORTH AMERICA HOLDINGS: **4.5%**

TOP 10 HOLDINGS PERCENTAGE (CONCENTRATION): **30.78%**

PORTFOLIO TURNOVER: **36.0%**   BENCHMARK: **20.0%**

BETA COEFFICIENT: **1.28**

R-SQUARED (1 YEAR): **67.24%**

1-YEAR RETURN: **37.74%**   BENCHMARK: **30.69%**

3-YEAR RETURN: **NA**   BENCHMARK: **3.34%**

TRACKING ERROR (PRICE VS. NAV)   1 YEAR: **13.99%**   ASSET CLASS MEDIAN: **10.41%**

$10,000 Invested at inception	2006	2007	2008	2009	2010	2011
	$—	$—	$11,225	$21,495	$26,930	$26,697

What's Under the Hood

Symbol	Name	Percentage of fund
914:HK	Anhui Conch Cement Co. Ltd.	3.85%
VALE	Vale SA	3.42%
CAT	Caterpillar Inc.	3.31%
1101	Taiwan Cement Corp.	3.21%
358:HK	Jiangxi Copper Co. Ltd.	3.17%
ABB:SE	Abb Ltd.	3.10%
MNOD:GB	GMK Noril'skiy nikel' OAO	2.93%
LTOD:GB	Larsen and Toubro Ltd.	2.84%
MUR:ZA	Murray and Roberts Holdings Ltd.	2.55%
1072:HK	Dongfang Electric Corp Ltd.	2.35%
ATCO_A:SE	Atlas Copco AB	2.26%
DIALOG:MY	Dialog Group Bhd	2.23%
CAP	Cap SA	2.17%
INTP:ID	Indocement Tunggal Prakarsa Tbk PT	2.10%
SMGR:ID	Semen Gresik (Persero) Tbk PT	2.06%
1618:HK	Metallurgical Corp Of China Ltd.	2.04%
WBO:ZA	Wilson Bayly Holmes Ovcon Ltd.	2.02%
MYPK3:BR	Iochpe Maxion SA	1.84%
2006	Tung Ho Steel Enterprise Corp.	1.73%
ARI	—	1.72%

Invesco PowerShares Capital Management LLC
301 West Roosevelt Road
Wheaton, IL 60187
(800) 803-0903
Website: *www.invescopowershares.com*

100 BEST STRATEGY: **FOUNDATION**

100 BEST CATEGORY: **STRATEGY/SECTOR**

SPDR FTSE/Macquarie Global 100 Infrastructure ETF

Ticker Symbol: GII ▫ Issuer: State Street Global Advisors (SSGA) ▫ Description: Equity Industry Specific Blend ▫ Geography: Global ▫ Morningstar Rating: 1 star ▫ Marco Polo XTF Rating: 2.4 ▫ Yield: 3.87% ▫ Expense Ratio: 0.59% (Benchmark: 0.60%)

Stated Purpose

The investment seeks to track the price and yield performance, before fees and expenses, of the Macquarie Global Infrastructure 100 Index. The fund invests at least 80 percent of assets in securities that comprise the index. The index measures the performance of companies within the infrastructure industry, principally those engaged in management, ownership, and operation of infrastructure and utility assets.

Our Take

We think one of the strongest investing themes of the age is and will be the replacement and efficiency enhancement of common infrastructure in developed countries. Much of this infrastructure—especially the kind you don't see or think about such as water pipes, sewer pipes, and electrical transmission infrastructure, needs to be replaced. A lot of it was first installed as much as 130 years ago.

In keeping with that theme, the SPDR FTSE/Macquarie Global 100 Infrastructure ETF tracks the 100 largest companies in the infrastructure industry and is a blend of infrastructure creators and infrastructure operators—primarily utilities. Some of these utilities, like Southern Company, are involved both in infrastructure creation and infrastructure operation. The utility emphasis provides a high current yield and a degree of defense against economic downturns. Currently, utility operators make up about 80 percent of the fund; it's also split about 50–50 between North American and international companies.

Why Should I Care?

This portfolio provides current income, some long-term growth prospects, and some defensiveness primarily for a foundation portfolio.

Upside

• Attractive yield
• Some international diversification
• Some defensive strength

Downside

• Vulnerable to interest rate hikes
• Some global economic sensitivity
• Maybe too dominated by utilities?

Just the Facts

INCEPTION DATE: **January 25, 2007**

TOTAL ASSETS: **$42.7 million**

AVERAGE DAILY VOLUME: **4,200**

TOTAL HOLDINGS: **99**

PERCENT NORTH AMERICA HOLDINGS: **49.7%**

TOP 10 HOLDINGS PERCENTAGE (CONCENTRATION): **31.76%**

PORTFOLIO TURNOVER: **6.0%**   BENCHMARK: **20.0%**

BETA COEFFICIENT: **0.748**

R-SQUARED (1 YEAR): **54.58%**

1-YEAR RETURN: **21.86%**   BENCHMARK: **30.69%**

3-YEAR RETURN: **-5.1%**   BENCHMARK: **3.34%**

TRACKING ERROR (PRICE VS. NAV)   1 YEAR: **9.31%**   ASSET CLASS MEDIAN: **10.41%**

$10,000 Invested at inception	2006	2007	2008	2009	2010	2011
	$—	$12,125	$8,316	$9,236	$9,341	$9,840

What's Under the Hood

Symbol	Name	Percentage of fund
GSZ:FR	Gdf Suez SA	4.82%
EOAN:DE	EON AG	4.58%
ENEL:IT	Enel SpA	3.53%
IBE:ES	Iberdrola SA	3.16%
NG_:GB	National Grid PLC	2.99%
SO	Southern Co.	2.91%
TRP:CA	TransCanada Corp.	2.54%
EXC	Exelon Corp.	2.53%
D	Dominion Resources Inc.	2.45%
CNA:GB	Centrica PLC	2.25%
ENB:CA	Enbridge Inc.	2.21%
DUK	Duke Energy Corp.	2.15%
NEE	NextEra Energy Inc.	2.02%
RWE:DE	Rwe AG	1.81%
SSE:GB	Scottish and Southern Energy PLC	1.74%
FE	Firstenergy Corp.	1.62%

Symbol	Name	Percentage of fund
WMB	Williams Companies Inc.	1.61%
AEP	American Electric Power Co Inc.	1.54%
SE	Spectra Energy Corp.	1.51%
PEG	Public Service Enterprise Group Inc.	1.45%

State Street Global Advisors
State Street Financial Center
1 Lincoln Street
Boston, MA 02111–2900
Phone: (617) 786-3000
Website: *www.spdrs.com*

100 BEST STRATEGY: **FOUNDATION/ROTATIONAL**

100 BEST CATEGORY: **STRATEGY/SECTOR**

Market Vectors Gold Miners ETF

Ticker Symbol: GDX ▫ Issuer: Van Eck Associates ▫ Description: Equity Industry Specific Large/Mid Cap Fund ▫ Geography: Global ▫ Morningstar Rating: 2 stars ▫ Marco Polo XTF Rating: 6.0 ▫ Yield: 0.67% ▫ Expense Ratio: 0.55% (Benchmark: 0.60%)

Stated Purpose

The investment seeks to replicate as closely as possible, before fees and expenses, the price and yield performance of the NYSE Arca Gold Miners Index. The fund generally normally invests at least 80 percent of its total assets in common stocks and American Depositary Receipts (ADRs) of companies involved in the gold mining industry.

Our Take

One doesn't have to ponder long these days to understand the allure of gold, with today's volatile economy and questions about the long-term oversupply and viability of paper currency. We won't go into that discussion here, but suffice it to say a great many investors these days want at least some gold in their portfolio.

Those investors can buy gold bars, but then they have to store them. Or they can buy gold through a fund that owns the stuff directly, like the iShares Comex Gold Trust (IAU)—another *100 Best ETF*, but then come the vagaries of daily price movements and those of commodity fund ownership in general. So a third way to make a stake in gold is to buy the companies that mine it.

The Market Vectors Gold Miners ETF owns companies that do just that—mine gold. Now you have a layer of management helping to run your show by making profits mining gold, which may (or may not) bring more return than the gold itself. You have the promise of more gold in the ground—somewhere—which could also bring a growth opportunity somewhere down the road. But now you also have companies that need to be valued, always an imprecise process. Pick your poison.

The Market Vectors Gold Miners ETF invests in primarily larger, steadier, less speculative names in the business, and is about 80 percent concentrated in North America. If you want a more aggressive ride, see the sister Market Vectors Junior Gold Miners (GDXJ), also on our *100 Best ETFs* list.

Why Should I Care?

For a relatively straightforward gold play in a foundation portfolio, or for a defensive play during periods of unusual market volatility, the Market Vectors Gold Miners ETF makes sense.

Upside
- Defensive gold play
- Some growth prospects
- Avoids commodity fund downsides

Downside
- Will gold continue to soar?
- Little diversification
- Doesn't track very well

Just the Facts

INCEPTION DATE: **May 16, 2006**

TOTAL ASSETS: **$6.8 billion**

AVERAGE DAILY VOLUME: **11.7 million**

TOTAL HOLDINGS: **32**

PERCENT NORTH AMERICA HOLDINGS: **78.8%**

TOP 10 HOLDINGS PERCENTAGE (CONCENTRATION): **71.87%**

PORTFOLIO TURNOVER: **3.0%**   BENCHMARK: **20.0%**

BETA COEFFICIENT: **NA**

R-SQUARED (1 YEAR): **NA**

1-YEAR RETURN: **5.75%**   BENCHMARK: **30.69%**

3-YEAR RETURN: **4.42%**   BENCHMARK: **3.34%**

TRACKING ERROR (PRICE VS. NAV)   1 YEAR: **25.35%**   ASSET CLASS MEDIAN: **10.41%**

$10,000 Invested at inception	2006	2007	2008	2009	2010	2011
	$10,339	$12,092	$8,880	$12,190	$16,306	$14,525

What's Under the Hood

Symbol	Name	Percentage of fund
ABX	Barrick Gold Corp.	15.59%
GG	Goldcorp Inc.	12.61%
NEM	Newmont Mining Corp.	9.00%
KGC	Kinross Gold Corp.	6.09%
AU	Anglogold Ashanti Ltd.	5.28%
SLW	Silver Wheaton Corp.	4.87%
AUY	Yamana Gold Inc.	4.71%
EGO	Eldorado Gold Corp.	4.68%
BVN	Compania De Minas Buenaventura SAA	4.58%
GFI	Gold Fields Ltd.	4.50%
GOLD	Randgold Resources Ltd.	4.08%
AEM	Agnico Eagle Mines Ltd.	3.77%
IAG	IAMGOLD Corp.	3.70%
HMY	Harmony Gold Mining Co.	2.88%
NGD	New Gold Inc.	2.14%
RGLD	Royal Gold Inc.	1.72%
PAAS	Pan American Silver Corp.	1.61%
CDE	Coeur D Alene Mines Corp.	1.21%
SSRI	Silver Standard Resources Inc.	1.09%
HL	Hecla Mining Co.	1.07%

Van Eck Global
335 Madison Avenue, 19th Floor
New York, NY 10017
(212) 293-2000
Website: *www.vaneck.com*

100 BEST STRATEGY: **FOUNDATION/ROTATIO**

100 BEST CATEGORY: **STRATEGY/SECTOR**

Market Vectors Junior Gold

Ticker Symbol: GDXJ ◻ Issuer: Van Eck Associates ◻ Descri
Small Cap Fund ◻ Geography: Global ◻ Morningstar Rating: Nh
Yield: 1.4% ◻ Expense Ratio: 0.54% (Benchmark: 0.60%)

Stated Purpose

The investment seeks to replicate, net of expenses, the Market Vectors Junior Gold Miners Index. The fund normally invests at least 80 percent of total assets in securities that comprise the index. The index tracks the overall performance of foreign and domestic publicly traded companies of small- and medium-capitalization that are involved primarily in the mining for gold and/or silver.

Our Take

Those of you who just read our take on the sister Market Vectors Gold Miners ETF (GDX) will find the following three paragraphs familiar:

One doesn't have to ponder long these days to understand the allure of gold, with today's volatile economy and questions about the long-term oversupply and viability of paper currency. We won't go into that discussion here, but suffice it to say a great many investors these days want at least some gold in their portfolio.

Those investors can buy gold bars, but then they have to store them. Or they can buy gold through

a fund that owns the s
like the iShares Comex Go
(IAU)—another *100 Best ETF*,
then come the vagaries of daily price
movements and those of commodity fund ownership in general. So a third way to make a stake in gold is to buy the companies that mine it.

The Market Vectors Junior Gold Miners ETF owns companies that do just that—mine gold. Now you have a layer of management helping to run your show by making profits mining gold, which may (or may not) bring more return than the gold itself. You have the promise of more gold in the ground—somewhere—which could also bring a growth opportunity somewhere down the road. But now you also have companies that need to be valued, always an imprecise process. Pick your poison.

Now here's the part that's different. The Market Vectors Junior Gold Miners ETF invests in the smaller gold miners out there—small-cap and mid-cap companies with a total market capitalization of less than $5 billion. Now, these aren't companies formed to mine ncle's former grubstake on—about 72 percent of panies fall into the mid-e—about $1 billion to $5 in market cap. Additionally, ou think these companies are ted somewhere in the jungles Africa or some other politically, ocially, and otherwise unstable place, about 88 percent of the holdings are in Canada and Australia. So, yes, you've never heard of most of these companies, and they are more speculative than those in the GDX fund. But they're bigger, more important, and more stable than you think, and they offer a stronger growth component.

Why Should I Care?
This fund makes sense to get exposure to gold with an additional layer of growth potential (albeit with some more risk). It also is a play on the stronger currencies of Canada and Australia, and makes sense as a "defensive/aggressive" foundation or rotational play.

Upside
- Defensive gold play
- Growth prospects
- Currency tailwind

Downside
- Will gold continue to soar?
- Relatively new and unproven
- High tracking error

Just the Facts
INCEPTION DATE: **November 10, 2009**

TOTAL ASSETS: **$2.0 billion**

AVERAGE DAILY VOLUME: **2.9 million**

TOTAL HOLDINGS: **74**

PERCENT NORTH AMERICA HOLDINGS: **76.71%**

TOP 10 HOLDINGS PERCENTAGE (CONCENTRATION): **33.71%**

PORTFOLIO TURNOVER: **48.0%**   BENCHMARK: **20.0%**

BETA COEFFICIENT: **NM**

R-SQUARED (1 YEAR): **NM**

1-YEAR RETURN: **33.36%**   BENCHMARK: **30.69%**

3-YEAR RETURN: **NA**   BENCHMARK: **3.34%**

TRACKING ERROR (PRICE VS. NAV)   1 YEAR: **33.22%**   ASSET CLASS MEDIAN: **10.41%**

$10,000 Invested at inception	2006	2007	2008	2009	2010	2011
	$—	$—	$—	$9,521	$15,786	$13,345

What's Under the Hood

Symbol	Name	Percentage of fund
FR:CA	First Majestic Silver Corp.	4.63%
SSRI	Silver Standard Resources Inc.	4.28%
AGI:CA	Alamos Gold Inc.	4.20%
AUQ	Aurico Gold Inc.	4.17%
SVM:CA	Silvercorp Metals Inc.	3.63%
PRU:AU	Perseus Mining Ltd.	2.83%
MML:AU	Medusa Mining Ltd.	2.57%
KCN:AU	Kingsgate Consolidated Ltd.	2.44%
MFN	Minefinders Corp Ltd.	2.37%
NSU:CA	Nevsun Resources Ltd.	2.30%
XG:CA	Extorre Gold Mines Ltd.	2.16%
KGI:CA	Kirkland Lake Gold Inc.	2.02%
NXG	Northgate Minerals Corp.	1.93%
SGR:CA	San Gold Corp.	1.92%
ARZ:CA	Aurizon Mines Ltd.	1.84%
ARZ:CA	Aurizon Mines Ltd.	1.84%
GBG:CA	Great Basin Gold Ltd.	1.78%
BTO:CA	B2gold Corp.	1.78%
DPM:CA	Dundee Precious Metals Inc.	1.70%
R:CA	Romarco Minerals Inc.	1.69%

Van Eck Global
335 Madison Avenue, 19th Floor
New York, NY 10017
(212) 293-2000
Website: *www.vaneck.com*

PowerShares Dynamic Networking Portfolio

Ticker Symbol: PXQ ❑ Issuer: Invesco ❑ Description: Equity Industry Specific Blend ❑ Geography: U.S. ❑ Morningstar Rating: 5 stars ❑ Marco Polo XTF Rating: 4.0 ❑ Yield: nil ❑ Expense Ratio: 0.63% (Benchmark: 0.60%)

Stated Purpose

The investment seeks to replicate, net of expenses, the Dynamic Semiconductors Intellidex Index. The fund normally invests at least 90 percent of its assets in common stocks that comprise the index. The index includes companies that are principally engaged in the development, manufacture, sale, or distribution of products, services, or technologies that support the flow of electronic information.

Our Take

There is little argument that we are in the midst of a global revolution in technology and the application of technology to our daily lives. The persistent question for investors is "How best to invest in it?"

We think most technology funds are too broad based, consisting of an assortment of companies marketing emerging technologies counterbalanced to the downside by companies selling aging technologies. Emerging cloud computing stars are mixed with aging PC technologies, the HPs and Microsofts of the world; smartphones

mixed with dumb phones—well, you get the idea.

We also think networking is one of the "where it's going" sectors in technology and will be for some time. This sector not only consists of the Internet and other plumbing necessary to hook the world together, both with wires and with wireless pathways, but it also includes the "cloud." This isn't so well defined today but we envision a point where computing becomes almost like using a public utility—you need your taxes done, you simply log on and use a tax software program out there in cyberspace, while the meter runs and bills you for the usage. No expensive hardware, no software requiring constant updates.

So that's the vision, and the PowerShares Dynamic Networking Portfolio helps us get there. It's an attractive portfolio, and not surprisingly you'll see many of these names on our *100 Best Aggressive Stocks* list and our *100 Best Technology Stocks* lists. How the fund created a stock list like this without heavyweight Cisco on the list we're not sure, but we applaud the omission of this somewhat troubled player in favor of the more up and coming parts of the industry.

Why Should I Care?

The PowerShares Dynamic Networking Portfolio makes sense for more aggressive, growth-oriented applications in a foundation or rotational portfolio.

Upside

- Solid list of leading companies
- Focused, not too diversified
- Very strong recent performance

Downside

- Vulnerable to technology shifts
- Do they really need 0.63 percent to manage thirty-one holdings?
- Could be expensive to buy now

Just the Facts

INCEPTION DATE: **June 23, 2005**

TOTAL ASSETS: **$157.0 billion**

AVERAGE DAILY VOLUME: **64,400**

TOTAL HOLDINGS: **31**

PERCENT NORTH AMERICA HOLDINGS: **100%**

TOP 10 HOLDINGS PERCENTAGE (CONCENTRATION): **46.67%**

PORTFOLIO TURNOVER: **61%**   BENCHMARK: **20.0%**

BETA COEFFICIENT: **1.32**

R-SQUARED (1 YEAR): **81.27%**

1-YEAR RETURN: **55.36%**   BENCHMARK: **30.69%**

3-YEAR RETURN: **23.03%**   BENCHMARK: **3.34%**

TRACKING ERROR (PRICE VS. NAV)   1 YEAR: **16.28%**   ASSET CLASS MEDIAN: **10.41%**

$10,000 Invested at inception	2006	2007	2008	2009	2010	2011
	$12,060	$12,383	$7,138	$12,500	$18,241	$19,370

What's Under the Hood

Symbol	Name	Percentage of fund
VMW	VMware Inc.	5.71%
SYMC	Symantec Corp.	5.49%
QCOM	Qualcomm Inc.	5.29%
MSI	Motorola Solutions Inc.	5.22%

Symbol	Name	Percentage of fund
APH	Amphenol Corp.	5.02%
FFIV	F5 Networks Inc.	4.59%
CTXS	Citrix Systems Inc.	4.58%
ELMG	EMS Technologies Inc.	3.94%
VHC	Virnetx Holding Corp.	3.81%
JNPR	Juniper Networks Inc.	3.50%
ARRS	ARRIS Group Inc.	3.22%
BDC	Belden Inc.	3.12%
PLPC	Preformed Line Products Co.	2.88%
QLGC	QLogic Corp.	2.85%
WBSN	Websense Inc.	2.82%
OPLK	Oplink Communications Inc.	2.81%
VDSI	Vasco Data Security International Inc.	2.73%
SWI	Solarwinds Inc.	2.72%
TKLC	Tekelec	2.63%
MOLX	Molex Inc.	2.61%

Invesco PowerShares Capital Management LLC
301 West Roosevelt Road
Wheaton, IL 60187
(800) 803-0903
Website: *www.invescopowershares.com*

100 BEST STRATEGY: **FOUNDATION/ROTATIONAL**

100 BEST CATEGORY: **STRATEGY/SECTOR**

Vanguard Information Technology Index Fund

Ticker Symbol: VGT ▫ Issuer: Vanguard ▫ Description: Equity Industry Specific Blend ▫ Geography: U.S. ▫ Morningstar Rating: 3 stars ▫ Marco Polo XTF Rating: 8.0 ▫ Yield: 0.56% ▫ Expense Ratio: 0.24% (Benchmark: 0.60%)

Stated Purpose

The investment seeks to replicate, net of expenses, the MSCI U.S. Investable Market Information Technology 25/50 Index. The fund invests all, or substantially all, of its assets in the stocks that make up the index. The index consists of all capitalizations of stock in the technology sector. It includes companies involved in technology, software, Internet applications systems, databases, consulting, data processing, and outsourced services.

Our Take

We're in the information age, no doubt, so it makes sense to invest in information technology, right? For those who want a solid and broad-based information technology play, the Vanguard Information Technology Index Fund makes sense.

It's hard to know what the next emerging super-trend—or company—will be in the technology space. This portfolio gives a very broad exposure (416 holdings) but concentrates the exposure as a cap-weighted fund in the biggest and brightest stars—Apple, IBM, Microsoft, Google, Oracle, Intel. Anyone who expects these companies to continue to wield their power and not only capitalize on the industry but continue to define it will want to come here. The fund provides a comprehensive blend of tech developers, tech sellers, hardware and software makers, and the companies like Qualcomm, Intel, and Corning that make all the piece parts to make the whole thing work. Vanguard brings better returns than most competitors to you at a very attractive cost.

Why Should I Care?

For an investor wanting a broad, relatively risk-free tech play that doesn't require too much specific knowledge of the industry, this fund makes sense either for a more aggressive portion of a foundation portfolio or as a rotational play.

Upside

- Solid, mainstream winners
- Low expense ratio
- Not just pure computing—Visa, Mastercard, ADP, etc.

Downside

- A lot of "heavy old" tech—HP, Microsoft, Cisco, etc.
- Overdiversified?
- Cap weighting may snuff out more leading-edge plays

Just the Facts

INCEPTION DATE: **January 26, 2004**

TOTAL ASSETS: **$1.8 billion**

AVERAGE DAILY VOLUME: **131,200**

TOTAL HOLDINGS: **416**

PERCENT NORTH AMERICA HOLDINGS: **96.5%**

TOP 10 HOLDINGS PERCENTAGE (CONCENTRATION): **55.1%**

PORTFOLIO TURNOVER: **9.0%**   BENCHMARK: **20.0%**

BETA COEFFICIENT: **1.30**

R-SQUARED (1 YEAR): **93.23%**

1-YEAR RETURN: **28.75%**   BENCHMARK: **30.69%**

3-YEAR RETURN: **7.01%**   BENCHMARK: **3.34%**

TRACKING ERROR (PRICE VS. NAV)   1 YEAR: **6.36%**   ASSET CLASS MEDIAN: **10.41%**

$10,000 Invested at inception	2006	2007	2008	2009	2010	2011
	$10,948	$12,590	$7,198	$11,642	$15,126	$13,514

What's Under the Hood

Symbol	Name	Percentage of fund
AAPL	Apple Inc.	13.44%
IBM	International Business Machines Corp.	8.29%
MSFT	Microsoft Corp.	7.74%
GOOG	Google Inc.	5.66%
ORCL	Oracle Corp.	4.62%
INTC	Intel Corp.	4.58%
QCOM	Qualcomm Inc.	3.36%
CSCO	Cisco Systems Inc.	3.30%
HPQ	Hewlett Packard Co.	2.86%
EMC	EMC Corp.	2.02%
V	Visa Inc.	1.58%
EBAY	eBay Inc.	1.43%
ACN	Accenture Public Ltd. Co.	1.42%
TXN	Texas Instruments Inc.	1.30%
MA	Mastercard Inc.	1.26%
DELL	Dell Inc.	1.05%
ADP	Automatic Data Processing Inc.	0.95%
GLW	Corning Inc.	0.93%
CTSH	Cognizant Technology Solutions Corp.	0.79%
BRCM	Broadcom Corp.	0.67%

Vanguard
P.O. Box 1110
Valley Forge, PA 19482–1110
(877) 241-1395
Website: *www.vanguard.com*

100 BEST STRATEGY: **FOUNDATION/ROTATIONAL**

100 BEST CATEGORY: **STRATEGY/SECTOR**

WisdomTree Global Natural Resources Fund

Ticker Symbol: GNAT ❑ Issuer: WisdomTree Investments ❑ Description: Equity Sector Blend ❑ Geography: Global ❑ Morningstar Rating: 4 stars ❑ Marco Polo XTF Rating: 4.4 ❑ Yield: 2.90% ❑ Expense Ratio: 0.58% (Benchmark: 0.60%)

Stated Purpose

The investment seeks to track the price and yield performance, before fees and expenses, of the Wisdom-Tree Global Natural Resources Index. The fund employs a "passive management"—or indexing—investment approach designed to track the performance of the Wis-domTree Global Natural Resources Index. It attempts to invest all or substantially all of its assets in the stocks that make up the index.

Our Take

A persistently growing world population, and a growth in the standard of living and size of emerging economies in particular, and a finite amount of most elementary natural resources combine to make a pretty strong case for investing in natural resources, particularly for the long term.

While it makes sense to invest in energy resources, where the supply is particularly finite and the demand is seemingly insatiable, it also makes sense to invest in a broader base of resources and commodities. The WisdomTree Global Natural Resources Fund gives a

fairly broad, though still energy-weighted, natural resource base. By investing in companies, it avoids the short-term swings and downsides of investing in commodities directly.

The fund is about 50 percent invested in oil and gas, 31 percent in metals and mining, 6 percent in energy services, 6 percent in chemicals, and 3 percent in agriculture. In selecting the 100 largest global companies in the natural resources business, it gives a good international exposure, particularly in Canada, Australia, Russia, and Mexico. Further, the fund aims at capturing dividend yields and is weighted by those yields, so it throws off more income than most comparable choices. Those wanting a little less oil and gas exposure might want to check out our other pick in this sector, the SPDR S&P Global Natural Resources ETF (GNR).

Why Should I Care?

The WisdomTree Global Natural Resources portfolio gives a good broad-based exposure to natural resource commodities, with a healthy amount of international exposure and an attractive yield. It makes sense as a long-term foundation investment and also as a rotational play when such commodities are on the rise.

Upside

- Diverse natural resource and international exposure

- Attractive yield, dividend emphasis
- Held up fairly well in commodity down cycle

Downside

- Vulnerable to commodity price swings
- Relatively high cost
- Small size and liquidity

Just the Facts

INCEPTION DATE: October 13, 2006

TOTAL ASSETS: $45.5 million

AVERAGE DAILY VOLUME: 13,600

TOTAL HOLDINGS: 95

PERCENT NORTH AMERICA HOLDINGS: 29.32%

TOP 10 HOLDINGS PERCENTAGE (CONCENTRATION): 28.96%

PORTFOLIO TURNOVER: 32.0%   BENCHMARK: 20.0%

BETA COEFFICIENT: 1.41

R-SQUARED (1 YEAR): 79.66%

1-YEAR RETURN: 46.48%   BENCHMARK: 30.69%

3-YEAR RETURN: -3.94%%   BENCHMARK: 3.34%

TRACKING ERROR (PRICE VS. NAV)   1 YEAR: 11.85%   ASSET CLASS MEDIAN: 10.41%

$10,000 Invested at inception	2006	2007	2008	2009	2010	2011
	$10,572	$13,249	$8,012	$11,625	$11,901	$12,861

What's Under the Hood

Symbol	Name	Percentage of fund
KIO:ZA	Kumba Iron Ore Ltd.	4.09%
ANTO:GB	Antofagasta Plc	3.16%
RDSB:GB	Royal Dutch Shell Plc	3.00%
CPG:CA	Crescent Point Energy Corp.	2.83%
ENI:IT	Eni SpA	2.70%
FP:FR	Total SA	2.65%
SCCO	Southern Copper Corp.	2.63%
PE_OLES__:MX	Industrias Penoles SAB de CV	2.51%
DO	Diamond Offshore Drilling Inc.	2.34%
COS:CA	Canadian Oil Sands Ltd.	2.20%
STL:NO	Statoil ASA	2.10%
REP:ES	Repsol YPF SA	1.94%
ICL:IL	ICL Israel Chemicals Ltd.	1.82%
RDSA:GB	Royal Dutch Shell Plc	1.79%
LKOD:GB	NEFTYANAYA KOMPANIYA LUKOIL OAO	1.68%
MNOD:GB	GMK Noril'skiy nikel' OAO	1.67%
BHP:AU	BHP Billiton Ltd.	1.65%
STO:AU	Santos Ltd.	1.57%
COP	ConocoPhillips	1.56%
IOICORP:MY	IOI Corporation Bhd	1.53%

WisdomTree Investments
380 Madison Avenue, 21st Floor
New York, NY 10017
(866) 909-9473
Website: *www.wisdomtree.com*

100 BEST STRATEGY: **FOUNDATION/ROTATIONAL**

100 BEST CATEGORY: **STRATEGY/SECTOR**

SPDR S&P Global Natural Resources ETF

Ticker Symbol: GNR ▫ Issuer: State Street Global Advisors (SSGA) ▫ Description: Equity Sector Blend ▫ Geography: Global ▫ Morningstar Rating: NR ▫ Marco Polo XTF Rating: 4.4 ▫ Yield: 0.99% ▫ Expense Ratio: 0.40% (Benchmark: 0.60%)

Stated Purpose

The investment seeks to replicate, net of expenses, the S&P Global Natural Resources Index. The fund invests at least 80 percent of assets in securities comprising the index. The index is comprised of ninety of the largest U.S. and foreign publicly traded companies, based on market capitalization, in natural resources and commodities.

Our Take

The argument for the continued global demand and scarcity of most natural resources is pretty compelling, and it probably makes sense, through one vehicle or another, to have some investment exposure to this long-term play. The SPDR S&P Global Natural Resources ETF is one of the most diverse and efficient ways to do this.

The equal-weighted GNR fund is about 33 percent oil and gas, 31 percent metals and mining, 19 percent chemicals, 8 percent agriculture, and 4 percent forest products—a good blend in our estimation. It brings plenty of international diversification, with twenty-one countries

represented overall and strong concentrations in Canada, Australia, and Russia. The expense ratio of 0.40 percent and the broader commodity diversification compare favorably with our other pick in this arena, the WisdomTree Global Natural Resources Fund (GNAT)—although that fund has a more enticing yield.

Why Should I Care?

This fund brings the broadest and most effectively diversified natural resources play for a long-term foundation holding or a short-term rotational holding in periods of commodity price rises.

Upside

- Broad commodities, not just oil and gas
- Reasonable expenses
- Safety: right amount of diversification

Downside

- Vulnerable to commodity cycles
- Relatively new and unproven
- Equal weighting may not follow winners long enough

Just the Facts

INCEPTION DATE: **September 13, 2010**

TOTAL ASSETS: **$169.5 million**

AVERAGE DAILY VOLUME: **13,600**

TOTAL HOLDINGS: **91**

PERCENT NORTH AMERICA HOLDINGS: **43.02%**

TOP 10 HOLDINGS PERCENTAGE (CONCENTRATION): **34.03%**

PORTFOLIO TURNOVER: **NA**   BENCHMARK: **NA**

BETA COEFFICIENT: **NA**

R-SQUARED (1 YEAR): **NA**

1-YEAR RETURN: **NA**   BENCHMARK: **30.69%**

3-YEAR RETURN: **NA**   BENCHMARK: **3.34%**

TRACKING ERROR (PRICE VS. NAV)   1 YEAR: **NA**   ASSET CLASS MEDIAN: **10.41%**

$10,000 Invested at inception	2006	2007	2008	2009	2010	2011
	$—	$—	$—	$—	$11,616	$11,827

What's Under the Hood

Symbol	Name	Percentage of fund
BHP:AU	BHP Billiton Ltd.	4.92%
XOM	Exxon Mobil Corp.	4.84%
POT	Potash Corp Of Saskatchewan Inc.	4.41%
MON	Monsanto Co.	3.49%
F34:SG	Wilmar International Ltd.	2.98%
MOS	Mosaic Co.	2.79%
SYNN	Syngenta AG	2.76%
CVX	Chevron Corp	2.72%
OGZD:GB	Gazprom OAO	2.55%
AAL:GB	Anglo American Plclc	2.51%
XTA:GB	Xstrata PLC	2.47%
FCX	Freeport McMoRan Copper and Gold Inc.	1.93%
MT	—	1.90%
PBR	Petroleo Brasileiro SA Petrobras	1.88%
BP_:GB	BP PLC	1.86%
ABX	Barrick Gold Corp.	1.79%

Symbol	Name	Percentage of fund
ADM	Archer Daniels Midland Co.	1.78%
FP:FR	Total SA	1.73%
RDSA:GB	Royal Dutch Shell Plc	1.72%
VALE	Vale SA	1.55%

State Street Global Advisors
State Street Financial Center
1 Lincoln Street
Boston, MA 02111–2900
Phone: (617) 786-3000
Website: *www.spdrs.com*

100 BEST STRATEGY: **FOUNDATION**

100 BEST CATEGORY: **STRATEGY/SECTOR**

WisdomTree Large Cap Value Fund

Ticker Symbol: EZY ▫ Issuer: WisdomTree Investments ▫ Description: Equity Large Cap Style Selection ▫ Geography: U.S. ▫ Morningstar Rating: 3 stars ▫ Marco Polo XTF Rating: 7.5 ▫ Yield: 1.26% ▫ Expense Ratio: 0.38% (Benchmark: 0.60%)

Stated Purpose

The investment seeks to track the price and yield performance, before fees and expenses, of the WisdomTree Large Cap Value Index. The fund employs a "passive management"— or indexing—investment approach designed to track the performance of the WisdomTree Large Cap Value Index. It attempts to invest all or substantially all of its assets in the stocks that make up the index.

Our Take

More and more investors today (including us) are following time-honored value principles for making our investments, following in the footsteps of Warren Buffett and Benjamin Graham—and by the way, your coauthor Peter, who wrote *Value Investing for Dummies*. Yes, we like value, particularly when it includes a growth component— growth is *part of* value, not the antithesis of it, in our view.

For a broad but fairly strategic view on value, we chose the WisdomTree Large Cap Value Fund to carry the torch for those venerable large-cap names high on the value charts. To best understand its mechanics, we may as well quote WisdomTree's own take on their proprietary WisdomTree Large Cap Value Index. It is "a fundamentally weighted index that measures the performance of large-cap value companies. . . . The Index consists of U.S. companies that have positive cumulative earnings over the past four fiscal quarters. WisdomTree creates a 'value' score for each company based on the company's Price to Earnings Ratio, Price to Sales Ratio, and Price to Book Value and 1-year change in stock price. The top 30 percent of companies with the highest value scores within the 1000 largest companies by market capitalization are included in the Index. Companies are weighted in the Index annually based on earnings."

We like the earnings weighting and the inclusion of the stock price, both elements of growth to add to the traditional price-to-something ratios. We also like the resulting portfolio and expense profile.

Why Should I Care?

This fund would make a good core holding for the equity portion of a foundation portfolio.

Upside

- Enhanced value approach considers growth
- Relatively low expense ratio
- Highly diversified

Downside

- Didn't do well in 2008 downturn—too much energy?
- Small and not so liquid
- Couldn't the yield be better?

Just the Facts

INCEPTION DATE: **February 23, 2007**

TOTAL ASSETS: **$25.7 million**

AVERAGE DAILY VOLUME: **2,400**

TOTAL HOLDINGS: **303**

PERCENT NORTH AMERICA HOLDINGS: **100%**

TOP 10 HOLDINGS PERCENTAGE (CONCENTRATION): **45.11%**

PORTFOLIO TURNOVER: **6.0%**   BENCHMARK: **20.0%**

BETA COEFFICIENT: **1.15**

R-SQUARED (1 YEAR): **97.17%**

1-YEAR RETURN: **36.59%**   BENCHMARK: **30.69%**

3-YEAR RETURN: **3.66%**   BENCHMARK: **3.34%**

TRACKING ERROR (PRICE VS. NAV)   1 YEAR: **3.58%**   ASSET CLASS MEDIAN: **10.41%**

$10,000 Invested at inception	2006	2007	2008	2009	2010	2011
	$—	$10,262	$6,020	$7,770	$8,873	$9,641

What's Under the Hood

Symbol	Name	Percentage of fund
XOM	Exxon Mobil Corp.	13.36%
CVX	Chevron Corp.	8.82%
T	AT&T Inc.	8.17%
COP	ConocoPhillips	3.33%
VZ	Verizon Communications Inc.	3.06%
UNH	UnitedHealth Group Inc.	2.48%
CMCSA	Comcast Corp.	1.67%
NWSA	News Corp.	1.45%
DD	E I Du Pont De Nemours and Co.	1.38%
TRV	Travelers Companies Inc.	1.35%
WLP	Wellpoint Inc.	1.31%
COF	Capital One Financial Corp.	1.27%
CAT	Caterpillar Inc.	1.14%
DOW	Dow Chemical Co.	1.02%
CB	Chubb Corp.	1.00%
HAL	Halliburton Co.	1.00%
HES	Hess Corp.	0.96%
AET	Aetna Inc.	0.87%
NOV	National Oilwell Varco Inc.	0.84%
VIA/B	Viacom Inc.	0.84%

WisdomTree Investments
380 Madison Avenue, 21st Floor
New York, NY 10017
(866) 909- 9473
Website: *www.wisdomtree.com*

100 BEST STRATEGY: **FOUNDATION/ROTATIONAL/OPPORTUNISTIC**

100 BEST CATEGORY: **STRATEGY/SECTOR**

PowerShares Global Wind Energy Portfolio

Ticker Symbol: PWND ❑ Issuer: Invesco ❑ Description: Equity Industry Selection ❑ Geography: Global ❑ Morningstar Rating: NR ❑ Marco Polo XTF Rating: 1.2 ❑ Yield: nil ❑ Expense Ratio: 0.75% (Benchmark: 0.60%)

Stated Purpose

The fund seeks investment results that correspond (before fees and expenses) generally to the price and yield performance of the NASDAQ OMX Clean Edge Global Wind Energy Index. The fund normally invests at least 90 percent of total assets in the securities and depositary receipts based on the securities included in the underlying index. It anticipates that the majority of investments are in securities that comprise the underlying index rather than in depositary receipts. The fund normally invests at least 80 percent of total assets in securities of companies engaged in the wind energy industry.

Our Take

For those of you subscribing to the Bob Dylan lyrics, "The answer, my friend, is blowing in the wind," here's a fund for you. The PowerShares Global Wind Energy Portfolio, as the name plainly states, tracks companies aligned to the wind power industry.

The global portfolio includes both wind power producers and businesses that manufacture the pieces and parts for wind power; the mix is about 50–50 in this regard. As you can see from the Top 20 holdings list, there is a fair amount of exposure to China and other international players, where wind power has blown in to a greater degree than in the United States. The top three countries, interestingly, are China, Portugal, and Italy. Aside from China, about 57 percent of the holdings are in Europe.

As you can see from the price performance, wind power hasn't really caught on like many thought it would, at least as a profitable business model. The fund might do better if it held companies such as Otter Tail Corporation, an upper Midwest utility (and a *100 Best Stock*), that use wind power and make wind power components but don't do so as the majority of their business.

Still, at current prices, this fund is cheap, and could be an interesting opportunity if wind gains traction, and we think that may be more likely with the recent problems in the nuclear sector.

Why Should I Care?

This fund makes sense as a more aggressive alternative energy play and could be played for long-term gain or as a short-term turnaround play.

Upside

- Focused, but covers industry well
- International exposure
- Deep discount to original value

Downside

- Long road to profitability for component companies
- High expense ratio
- Size and liquidity

Just the Facts

INCEPTION DATE: **July 1, 2008**

TOTAL ASSETS: **$24.0 million**

AVERAGE DAILY VOLUME: **12,300**

TOTAL HOLDINGS: **31**

PERCENT NORTH AMERICA HOLDINGS: **17.42%**

TOP 10 HOLDINGS PERCENTAGE (CONCENTRATION): **85.24%**

PORTFOLIO TURNOVER: **41.0%**   BENCHMARK: **20.0%**

BETA COEFFICIENT: **1.25**

R-SQUARED (1 YEAR): **43.11**

1-YEAR RETURN: **-1.24%**   BENCHMARK: **30.69%**

3-YEAR RETURN: **NA**   BENCHMARK: **3.34%**

TRACKING ERROR (PRICE VS. NAV)   1 YEAR: **22.54%**   ASSET CLASS MEDIAN: **10.41%**

$10,000 Invested at inception	2006	2007	2008	2009	2010	2011
	$—	$—	$4,950	$6,688	$4,304	$4,239

What's Under the Hood

Symbol	Name	Percentage of fund
EDPR:PT	EDP Renovaveis SA	10.98%
EGPW:IT	Enel Green Power SpA	10.05%
916:HK	China Longyuan Power Group Corp Ltd.	9.67%
VWS:DK	Vestas Wind Systems A/S	8.81%
HSN:GB	Hansen Transmissions International NV	6.70%
INE:CA	Innergex Renewable Energy Inc.	4.72%
RPW:DE	REpower Systems SE	4.59%
MY	China Ming Yang Wind Power Group Ltd.	3.81%
GAM:ES	GameSA Corporacion Tecnologica SA	3.67%
182:HK	China WindPower Group Ltd.	3.63%
AMSC	American Superconductor Corp.	3.50%
NDX1:DE	Nordex Se	3.41%
ZOLT	Zoltek Companies Inc.	3.28%
658:HK	China High Speed Transmission Equipment Group Co Ltd.	3.18%
GUR:CH	Gurit Holding AG	2.74%
IFN:AU	Infigen Energy Ltd.	2.71%
TEO:FR	Theolia SA	1.80%
EOAN:DE	EON AG	1.67%
SIE:DE	Siemens AG	1.65%
GE	General Electric Co.	1.64%

Invesco PowerShares Capital Management LLC
301 West Roosevelt Road
Wheaton, IL 60187
(800) 803-0903
Website: *www.invescopowershares.com*

Market Vectors Global Alternative Energy Fund

Ticker Symbol: GEX ❑ Issuer: Van Eck Associates ❑ Description: Equity Industry Selection ❑ Geography: Global ❑ Morningstar Rating: 1 star ❑ Marco Polo XTF Rating: 4.3 ❑ Yield: 1.04% ❑ Expense Ratio: 0.60% (Benchmark: 0.60%)

Stated Purpose

The investment seeks to replicate as closely as possible, before fees and expenses, the price and yield performance of the Ardour Global Index. The fund normally invests at least 80 percent of total assets in stocks in proportion to their weightings in the index. It invests at least 30 percent of assets in securities of non-U.S. companies located in at least three different countries.

Our Take

In truth, this is one of the weaker "stated purpose" statements we've seen, and we'd be happy to offer our services as freelance writers to help Market Vectors put more information into it.

That aside, during the years 2007 and 2008 environmental concerns and alternative energy hit the forefront. The early 2008 release of personal finance guru David Bach's book *Go Green, Live Rich* was probably the apex of this cycle. And several new "green" ETFs were created to take advantage of this trend. While we're not "greenies" by nature, we do believe that alternative energy sooner or later will become a viable industry (it has to). The question really is when and in what form.

That question makes funds such as the Market Vectors Global Alternative Energy Fund really the way to go to invest in this opportunity. Who's to say that solar or wind or biomass or fuel cells will really become the way of the future? And who's to say whether thin-film solar panels or some other yet-to-be-discovered substrate will win out? It could be that the winning path will simply be in producing devices that make energy use more efficient, like Cree and Itron on this list (and on our *100 Best Aggressive* and *100 Best Technology* lists as well). So it makes sense to cover the bases if you want to invest in this industry.

The recent poor price performance of this fund probably makes it a good opportunity; aside from that, it is a good way for patient investors to play the future—whatever that might turn out to be. Those investors should hope that oil prices go through the roof.

Why Should I Care?

This fund makes sense as a more aggressive alternative energy play and could be played for long-term gain or as a short-term turnaround play.

Upside

• Good exposure to strategic sector
• Decent size and liquidity for this type of fund
• Deep discount to original price

Downside

• Not diversified enough? These thirty-one companies may not have the answer
• Very poor recent price performance—also an opportunity?
• Desired results may take a while

Just the Facts

INCEPTION DATE: **May 3, 2007**

TOTAL ASSETS: **$133.70 million**

AVERAGE DAILY VOLUME: **53,200**

TOTAL HOLDINGS: **31**

PERCENT NORTH AMERICA HOLDINGS: **46.17%**

TOP 10 HOLDINGS PERCENTAGE (CONCENTRATION): **55.44%**

PORTFOLIO TURNOVER: **30.0%**   BENCHMARK: **20.0%**

BETA COEFFICIENT: **1.38**

R-SQUARED (1 YEAR): **59.92%**

1-YEAR RETURN: **2.10%**   BENCHMARK: **30.69%**

3-YEAR RETURN: **-28.09%**   BENCHMARK: **3.34%**

TRACKING ERROR (PRICE VS. NAV)   1 YEAR: **17.72%**   ASSET CLASS MEDIAN: **10.41%**

$10,000 Invested at inception	2006	2007	2008	2009	2010	2011
	$—	$14,476	$5,650	$6,155	$4,964	$4,622

What's Under the Hood

Symbol	Name	Percentage of fund
FSLR	First Solar Inc.	9.98%
VWS:DK	Vestas Wind Systems A/S	6.91%
PPO	Polypore International Inc.	6.08%
CREE	Cree Inc.	5.80%
EGPW:IT	Enel Green Power SpA	5.73%
6370:JP	Kurita Water Industries Ltd.	5.40%
VER:AT	VERBUND AG	5.19%
CVA	Covanta Holding Corp.	3.89%
CZZ	Cosan Ltd.	3.88%
IRF	International Rectifier Corp.	3.29%
ITRI	Itron Inc.	3.19%
WFR	MEMC Electronic Materials Inc.	3.09%
916:HK	China Longyuan Power Group Corp Ltd.	3.01%
VECO	Veeco Instruments Inc.	2.92%
ENS	EnerSys	2.81%
EDPR:PT	EDP Renovaveis SA	2.67%
GAM:ES	GameSA Corporacion Tecnologica SA	2.66%
TSL	Trina Solar Ltd.	2.51%
1072:HK	Dongfang Electric Corp Ltd.	2.43%
TSLA	Tesla Motors Inc.	2.30%

Van Eck Global
335 Madison Avenue, 19th Floor
New York, NY 10017
(212) 293-2000
Website: *www.vaneck.com*

100 BEST STRATEGY: **FOUNDATION/ROTATIONAL/OPPORTUNISTIC**

100 BEST CATEGORY: **STRATEGY/SECTOR**

First Trust NASDAQ Clean Edge Smartgrid Infrastructure Core Index Fund

Ticker Symbol: GRID ❑ Issuer: First Trust Advisors ❑ Description: Equity Industry Selection ❑ Geography: Global ❑ Morningstar Rating: NR ❑ Marco Polo XTF Rating: NR ❑ Yield: 0.85% ❑ Expense Ratio: 0.70% (Benchmark: 0.60%)

Stated Purpose

The fund seeks investment results that correspond generally to the price and yield (before the fund's fees and expenses) of an equity index called the NASDAQ OMX Clean Edge Smartgrid Infrastructure Index. The fund normally invests at least 90 percent of assets in common stocks that comprise the index or in depositary receipts representing securities in the index. The index is designed to act as a transparent and liquid benchmark for the grid and electric energy infrastructure sector.

Our Take

Now here's a fund with a groovy name, and we like groovy names, right? Well, maybe for a pop band or a movie, but it doesn't move the needle for an ETF selection. Aren't you relieved?

What we *do* like is funds aligned around an industry that we see as critically important to our future. The future is hard to predict, but lots of money has been made by those who get it right, especially when they get it right before everyone else does.

What we have with this First Trust fund (we won't spell out the entire name again) is a serious and focused play on one of the most underrated future "problems" we face: the replacement of all that infrastructure we don't see or think about much . . . water pipes, sewer pipes, and, in this case, electrical transmission lines. Most of the infrastructure to move electricity around was created fifty to seventy years ago, and we think it not only needs to be replaced but also upgraded to make the "grid" more efficient. The energy savings could be huge.

Only problem is, such improvements cost a lot of money. Utilities and in some places, governments, have to come up with the cash. So that's slowed things down a bit. But this portfolio captures a number of companies that make the piece parts (GE, General Cable, etc.) and that add the efficiency (Itron, Power One). We think the light will go on and burn brightly, we're just not sure exactly when. This fund is a good way to keep your hand on the switch.

Why Should I Care?
This fund makes sense to hold in anticipation of long-term cycle of energy infrastructure replacement; recent prices also make it an attractive short-term turnaround play.

Upside
- Aligns around an obvious market need

- Focused
- Deep discount may signal opportunity

Downside
- Major infrastructure investments can take a long time
- High expenses
- Small and illiquid

Just the Facts
INCEPTION DATE: **November 16, 2009**

TOTAL ASSETS: **$26.4 million**

AVERAGE DAILY VOLUME: **3,400**

TOTAL HOLDINGS: **38**

PERCENT NORTH AMERICA HOLDINGS: **59.68%**

TOP 10 HOLDINGS PERCENTAGE (CONCENTRATION): **52.14%**

PORTFOLIO TURNOVER: **50.0%**   BENCHMARK: **20.0%**

BETA COEFFICIENT: **1.45**

R-SQUARED (1 YEAR): **77.77%**

1-YEAR RETURN: **21.39%**   BENCHMARK: **30.69%**

3-YEAR RETURN: **NA**   BENCHMARK: **3.34%**

TRACKING ERROR (PRICE VS. NAV)   1 YEAR: **12.58%**   ASSET CLASS MEDIAN: **10.41%**

$10,000 Invested at inception	2006	2007	2008	2009	2010	2011
	$—	$—	$—	$10,750	$10,723	$11,206

What's Under the Hood

Symbol	Name	Percentage of fund
5333:JP	NGK Insulators Ltd.	9.51%
PWR	Quanta Services Inc.	8.02%
REE:ES	RED ELECTRICA DE ESPANA SAU	7.49%
SU:FR	Schneider Electric SA	7.42%
PRY:IT	Prysmian SpA	7.24%
BGC	General Cable Corp.	4.41%
ELT	Elster Group SE	4.32%
ITC	ITC Holdings Corp.	4.19%
ITRI	Itron Inc.	3.62%
ESE	ESCO Technologies Inc.	3.58%
S92:DE	SMA Solar Technology AG	3.53%
PWER	Power One Inc.	2.90%
AZZ	AZZ Inc.	2.43%
NG_:GB	National Grid PLC	2.07%
SIE:DE	Siemens AG	2.01%
GE	General Electric Co.	1.99%
ABBN:CH	Abb Ltd.	1.94%
HUB/B	Hubbell Inc.	1.92%
MYRG	MYR Group Inc.	1.90%
VMI	Valmont Industries Inc.	1.82%

FirstTrust Portfolios L.P.
120 E. Liberty Drive, Suite 400
Wheaton, IL 60187
(800) 621-1675
Website: *www.ftportfolios.com*

100 BEST STRATEGY: **FOUNDATION**

100 BEST CATEGORY: **STRATEGY/SECTOR**

Focus Morningstar Health Care Index ETF

Ticker Symbol: FHC ❑ Issuer: FocusShares ❑ Description: Equity Sector Selection ❑ Geography: U.S. ❑ Morningstar Rating: NR ❑ Marco Polo XTF Rating: NR ❑ Yield: 0.60% ❑ Expense Ratio: 0.19% (Benchmark: 0.60%)

Stated Purpose

The investment seeks to replicate, net of expenses, the Morningstar Health Care Index. The index is determined on the basis of capital value of component securities that are publicly held, which typifies a "float adjusted" capitalization index and a subset of the Morningstar U.S. Market Index. It consists of companies involved in biotechnology, pharmaceuticals, research services, home health care, hospitals, long-term care facilities, and medical equipment and supplies. The fund invests 90 percent of assets in securities of the underlying index.

Our Take

For better or for worse, health care has become a huge and growing industry. Demographics have combined with technology and a complex not unlike the classic "military-industrial complex"—only this time with insurers thrown in—to remove most considerations of price and virtually guarantee long-term viability and growth.

Okay, off the soap box—but regardless of politics we think the health care industry is here to stay and to grow. The emphasis may shift from demographics and technology to efficiency, but one way or another, these companies will continue to make money.

We wanted a fund to provide a broad exposure to health care providers, suppliers, pharmaceutical makers, and deliverers of alternative care. We wanted some companies thriving on current practices as well as future technologies, such as biotech and systems design and integration. The Focus Morningstar Health Care Index ETF, in our view, provides the best mix and does it at a very reasonable cost: 0.19 percent.

Those wanting a more aggressive, technology-based health care play, see our PowerShares S&P Small Cap Health Care Portfolio choice (PSCH).

Why Should I Care?

This portfolio makes sense for a broad and long-term participation in the health care industry, primarily for a foundation portfolio.

Upside

- Broad exposure to broadest definition of industry
- Very low expense ratio, cheaper than alternatives
- Old technology, new technology

Downside

- New and unproven
- Current yield could be higher
- Too heavy with drug companies?

Just the Facts

INCEPTION DATE: **March 29, 2011**

TOTAL ASSETS: **$5.4 million**

AVERAGE DAILY VOLUME: **2,900**

TOTAL HOLDINGS: **133**

PERCENT NORTH AMERICA HOLDINGS: **98.18%**

TOP 10 HOLDINGS PERCENTAGE (CONCENTRATION): **51.04%**

PORTFOLIO TURNOVER: **NA**   BENCHMARK: **20.0%**

BETA COEFFICIENT: **NA**

R-SQUARED (1 YEAR): **NA**

1-YEAR RETURN: **NA**   BENCHMARK: **30.69%**

3-YEAR RETURN: **NA**   BENCHMARK: **3.34%**

TRACKING ERROR (PRICE VS. NAV)   1 YEAR: **NA**   ASSET CLASS MEDIAN: **10.41%**

$10,000 Invested at inception	2006	2007	2008	2009	2010	2011
	$—	$—	$—	$—	$—	$10,718

What's Under the Hood

Symbol	Name	Percentage of fund
JNJ	Johnson & Johnson	11.68%
PFE	Pfizer Inc.	10.22%
MRK	Merck & Co Inc.	6.91%
ABT	Abbott Laboratories	5.20%
UNH	Unitedhealth Group Inc.	3.60%
AMGN	Amgen Inc.	3.36%
BMY	Bristol Myers Squibb Co.	3.25%

Symbol	Name	Percentage of fund
MDT	Medtronic Inc.	2.57%
LLY	Eli Lilly and Co.	2.48%
GILD	Gilead Sciences Inc.	2.22%
BAX	Baxter International Inc.	2.20%
CELG	Celgene Corp.	1.84%
ESRX	Express Scripts Inc.	1.75%
MHS	Medco Health Solutions Inc.	1.66%
AGN	Allergan Inc.	1.65%
WLP	Wellpoint Inc.	1.65%
COV	Covidien Plc	1.65%
TMO	Thermo Fisher Scientific Inc.	1.52%
BIIB	Biogen Idec Inc.	1.52%
VMI	Valmont Industries Inc.	1.82%

Invesco PowerShares Capital Management LLC
301 West Roosevelt Road
Wheaton, IL 60187
(800) 803-0903
Website: *www.invescopowershares.com*

100 BEST STRATEGY: **FOUNDATION/ROTATIONAL**

100 BEST CATEGORY: **STRATEGY/SECTOR**

PowerShares S&P Small Cap Health Care Portfolio

Ticker Symbol: PSCH ▫ Issuer: Invesco ▫ Description: Equity Sector Small Cap Selection ▫ Geography: U.S. ▫ Morningstar Rating: NR ▫ Marco Polo XTF Rating: 8.0 ▫ Yield: nil ▫ Expense Ratio: 0.29% (Benchmark: 0.60%)

Stated Purpose

The investment seeks to replicate, net of expenses, the S&P Small Cap 600 Capped Health Care Index. The fund invests at least 90 percent of its total assets in common stocks that comprise the index. The index is comprised of common stocks of U.S. health care companies. It is a subset of the S&P Small Cap 600 index that reflects the U.S. small-cap market. The fund is nondiversified.

Our Take

For those believing in the long-term future of the health care industry, and particularly in those technologies that will make it more effective and efficient, the PowerShares S&P Small Cap Health Care Portfolio might make sense.

As a small-cap fund, you're pretty much automatically getting the rising and growing companies with new ideas (as well as a few that don't work). With seventy holdings, there is enough focus on the good ones and small enough exposure to the bad ones to make this mix work well. The first-year growth of 45.2 percent suggests that indeed, it is working well, at least so far.

This fund could be risky, especially if belt tightening really takes hold in the health care sector. Spending on new health care technologies could be curtailed, and you might be safer in a fund with holdings in the traditional drug, hospital, and other sectors, like the Focus Morningstar Health Care Index ETF (FHC) also found on our list.

Why Should I Care?

This fund could work either as a long-term foundation play, as a shorter-term rotational play in either small-cap stocks or health care stocks or both.

Upside

- Compelling exposure to growth segment of growing industry
- Low expense ratio
- Right amount of diversification

Downside

- New and unproven
- Health care cost initiatives could hurt
- Small-cap funds always riskier

Just the Facts

INCEPTION DATE: **April 7, 2010**

TOTAL ASSETS: **$158.7 million**

AVERAGE DAILY VOLUME: **13,500**

TOTAL HOLDINGS: **70**

PERCENT NORTH AMERICA HOLDINGS: **100%**

TOP 10 HOLDINGS PERCENTAGE (CONCENTRATION): **36.76%**

PORTFOLIO TURNOVER: **14.0%**   BENCHMARK: **20.0%**

BETA COEFFICIENT: **0.91**

R-SQUARED (1 YEAR): **51.07%**

1-YEAR RETURN: **45.20%**   BENCHMARK: **30.69%**

3-YEAR RETURN: **NA**   BENCHMARK: **3.34%**

TRACKING ERROR (PRICE VS. NAV)   1 YEAR: **12.65%**   ASSET CLASS MEDIAN: **10.41%**

$10,000 Invested at inception	2006	2007	2008	2009	2010	2011
	$—	$—	$—	$—	$11,113	$13,256

What's Under the Hood

Symbol	Name	Percentage of fund
REGN	Regeneron Pharmaceuticals Inc.	6.74%
HS	Healthspring Inc.	4.74%
SLXP	Salix Pharmaceuticals Ltd.	3.86%
HMSY	HMS Holdings Corp.	3.64%
CBST	Cubist Pharmaceuticals Inc.	3.47%
QCOR	Questcor Pharmaceuticals Inc.	3.26%
QSII	Quality Systems Inc.	2.99%
HAE	Haemonetics Corp.	2.87%
CNC	Centene Corp.	2.79%
MGLN	Magellan Health Services Inc.	2.77%
ZOLL	Zoll Medical Corp.	2.60%
ALGN	Align Technology Inc.	2.59%
WST	West Pharmaceutical Services Inc.	2.50%
VPHM	Viropharma Inc.	2.34%
PSSI	PSS World Medical Inc.	2.26%
CHE	Chemed Corp.	2.20%
PRXL	PAREXEL International Corp.	2.06%
PRX	Par Pharmaceutical Companies Inc.	2.00%
NUVA	Nuvasive Inc.	1.93%
MWIV	MWI Veterinary Supply Inc.	1.91%

Invesco PowerShares Capital Management LLC
301 West Roosevelt Road
Wheaton, IL 60187
(800) 803-0903
Website: *www.invescopowershares.com*

100 BEST STRATEGY: **FOUNDATIONAL/ROTATIONAL**

100 BEST CATEGORY: **STRATEGY/SECTOR**

SPDR S&P Biotech ETF

Ticker Symbol: XBI ▫ Issuer: State Street Global Advisors ▫ Description: Equity Industry Selection ▫ Geography: U.S. ▫ Morningstar Rating: 3 stars ▫ Marco Polo XTF Rating: 8.8 ▫ Yield: nil ▫ Expense Ratio: 0.35% (Benchmark: 0.60%)

Stated Purpose

The investment seeks to replicate, net of expenses, the S&P Biotechnology Select Industry Index. The fund generally invests substantially all, but at least 80 percent, of its assets in the securities comprising the index. The index represents the biotechnology subindustry portion of the S&P Total Market Index.

Our Take

This is one of the clearer examples of where ETF investing makes sense. Unless you hold a PhD in biochemistry or something similar, how can you possibly know which of the forty-four (or many more) companies in the biotech industry it really makes sense to own? If you say, "I believe in 'better living through biotech' as a concept but just don't know how to invest in it," then this fund is for you.

The SPDR S&P Biotech ETF brings a fairly focused (forty-four names) list of companies, many of which are larger and more familiar like Amgen, Biogen, and Celgene. Others are less familiar and smaller. We also like the 0.35 percent expense

ratio, low for this type of holding and less than most of its competitors. The equal weighting scheme may diminish long-term returns somewhat, but returns have been okay for the past few years, and equal weighting will help if some of the smaller names uncover big markets and take off.

Why Should I Care?

This fund probably makes sense for investors of the mind that technology solutions will become increasingly important in medicine and to a lesser extent in agriculture and maybe energy—really, anywhere organic molecules are present. It's probably a long-term proposition, so it fits best in a foundation portfolio.

Upside

- Good way to invest in complex sector
- Low expense ratio
- Somewhat recession resistant

Downside

- Lots of unproven technologies
- Active management might be better in this kind of industry
- Might have to be patient

Just the Facts

INCEPTION DATE: **January 31, 2006**

TOTAL ASSETS: **$642.6 million**

AVERAGE DAILY VOLUME: **232,100**

TOTAL HOLDINGS: **44**

PERCENT NORTH AMERICA HOLDINGS: **33.36%**

TOP 10 HOLDINGS PERCENTAGE (CONCENTRATION): **80.0%**

PORTFOLIO TURNOVER: **20.0%**   BENCHMARK: **20.0%**

BETA COEFFICIENT: **1.01**

R-SQUARED (1 YEAR): **51.46%**

1-YEAR RETURN: **40.92%**   BENCHMARK: **30.69%**

3-YEAR RETURN: **8.43%**   BENCHMARK: **3.34%**

TRACKING ERROR (PRICE VS. NAV)   1 YEAR: **13.30%**   ASSET CLASS MEDIAN: **10.41%**

$10,000 Invested at inception	2006	2007	2008	2009	2010	2011
	$9,291	$11,995	$10,938	$10,990	$12,923	$14,965

What's Under the Hood

Symbol	Name	Percentage of fund
ALXN	Alexion Pharmaceuticals Inc.	3.72%
ARIA	Ariad Pharmaceuticals Inc.	3.70%
BMRN	BioMarin Pharmaceutical Inc.	3.57%
SPPI	Spectrum Pharmaceuticals Inc.	3.54%
BIIB	Biogen Idec Inc.	3.32%
VRTX	Vertex Pharmaceuticals Inc.	3.20%
GILD	Gilead Sciences Inc.	3.13%
CELG	Celgene Corp.	3.03%
VRUS	Pharmasset Inc.	3.03%
CEPH	Cephalon Inc.	2.99%
SVNT	Savient Pharmaceuticals Inc.	2.99%
ITMN	Intermune Inc.	2.98%
UTHR	United Therapeutics Corp.	2.95%
INCY	Incyte Corp.	2.95%
AMLN	Amylin Pharmaceuticals Inc.	2.90%
REGN	Regeneron Pharmaceuticals Inc.	2.89%

Symbol	Name	Percentage of fund
CBST	Cubist Pharmaceuticals Inc.	2.89%
CPHD	Cepheid	2.87%
AMGN	Amgen Inc.	2.81%
DNDN	Dendreon Corp.	2.81%

State Street Global Advisors
State Street Financial Center
1 Lincoln Street
Boston, MA 02111–2900
Phone: (617) 786-3000
Website: *www.spdrs.com*

100 BEST STRATEGY: **FOUNDATIONAL/ROTATIONAL**

100 BEST CATEGORY: **STRATEGY/SECTOR**

SPDR Energy Select Sector Fund

Ticker Symbol: XLE ▫ Issuer: State Street Global Advisors ▫ Description: Equity Sector Selection ▫ Geography: U.S. ▫ Morningstar Rating: 4 star ▫ Marco Polo XTF Rating: 9.6 ▫ Yield: 1.33% ▫ Expense Ratio: 0.20% (Benchmark: 0.60%)

Stated Purpose

The investment seeks to replicate, net of expenses, the Energy Select Sector Index. The fund generally invests substantially all, but at least 95 percent, of its assets in the securities comprising the index. The index includes companies from the following industries: oil, gas and consumable fuels; and energy equipment and services. The fund bears a higher level of risk than more broadly diversified funds as it is subject to both sector risk and nondiversification risk, which generally result in greater price fluctuations than the overall market. The fund is nondiversified.

Our Take

You believe in the long-term health of the traditional petroleum industry. Growing demand, shrinking supply, higher prices. You also know that most petroleum these days comes from somewhere outside of the United States portion of the World Atlas, but you want the relative safety, security, and understandability of U.S. companies guiding your way. You also want size, liquidity, and experience; that is, a fund without any surprises that you can move easily into or out of at a moment's notice.

The SPDR Energy Select Sector Fund may be just the fund for you. With $9.0 billion in assets and a thirteen-year track record, it has been the energy selection for a lot of other people too. It is definitely a large-cap fund, and it will generally track the price of oil and gas and the long-term success of the industry more than just a few companies or countries that might "strike it rich."

The portfolio is about what you would expect it to be, headed up by big familiar names and working its way down to some of the more intermediate players. But, again, no surprises here either. The portfolio is 77 percent oil and gas producers and 23 percent energy equipment and services.

Why Should I Care?

The SPDR Energy Select Sector Fund works for investors looking for a steady and solid long-term energy play in a foundation portfolio, as well as rotational investors looking to capitalize on shorter-term energy price swings.

Upside

- Blue chip energy companies—strong finances
- Covers the industry
- Low expense ratio

Downside

- Vulnerable to energy price swings
- Could yield be higher?
- Assumes oil is forever—no alternative energy plays

Just the Facts

INCEPTION DATE: **December 18, 1998**

TOTAL ASSETS: **$9.0 billion**

AVERAGE DAILY VOLUME: **22.4 million**

TOTAL HOLDINGS: **43**

PERCENT NORTH AMERICA HOLDINGS: **98.55%**

TOP 10 HOLDINGS PERCENTAGE (CONCENTRATION): **53.34%**

PORTFOLIO TURNOVER: **7.58%**   BENCHMARK: **20.0%**

BETA COEFFICIENT: **1.15**

R-SQUARED (1 YEAR): **75.71%**

1-YEAR RETURN: **53.99%**   BENCHMARK: **30.69%**

3-YEAR RETURN: **-3.50%**   BENCHMARK: **3.34%**

TRACKING ERROR (PRICE VS. NAV)   1 YEAR: **9.20%**   ASSET CLASS MEDIAN: **10.41%**

$10,000 Invested at inception	2006	2007	2008	2009	2010	2011
	$19,475	$26,533	$16,252	$19,760	$24,452	$26,715

What's Under the Hood

Symbol	Name	Percentage of fund
XOM	Exxon Mobil Corp.	16.63%
CVX	Chevron Corp.	13.39%
SLB	Schlumberger NV	8.02%
COP	ConocoPhillips	4.72%
OXY	Occidental Petroleum Corp.	4.37%
HAL	Halliburton Co.	3.76%
APA	Apache Corp.	3.43%
APC	Anadarko Petroleum Corp.	3.00%
BHI	Baker Hughes Inc.	2.80%
NOV	National Oilwell Varco Inc.	2.71%
DVN	Devon Energy Corp.	2.41%
EOG	Eog Resources Inc.	2.09%
CHK	Chesapeake Energy Corp.	1.89%
WMB	Williams Companies Inc.	1.65%
HES	Hess Corp.	1.62%
MRO	Marathon Oil Corp.	1.62%
EP	El Paso Corp.	1.56%
PXD	Pioneer Natural Resources Co.	1.54%
NBL	Noble Energy Inc.	1.50%
SE	Spectra Energy Corp.	1.48%

State Street Global Advisors
State Street Financial Center
1 Lincoln Street
Boston, MA 02111–2900
Phone: (617) 786-3000
Website: *www.spdrs.com*

100 BEST STRATEGY: **FOUNDATION/ROTATIONAL**

100 BEST CATEGORY: **STRATEGY/SECTOR**

PowerShares S&P Small Cap Energy Portfolio

Ticker Symbol: PSCE ❑ Issuer: Invesco ❑ Description: Equity Sector Small Cap Selection ❑ Geography: U.S. ❑ Morningstar Rating: NR ❑ Marco Polo XTF Rating: 6.3 ❑ Yield: NA ❑ Expense Ratio: 0.29% (Benchmark: 0.60%)

Stated Purpose

The investment seeks to replicate, net of expenses, the S&P Small Cap 600 Capped Energy Index. The fund invests at least 90 percent of its assets in common stocks that comprise the index. The index is comprised of common stocks of U.S. energy companies that are engaged in producing, distributing, or servicing energy-related products. It is a subset of the S&P Small Cap 600 Index that reflects the U.S. small-cap market.

Our Take

Investors in the PowerShares S&P Small Cap Energy Portfolio believe two things. One is that energy is strategic to our collective future and the supply/demand balance will only worsen over time, increasing prices and profitability for those who explore for, produce, and distribute energy products. Second is that small-cap, emerging companies are the best way to play this and that small-cap stocks in general tend to have the greatest growth potential for the future.

We like both theories. With this fund, you get exposure to a lot of small companies you've probably never heard of but that could well be the up and comers in the industry, if not outright acquisition candidates by the major oil firms. It may not take an expert or a fund to invest in Exxon Mobil or ConocoPhillips, but you might well want to have a diverse portfolio and the discipline of set selection criteria behind you when you enter this space. Analyzing an individual small-cap oil company is pretty difficult and risky, for they don't usually know what they really have.

The fund is about evenly split between energy producers and energy-producing equipment. Recent returns have been exceptional with a low cost to boot.

Why Should I Care?

This fund makes sense as a long-term and fairly aggressive part of a foundation portfolio; it also works as a rotational play during periods of demand increases and/or supply shortages.

Upside

- Aggressive energy exposure
- Focused but still diverse; takes tough decisions out of your hands
- Exceptional historical returns at low cost

Downside

- Vulnerable to energy price swings
- New and unproven
- Could be a bit more diversified?

Just the Facts

INCEPTION DATE: **April 7, 2010**

TOTAL ASSETS: **$104.5 million**

AVERAGE DAILY VOLUME: **58,300**

TOTAL HOLDINGS: **22**

PERCENT NORTH AMERICA HOLDINGS: **100%**

TOP 10 HOLDINGS PERCENTAGE (CONCENTRATION): **65.0%**

PORTFOLIO TURNOVER: **16.0%**   BENCHMARK: **20.0%**

BETA COEFFICIENT: **1.24**

R-SQUARED (1 YEAR): **45.24%**

1-YEAR RETURN: **80.10%**   BENCHMARK: **30.69%**

3-YEAR RETURN: **NA**   BENCHMARK: **3.34%**

TRACKING ERROR (PRICE VS. NAV)   1 YEAR: **18.98%**   ASSET CLASS MEDIAN: **10.41%**

$10,000 Invested at inception	2006	2007	2008	2009	2010	2011
	$—	$—	$—	$—	$13,066	$15,121

What's Under the Hood

Symbol	Name	Percentage of fund
INT	World Fuel Services Corp.	10.94%
LUFK	Lufkin Industries Inc.	10.19%
CKH	SEACOR Holdings Inc.	8.92%
GPOR	Gulfport Energy Corp.	6.32%
IO	Ion Geophysical Corp.	5.04%
PDC	Pioneer Drilling Co.	5.04%
BAS	Basic Energy Services Inc.	4.84%
BRS	Bristow Group Inc.	4.78%
SGY	Stone Energy Corp.	4.74%
SFY	Swift Energy Co.	4.67%

Symbol	Name	Percentage of fund
TTI	Tetra Technologies Inc.	4.61%
PETD	Petroleum Development Corp.	4.38%
MCF	Contango Oil and Gas Co.	4.16%
AREX	Approach Resources Inc.	3.79%
HOS	Hornbeck Offshore Services Inc.	3.25%
PVA	Penn Virginia Corp.	3.07%
GIFI	Gulf Island Fabrication Inc.	2.55%
GEOI	Georesources Inc.	2.43%
PQ	Petroquest Energy Inc.	2.32%
OYOG	OYO Geospace Corp.	2.29%

Invesco PowerShares Capital Management LLC
301 West Roosevelt Road
Wheaton, IL 60187
(800) 803-0903
Website: *www.invescopowershares.com*

100 BEST STRATEGY: **FOUNDATION/ROTATIONAL**

100 BEST CATEGORY: **STRATEGY/SECTOR**

PowerShares Water Resources Portfolio

Ticker Symbol: PHO ❑ Issuer: Invesco ❑ Description: Equity Industry Selection ❑ Geography: Global ❑ Morningstar Rating: 2 stars ❑ Marco Polo XTF Rating: 3.2 ❑ Yield: 0.89% ❑ Expense Ratio: 0.64% (Benchmark: 0.60%)

Stated Purpose

The investment seeks to replicate, net of expenses, the Palisades Water Index. The fund normally invests at least 90 percent of its total assets in American Depository Receipts and common stocks that comprise the index. The index includes companies that are involved in the provision of potable water, the treatment of water, and the technology and services that are directly related to water consumption.

Our Take

As the saying goes, "Water, water everywhere." Well, not quite everywhere, especially where and when you need it. And we believe the proposition of getting water where it has to go when it has to get there offers some interesting long-term growth prospects.

The demand for clean drinking water (and industrial and agricultural water, for that matter) is growing steadily as the world develops and spreads into inhospitable places like Las Vegas. But the real issue—and you've probably picked it up by reading a few of our other *100 Best ETF* selections—is that the existing water delivery infrastructure, much of which was installed in the nineteenth century, is getting old and needs to be replaced. Out of sight, out of mind? Hardly.

There are a few water-oriented funds out there, but many of them specialize in companies in business to deliver "clean" water, that is, the chemicals and analytical tools to mitigate pollution (e.g., Nalco and Tetra Technologies on the list). We think that's important too, but were looking for a fund with companies that also provide the pieces and parts to deliver water and rebuild the infrastructure (Valmont, Ameron, Itron, and others). This PowerShares Water Resources Portfolio has both.

Recently diminished public sector spending has probably held this fund back a bit, and we're not sure that the equal weighting scheme delivers the most to investors in a long-term play. But the fund has a lot of larger and smaller holdings that play well into the theme.

Why Should I Care?

We like this fund mainly as a long-term holding for patient investors agreeing with us that water infrastructure is a long-term problem that must be fixed one way or another.

Upside

- Compelling long-term demand story
- Emerging market growth
- Focused and somewhat defensive

Downside

- Dependent on public spending
- High expense ratio
- Growth story could take a while to develop

Just the Facts

INCEPTION DATE: **December 6, 2005**

TOTAL ASSETS: **$1.2 billion**

AVERAGE DAILY VOLUME: **233,300**

TOTAL HOLDINGS: **33**

PERCENT NORTH AMERICA HOLDINGS: **83.18%**

TOP 10 HOLDINGS PERCENTAGE (CONCENTRATION): **41.15%**

PORTFOLIO TURNOVER: **13.0%**   BENCHMARK: **20.0%**

BETA COEFFICIENT: **1.36**

R-SQUARED (1 YEAR): **85.16%**

1-YEAR RETURN: **29.3%**   BENCHMARK: **30.69%**

3-YEAR RETURN: **-1.61%**   BENCHMARK: **3.34%**

TRACKING ERROR (PRICE VS. NAV)   1 YEAR: **8.49%**   ASSET CLASS MEDIAN: **10.41%**

$10,000 Invested at inception	2006	2007	2008	2009	2010	2011
	$12,239	$14,335	$9,724	$11,381	$12,891	$13,200

What's Under the Hood

Symbol	Name	Percentage of fund
NLC	Nalco Holding Co.	4.66%
VMI	Valmont Industries Inc.	4.61%
LNN	Lindsay Corp.	4.31%
TTEK	Tetra Tech Inc.	4.20%
AMN	Ameron International Corp.	4.17%
URS	URS Corp.	4.07%
ACM	AECOM Technology Corp.	4.04%
BMI	Badger Meter Inc.	3.74%
DHR	Danaher Corp.	3.64%
VE	Veolia Environnement Ve SA	3.56%
ITRI	Itron Inc.	3.50%
INSU	Insituform Technologies Inc.	3.43%
LAYN	Layne Christensen Co.	3.43%
GRC	Gorman Rupp Co.	3.37%
WTS	Watts Water Technologies Inc.	3.36%
PNR	Pentair Inc.	3.34%
ITT	ITT Corp.	3.32%
ROP	Roper Industries Inc.	3.70%

Invesco PowerShares Capital Management LLC
301 West Roosevelt Road
Wheaton, IL 60187
(800) 803-0903
Website: *www.invescopowershares.com*

100 BEST STRATEGY: **FOUNDATION/ROTATION/OPPORTUNISTIC**
100 BEST CATEGORY: **STRATEGY/SECTOR**

PowerShares Global Nuclear Energy Portfolio

Ticker Symbol: PKN ❏ Issuer: Invesco ❏ Description: Equity Industry Selection ❏ Geography: Global. ❏ Morningstar Rating: 3 stars ❏ Marco Polo XTF Rating: 0.9 ❏ Yield: 3.72% ❏ Expense Ratio: 0.75% (Benchmark: 0.60%)

Stated Purpose

The investment seeks results that correspond (before fees and expenses) generally to the price and yield performance of the index called the WNA Nuclear Energy IndexSM (the underlying index). The fund normally invests at least 90 percent of its total assets in stocks and American Depositary Receipts (ADRs) based on the securities that comprise the underlying index. It normally invests at least 80 percent of total assets in the nuclear energy industry. The fund is nondiversified.

Our Take

First off, we will admit that this fund will not appeal to everyone.

To believe in nuclear energy as an investment, you have to believe in three things. First, you must believe, as we do, that fossil fuels will need to be replaced sooner or later, and nuclear energy simply has scale that other alternatives have yet to achieve (we don't have a stat on how many square miles of solar panels it takes to produce the same amount of juice as a nuclear plant, but we could probably find or calculate one).

Second, you have to believe, as we do, that modern technology can work to make nuclear energy safer and easier to capitalize on. Most current nuclear plants were built before the time of widespread computer availability, and there have been advances in material science, cooling technology, and other key areas as well. A plant built today would be better than one built in the late 1960s, just as an aircraft or a spacecraft would be.

Third, you have to believe—and we're not sure about this one—that the ramifications from the recent March 2011 earthquake in Japan, while certainly sobering, won't cause the industry to falter long term. That disaster came at a time when the nuclear industry was just getting back on its feet again and gaining momentum after Chernobyl; now a lot of people and even some long-time government friends like Germany are starting to turn their backs on the atom.

If you believe the nuclear industry can get past this, there may be a major long-term opportunity. This fund contains not just nuclear energy equipment manufacturers, but also several nuclear-based utilities, so it pays a nice yield, which could in turn pay for your patience in waiting for things to get better for the nuclear industry.

Why Should I Care?

Such a fund, while not without risk, can make sense for a small portion of the foundation portfolio as an alternative energy play, as a rotational play when energy prices spike, or as an opportunistic play for a rebound when the news gets better for the industry.

Upside
- Attractive yield
- International exposure
- Long- and short-term alternative energy play

Downside
- Obvious nuclear risk
- Size and liquidity
- Radioactive expense ratio

Just the Facts

INCEPTION DATE: **April 3, 2008**

TOTAL ASSETS: **$25.4 million**

AVERAGE DAILY VOLUME: **12,300**

TOTAL HOLDINGS: **64**

PERCENT NORTH AMERICA HOLDINGS: **45.19%**

TOP 10 HOLDINGS PERCENTAGE (CONCENTRATION): **30.34%**

PORTFOLIO TURNOVER: **12.0%**   BENCHMARK: **20.0%**

BETA COEFFICIENT: **1.24**

R-SQUARED (1 YEAR): **75.60%**

1-YEAR RETURN: **18.21%**   BENCHMARK: **30.69%**

3-YEAR RETURN: **-8.96%**   BENCHMARK: **3.34%**

TRACKING ERROR (PRICE VS. NAV)   1 YEAR: **11.30%**   ASSET CLASS MEDIAN: **10.41%**

$10,000 Invested at inception	2006	2007	2008	2009	2010	2011
	$—	$—	$5,747	$7,360	$8,565	$7,807

What's Under the Hood

Symbol	Name	Percentage of fund
AREVA:FR	Areva SA	4.66%
6502:JP	Toshiba Corp.	4.61%
DML:CA	Denison Mines Corp.	4.31%
1963:JP	JGC CORP	4.20%
UUU:CA	Uranium One Inc.	4.17%
5802:JP	Sumitomo Electric Industries Ltd.	4.07%
EXC	Exelon Corp.	4.04%
CCO:CA	Cameco Corp.	3.74%
EOAN:DE	EON AG	3.64%
EMR	Emerson Electric Co.	3.56%
PDN:AU	Paladin Energy Ltd	3.50%
PH	Parker Hannifin Corp.	3.43%
DUK	Duke Energy Corp.	3.43%
6501:JP	Hitachi Ltd.	3.37%
GE	General Electric Co.	3.36%
FE	FirstEnergy Corp.	3.34%
A052690:KR	KEPCO Engineering & Construction	3.32%
USU	USEC Inc.	3.31%
EDF:FR	Electricite de France SA	3.26%
A034020:KR	Doosan Heavy Industries & Construction Co.	3.22%

Invesco PowerShares Capital Management LLC
301 West Roosevelt Road
Wheaton, IL 60187
(800) 803-0903
Website: *www.invescopowershares.com*

Country/Region

For those wishing a more targeted, and typically more aggressive, international exposure as compared to our International Equity/Index group, the following ten ETFs give exposure to specific countries (like Japan) or to narrowly defined regions, like the so-called "BRICs" (Brazil, Russia, India, China). Note that we've also woven in some strategy in a few cases, as with the Global X China Materials and Global X China Consumer Fund, where we chickened out on investing in the country as a whole but like these two important sectors. The WisdomTree Australia Dividend Fund picks up the Dividend theme with a 5.4 percent yield, the International diversification theme, and a currency appreciation theme all in one. Expenses for these relatively more specialized funds range from 0.50 to 0.65 percent.

100 BEST STRATEGY: FOUNDATION

100 BEST CATEGORY: COUNTRY/REGION

SPDR S&P BRIC 40 ETF

Ticker Symbol: BIK ▢ Issuer: State Street Global Advisors ▢ Description: Equity Region Selection ▢ Geography: Brazil, Russia, India, China ▢ Morningstar Rating: 3 stars ▢ Marco Polo XTF Rating: 4.6 ▢ Yield: 1.90% ▢ Expense Ratio: 0.50% (Benchmark: 0.60%)

Stated Purpose

The investment seeks to replicate as closely as possible, before fees and expenses, the total return performance of an equity index based upon the emerging markets of Brazil, Russia, India, and China. The fund uses a passive management strategy designed to track the total return performance of the S&P BRIC 40 Index. The BRIC 40 Index is a market capitalization weighted index designed to provide exposure to forty leading companies domiciled in the emerging markets of Brazil, Russia, India, and China that are listed on

the Hong Kong Stock Exchange, the London Stock Exchange, NAS-DAQ, and/or the NYSE.

Our Take

The appeal of investing in the so-called "BRICs" is pretty simple—it's where today's global growth is really centered. Of course, along with this growth comes a degree of risk; any rapidly growing economy will take a path through change—regulation, fiscal and monetary policy, environmental degradation and remedies, local corruption—you name it. From our somewhat isolated American front porch, it's hard to see how such changes and forces will affect the economies of these countries, let alone any single company.

That's why, to hitch your wagon to the BRICs, it makes sense to use a fund. The SPDR S&P BRIC 40 is just such a fund, and we think its concentration on the top forty companies gives you size with the degree of diversification necessary to participate in BRIC growth while limiting the risk. The BRIC 40 invests in companies that have largely become household names for anyone following the story of these countries.

The fund country breakdown is 45 percent China, 22 percent Brazil, 21 percent Russia, and 8 percent India. By sector it's 36 percent energy, 33 percent financials, 10 percent IT, 9 percent telecom, 9 percent materials, and 3 percent consumer. While we'd like to see a bit more of India, which

hasn't given rise to as many large companies as the other three, and a bit more in the consumer sector, as consumer wealth and standard of living grows in these countries, we generally like this mix.

Why Should I Care?

This fund makes the most sense for a more aggressive international exposure in a foundation portfolio.

Upside

- Balanced portfolio, safer than most BRIC
- Decent yield
- Easiest way to invest in BRIC

Downside

- Recent returns not stellar, stocks overpriced?
- The usual BRIC and emerging market risks
- Not enough India, consumer?

Just the Facts

INCEPTION DATE: **June 19, 2007**

TOTAL ASSETS: **$531.7 million**

AVERAGE DAILY VOLUME: **102,400**

TOTAL HOLDINGS: **41**

PERCENT NORTH AMERICA HOLDINGS: **0.0%**

TOP 10 HOLDINGS PERCENTAGE (CONCENTRATION): **52.44%**

PORTFOLIO TURNOVER: **9.0%**   BENCHMARK: **12.0%**

BETA COEFFICIENT: **0.66**

R-SQUARED (1 YEAR): **58.65%**

1-YEAR RETURN: **23.54%**   BENCHMARK: **30.69%**

3-YEAR RETURN: **0.13%**   BENCHMARK: **3.34%**

TRACKING ERROR (PRICE VS. NAV)   1 YEAR: **11.70%**   ASSET CLASS MEDIAN: **10.41%**

$10,000 Invested at inception	2006	2007	2008	2009	2010	2011
	$—	$13,533	$6,099	$11,050	$12,202	$12,539

What's Under the Hood

Symbol	Name	Percentage of fund
OGZD:GB	Gazprom OAO	8.95%
939:HK	China Construction Bank Corp.	6.09%
941:HK	China Mobile Ltd.	5.48%
PBR	Petroleo Brasiliero SA Petrobras	5.43%
ITUB	Itau Unibanco Holding SA	5.05%
BIDU	Baidu Inc.	4.88%
VALE	Vale SA	4.59%
1398:HK	Industrial and Commercial Bank of China	4.55%
BBD	Banco Bradesco SA	3.94%
883:HK	CNOOC Ltd.	3.77%
857:HK	PetroChina Co Ltd.	3.22%
INFY	Infosys Ltd.	3.22%
LKOD:GB	NEFTYANAYA KOMPANIYA LUKOIL OAO	3.06%
3988:HK	Bank of China Ltd.	2.97%
2628:HK	China Life Insurance Co Ltd.	2.69%
NVTK:GB	Novatek OAO	2.51%
ABV	Companhia De Bebidas Das Americas AMBEV	2.36%
MNOD:GB	GMK Noril'skiy nikel' OAO	2.21%
700:HK	Tencent Holdings Ltd.	2.20%
1088:HK	China Shenhua Energy Co. Ltd.	1.84%

State Street Global Advisors
State Street Financial Center
1 Lincoln Street
Boston, MA 02111–2900
Phone: (617) 786-3000
Website: *www.spdrs.com*

SPDR S&P Emerging Asia Pacific Fund

Ticker Symbol: GMF ❑ Issuer: State Street Global Advisors ❑ Description: Equity Region Selection ❑ Geography: Asia Pacific Region ❑ Morningstar rating: 4 stars ❑ Marco Polo XTF rating: 3.8 ❑ Yield: 1.52% ❑ Expense Ratio: 0.59% (Benchmark: 0.60%)

Stated Purpose

The investment seeks to replicate, net of expenses, the S&P Asia Pacific Emerging BMI Index. The fund invests at least 80 percent of its assets in the securities comprising the index. The index is a market capitalization weighted index that measures the investable universe of publicly traded companies in emerging Asian Pacific markets.

Our Take

It's hard to believe that it's been almost twenty years since the so-called "Asian tigers" hit economic prominence. Singapore, Malaysia, Thailand, Taiwan, Indonesia, India, and other developing nations rose in the wake of Japan's industrial and financial boom of the late 1980s. And for good reason: These countries offered inexpensive and largely skilled labor, natural resources in some cases, and a degree of cultural unity and alignment with Japan that allowed them to import some of that country's prosperity.

These countries boomed but eventually ran into fiscal and monetary problems of their own, especially as Japanese investment waned after that county's own setbacks. But we think the "Tigers" theme is still valid, and now we have China as the "new" Japan in its dominance of the region.

The SPDR S&P Emerging Asia Pacific Fund invests pretty much in this set of economies, with China thrown in for good measure. The country breakdown is 35 percent China, 27 percent Taiwan, 16 percent India, 7 percent Malaysia, and 5 percent Thailand. By sector: 26 percent financials, 20 percent IT, 13 percent energy, 10 percent materials. As such, the fund is attractive as a broad, diverse, and safe way to gain exposure to this economically influential part of the world.

Why Should I Care?

For a foundation portfolio the SPDR S&P Emerging Asia Pacific Fund offers a way to get a relatively more aggressive international exposure for the long term.

Upside

- Exposure to international strength without too much risk
- Reasonable yield
- Safety through diversification

Downside

- Vulnerable to weak dollar, local economic policy
- No Singapore? No consumer?
- Too much diversification? Hard to "beat the market"

Just the Facts

INCEPTION DATE: **March 19, 2007**

TOTAL ASSETS: **$714.2 million**

AVERAGE DAILY VOLUME: **100,400**

TOTAL HOLDINGS: **283**

PERCENT NORTH AMERICA HOLDINGS: **0.0%**

TOP 10 HOLDINGS PERCENTAGE (CONCENTRATION): **20.24%**

PORTFOLIO TURNOVER: **17.0%**   BENCHMARK: **12.0%**

BETA COEFFICIENT: **0.66**

R-SQUARED (ONE YEAR): **51.04%**

1-YEAR RETURN: **23.56%**   BENCHMARK: **30.69%**

3-YEAR RETURN: **18.90%**   BENCHMARK: **3.34%**

TRACKING ERROR (PRICE VS. NAV)   1 YEAR: **12.07%**   ASSET CLASS MEDIAN: **10.41%**

$10,000 Invested at inception	2006	2007	2008	2009	2010	2011
	$—	$14,484	$7,189	$12,504	$14,907	$14,874

What's Under the Hood

Symbol	Name	Percentage of fund
TSM	Taiwan Semiconductor Mfg	3.02%
939:HK	China Construction Bank Corp	2.41%
941:HK	China Mobile Ltd	2.35%
BIDU	Baidu Inc	2.07%
857:HK	PetroChina Co Ltd	1.87%
1398:HK	Industrial and Commercial Bank of China	1.83%
2498	HTC Corp	1.76%
RIGDS	Reliance Industries Ltd	1.64%
883:HK	CNOOC Ltd	1.61%
INFY	Infosys Ltd	1.58%
2628:HK	China Life Insurance Co Ltd	1.50%
2317	Hon Hai Precision Ind Co Ltd	1.28%

Symbol	Name	Percentage of fund
1301	Formosa Plastics Corp	1.20%
BHARTI	Bharti Airtel Ltd	1.16%
3988:HK	Bank of China Ltd	1.15%
1088:HK	China Shenhua Energy Co Ltd	1.13%
386:HK	China Petroleum & Chemical Corp	1.07%
700:HK	Tencent Holdings Ltd	0.98%
BBRI:ID	Bank Rakyat Indonesia (Persero) Tbk PT	0.98%
914:HK	Anhui Conch Cement Co Ltd	0.97%

State Street Global Advisors
State Street Financial Center
1 Lincoln St.
Boston, MA 02111–2900
Phone: (617) 786-3000
Website: *www.spdrs.com*

100 BEST STRATEGY: **FOUNDATION**

100 BEST CATEGORY: **COUNTRY/REGION**

WisdomTree Australia Dividend Fund

Ticker Symbol: AUSE ▫ Issuer: WisdomTree ▫ Description: Equity Country Selection ▫ Geography: Australia ▫ Morningstar Rating: 3 stars ▫ Marco Polo XTF Rating: 2.6 ▫ Yield: 5.90% ▫ Expense Ratio: 0.58% (Benchmark: 0.60%)

Stated Purpose

The investment seeks to replicate, net of expenses, the WisdomTree Australia Dividend Index. The index is a fundamentally weighted index that measures the performance of high-dividend yielding companies in Australia. The fund attempts to invest all, or substantially all, of its assets in the stocks that make up the index. It normally invests at least 95 percent of total assets in the component securities of the index.

Our Take

Like sailing, or throwing a Frisbee, it always works better when you have a tailwind. In that spirit, we think Australia is a pretty good place to invest right now. Why? First, because a good portion of its economy supports the fastest growing major economy in the world—China. While China may have its ups and downs with inflation and other economic twists inherent in a booming economy, Australia is a relatively smooth, established economy that just happens to be selling a lot of picks and shovels into the Chinese gold rush.

Second, and partly because of the first point, Australia's currency has been a bastion of strength against the U.S. dollar and many other world currencies. Their fiscal and monetary houses are in order; they are one of the few developed countries not having to buy (or borrow) their way out of a recession right now.

So we like Australian investments. We think investing in Australian companies is a better way to play this trade than simply investing in Australian currencies; it's safer and, in the case of the WisdomTree Australia Dividend Fund, you get a nice return of almost 6 percent right now. Assuming China doesn't implode—and we don't think it will—this fund offers current yield and growth potential through normal company growth and through currency appreciation— a nice trifecta to have on your side.

Why Should I Care?

The WisdomTree Australia Dividend Fund brings at once a solid current yield, growth prospects, and a favorable international exposure and is well suited for a foundation portfolio.

Upside

- Yield *and* growth
- Currency tailwind
- Not overloaded with mining shares

Downside

- Still affected by China's ups and downs
- Can Australian dollar keep appreciating?
- A bit small and illiquid

Just the Facts

INCEPTION DATE: **June 16, 2006**

TOTAL ASSETS: **$55.1 million**

AVERAGE DAILY VOLUME: **8,900**

TOTAL HOLDINGS: **69**

PERCENT NORTH AMERICA HOLDINGS: **1.08%**

TOP 10 HOLDINGS PERCENTAGE (CONCENTRATION): **28.85%**

PORTFOLIO TURNOVER: **46.0%**   BENCHMARK: **12.0%**

BETA COEFFICIENT: **1.07**

R-SQUARED (1 YEAR): **88.0%**

1-YEAR RETURN: **37.18%**   BENCHMARK: **30.69%**

3-YEAR RETURN: **8.51%**   BENCHMARK: **3.34%**

TRACKING ERROR (PRICE VS. NAV)   1 YEAR: **7.16%**   ASSET CLASS MEDIAN: **10.41%**

$10,000 Invested at inception	2006	2007	2008	2009	2010	2011
	$12,448	$15,133	$7,756	$14,184	$15,868	$16,637

What's Under the Hood

Symbol	Name	Percentage of fund
TLS:AU	Telstra Corp. Ltd.	3.82%
GFF:AU	Goodman Fielder Ltd.	3.76%
FGL:AU	Fosters Group Ltd.	2.96%
MTS:AU	Metcash Ltd.	2.92%
QBE:AU	QBE Insurance Group Ltd.	2.74%
MYR:AU	Myer Holdings Ltd.	2.72%
WBC:AU	Westpac Banking Corp.	2.68%
ANZ:AU	Australia and New Zealand Banking Group	2.51%
CBA:AU	Commonwealth Bank of Australia	2.45%
NAB:AU	National Australia Bank Ltd.	2.31%
DJS:AU	David Jones Ltd.	2.23%
LEI:AU	Leighton Hldg Ltd.	2.19%
OZL:AU	Oz Minerals Ltd.	2.01%
SHL:AU	Sonic Healthcare Ltd.	2.00%
JBH:AU	JB Hi Fi Ltd.	1.95%
AMC:AU	Amcor Ltd.	1.93%
TTS:AU	Tatts Group Ltd.	1.93%
MQG:AU	Macquarie Group Ltd.	1.91%
WES:AU	Wesfarmers Ltd.	1.88%
HVN:AU	Harvey Norman Holdings Ltd.	1.87%

WisdomTree Investments LLC
380 Madison Avenue, 21st Floor
New York, NY 10017
(866) 909- 9473
Website: *www.wisdomtree.com*

iShares MSCI Pacific Ex-Japan Index Fund

Ticker Symbol: EPP ▢ Issuer: BlackRock/iShares ▢ Description: Equity Region Selection ▢
Geography: Asia Pacific Region ▢ Morningstar Rating: 3 stars ▢ Marco Polo XTF Rating: 6.4 ▢
Yield: 3.65% ▢ Expense Ratio: 0.50% (Benchmark: 0.60%)

Stated Purpose

The investment seeks to replicate, net of expenses, the MSCI Pacific Ex-Japan Index. The fund generally invests at least 95 percent of its assets in the securities of the index and in depositary receipts (DRs) representing in the index. It at all times invests at least 90 percent of its assets in the securities of the underlying index or in DRs representing in the index. The index consists of stocks from the following four markets: Australia, Hong Kong, New Zealand, and Singapore.

Our Take

When looking for a fund investment, often you are trying to balance a series of investing objectives. "I want to invest in growth, but with a degree of safety, and I want some income too. I want some international exposure and want to invest overseas where things are good. But not too much risk, please, and let me avoid the countries that are in trouble."

If that sounds like you, perhaps an investment in the iShares MSCI Pacific Ex-Japan Index Fund is worth a look. This fund invests in the booming Asia-Pacific region, but carefully avoids the currently moribund Japan and the risky and volatile parts of China, bringing the best of the best in the four markets mentioned in the "stated purpose" statement. By the way, the mix is 61 percent Australia, 18 percent Hong Kong (well, yes, China, but the less "boomtown" part of it, we think), 12 percent Singapore, and the remaining 9 percent New Zealand.

So we're selling picks and shovels (and a lot of iron ore and coal and other stuff) into the Chinese gold rush, and we're also handling a lot of their money. By sector, the biggest weight is in financials (44 percent) and materials (20 percent). Because of the heavy financial weight, we have a fund that yields 3.7 percent. Beyond that, the strength of these currencies versus the U.S. dollar is another positive.

Why Should I Care?

EPP works as a relatively steady and high yielding international base for a foundation portfolio or as a relatively conservative rotational play on China growth and dollar weakness.

Upside

- Yield *and* growth, currency tailwind
- Best set of markets right now
- Large, liquid, and experienced

Downside

- Too exposed to financials?
- Mining stocks can be volatile
- Buy-in might be expensive

Just the Facts

INCEPTION DATE: **October 25, 2001**

TOTAL ASSETS: **$4.0 billion**

AVERAGE DAILY VOLUME: **946,100**

TOTAL HOLDINGS: **150**

PERCENT NORTH AMERICA HOLDINGS: **1.24%**

TOP 10 HOLDINGS PERCENTAGE (CONCENTRATION): **38.0%**

PORTFOLIO TURNOVER: **5.0%**   BENCHMARK: **12.0%**

BETA COEFFICIENT: **0.92**

R-SQUARED (1 YEAR): **82.26%**

1-YEAR RETURN: **34.88%**   BENCHMARK: **30.69%**

3-YEAR RETURN: **4.85%**   BENCHMARK: **3.34%**

TRACKING ERROR (PRICE VS. NAV)   1 YEAR: **7.82%**   ASSET CLASS MEDIAN: **10.41%**

$10,000 Invested at inception	2006	2007	2008	2009	2010	2011
	$29,421	$38,359	$19,165	$32,884	$38,281	$39,182

What's Under the Hood

Symbol	Name	Percentage of fund
BHP:AU	BHP Billiton Ltd.	9.67%
CBA:AU	Commonwealth Bank of Australia	5.55%
WBC:AU	Westpac Banking Corp.	4.47%
ANZ:AU	Australia and New Zealand Banking Group	3.94%
NAB:AU	National Australia Bank Ltd.	3.79%
RIO:AU	Rio Tinto Ltd.	2.53%

Symbol	Name	Percentage of fund
WOW:AU	Woolworths Ltd.	2.38%
NCM:AU	Newcrest Mining Ltd.	2.20%
WES:AU	Wesfarmers Ltd.	2.14%
1299:HK	AIA Group Ltd.	1.90%
WPL:AU	Woodside Petroleum Ltd.	1.74%
13:HK	Hutchison Whampoa Ltd.	1.65%
Z74:SG	Singapore Telecommunications Ltd.	1.48%
D05:SG	Dbs Group Holdings Ltd.	1.46%
1:HK	Cheung Kong (Holdings) Ltd.	1.41%
388:HK	Hong Kong Exchanges and Clearing Ltd.	1.40%
16:HK	Sun Hung Kai Properties Ltd.	1.40%
039:SG	Oversea Chinese Banking Corporation Ltd.	1.35%
U11:SG	United Overseas Bank Ltd.	1.32%
WDC:AU	Westfield Group	1.27%

BlackRock/iShares
525 Washington Boulevard, Suite 1405
Jersey City, NJ 07310
(800) 474-2737
Website: *www.ishares.com*

100 BEST STRATEGY: **ROTATIONAL/OPPORTUNISTIC**

100 BEST CATEGORY: **COUNTRY/REGION**

Global X China Materials Fund

Ticker Symbol: CHIM □ Issuer: Global X Mgt. □ Description: Equity Country Sector Selection □ Geography: China □ Morningstar Rating: NR □ Marco Polo XTF Rating: 0.5 □ Yield: 1.15% □ Expense Ratio: 0.65% (Benchmark: 0.60%)

Stated Purpose

The investment seeks to provide investment results that correspond generally to the price and yield performance, before fees and expenses, of the Solactive China Materials Index.

The fund normally invests at least 80 percent of total assets in the securities of the underlying index and in depository receipts based on the securities in the underlying index. It uses a replication strategy. The underlying index is a free float-adjusted, liquidity-tested and market capitalization-weighted index that is designed to measure the performance of the investable universe of companies in the Materials sector of the Chinese economy.

Our Take

Given the emerging eminence of China as the world's fastest-growing economy, it's hard not to direct us to one of the many country funds covering the Chinese investing landscape. Yet, we think there is a lot of inherent risk in China as the country's leadership struggles (if that's the right word) with a booming economy. Booms create busts; they also create economic distortions where certain sectors or industries come too much into favor, only to contract when economic reality takes over. Japanese real estate and finance is one example. We think Chinese real estate and finance will become another.

So we think the best way to play China is to carve out an economic segment that should prosper from the boom without being over-exposed to its frothiness. Regardless of what happens to the rest of the Chinese economy, we believe that manufacturing is there to stay. China has already captured so much manufacturing market share and has achieved "critical mass" with supply chains and technology to the point

that we doubt it will shift back to the original countries—the United States, Europe, and Japan—very soon. In that light, we think that companies that produce and supply materials into Chinese manufacturing will continue to prosper, thus we've chosen the CHIM fund as one of our two China picks (we also think the Chinese consumer economy will flourish; see our CHIQ pick—the Global X China Consumer Fund).

Beyond the rationale we just shared, we like the fact that this fund concentrates more in base manufacturing materials like copper, petrochemicals, and aluminum and less in infrastructure building materials like cement and steel, which could make it safer if the local economy falters. That said, if China changes its policy to let its currency appreciate, foreign sources for these materials will become more attractive.

Why Should I Care?

Long term, we think Chinese manufacturing is here to stay, and this supplier into that phenomenon makes sense in a foundation portfolio. Shorter term, you might choose to go for the ride in rotation or as a near-term opportunity.

Upside

- More of a sure thing in an uncertain economy
- Good way to buy companies you never heard of
- Decent yield for such a play

Downside

- Still exposed to China boom-bust cycles
- If China appreciates its currency —could hurt
- Very new, very small

Just the Facts

INCEPTION DATE: **January 14, 2010**

TOTAL ASSETS: **$3.8 million**

AVERAGE DAILY VOLUME: **5,800**

TOTAL HOLDINGS: **32**

PERCENT NORTH AMERICA HOLDINGS: **0.03%**

TOP 10 HOLDINGS PERCENTAGE (CONCENTRATION): **52.36%**

PORTFOLIO TURNOVER: **20.75%**　BENCHMARK: **12.0%**

BETA COEFFICIENT: **0.86**

R-SQUARED (1 YEAR): **48.39%**

1-YEAR RETURN: **18.52%**　BENCHMARK: **30.69%**

3-YEAR RETURN: **NA**　BENCHMARK: **3.34%**

TRACKING ERROR (PRICE VS. NAV)　1 YEAR: **15.04%**　ASSET CLASS MEDIAN: **10.41%**

$10,000 Invested at inception	2006	2007	2008	2009	2010	2011
	$—	$—	$—	$—	$12,312	$10,678

What's Under the Hood

Symbol	Name	Percentage of fund
2168:HK	Yingde Gases Group Co Ltd.	6.61%
358:HK	Jiangxi Copper Co Ltd.	5.72%
189:HK	Dongyue Group Ltd.	5.66%
2899:HK	Zijin Mining Group Co. Ltd.	5.64%
3983:HK	China Bluechemical Ltd.	5.23%
2600:HK	Aluminum Corp. Of China Ltd.	4.99%
1378	China Hongqiao Group Ltd.	4.89%
3993:HK	China Molybdenum Co. Ltd.	4.81%
1818:HK	Zhaojin Mining Industry Co. Ltd.	4.74%

Symbol	Name	Percentage of fund
338:HK	Sinopec Shanghai Petrochemical Co. Ltd.	4.71%
323:HK	Maanshan Iron & Steel Co. Ltd.	4.58%
347:HK	Angang Steel Co. Ltd.	4.41%
297:HK	Sinofert Holdings Ltd.	4.06%
267:HK	Citic Pacific Ltd.	4.01%
1393:HK	Hidili Industry International Development	3.96%
2626:HK	Hunan Nonferrous Metals Corp. Ltd.	3.91%
246:HK	Real Gold Mining Ltd.	2.94%
1033:HK	Sinopec Yizheng Chemical Fibre Co. Ltd.	2.71%
546:HK	Fufeng Group Ltd.	2.62%
769:HK	China Rare Earth Holdings Ltd.	2.11%

Global X Management Company LLC
410 Park Avenue, 4th Floor
New York, NY 10022
(888) 493-8631
Website: *www.globalxfunds.com*

100 BEST STRATEGY: **FOUNDATIONAL**

100 BEST CATEGORY: **COUNTRY/REGION**

Global X China Consumer Fund

Ticker Symbol: CHIQ ❑ Issuer: Global X Mgt. ❑ Description: Equity Country Sector Selection ❑ Geography: China ❑ Morningstar Rating: NR ❑ Marco Polo XTF Rating: 1.1 ❑ Yield: 1.04% ❑ Expense Ratio: 0.65% (Benchmark: 0.60%)

Stated Purpose

The investment seeks to provide results that correspond generally to the price and yield performance, before fees and expenses, of the Solactive China Consumer Index ("underlying index"). The fund normally invests at least 80 percent of total assets in the securities of the underlying index and in depositary receipts based on the securities in the underlying index. It uses a replication strategy. The underlying index is a free float-adjusted, liquidity-tested and market capitalization-weighted index that is designed to measure the performance of the investable universe of companies in the Consumer sector of the Chinese economy.

Our Take

If you just read our analysis of the Global X China Materials Fund (CHIM) you may find this next paragraph a bit familiar—because it is exactly the same. Here goes, anyway:

Given the emerging eminence of China as the world's fastest-growing economy, it's hard not to direct us to one of the many country funds covering the Chinese investing landscape. Yet, we think there is a lot of inherent risk in China as the country's leadership struggles (if that's the right word) with a booming economy. Booms create busts; they also create economic distortions where certain sectors or industries come too much into favor, only to contract when economic reality takes over. Japanese real estate and finance is one example. We think Chinese real estate and finance will become another.

So we think the best way to play China is to carve out an economic segment that should prosper from the boom without being overexposed to its frothiness. In this case, we believe the Chinese consumer economy, along with the material supply sector, will prosper. Why? Because the Chinese government is deliberately trying to get its consumers to spend. Why are they doing that? To help balance trade and the economy and to improve the overall standard of living in the country. Too, the middle class is growing rapidly. Chinese consumer goods companies, retailers, media, and marketing companies should all benefit from these trends. That's most of what you'll find in this fund.

Why Should I Care?

For the long term, the Chinese consumer will spend more on an improving standard of living; this trend should bode well for a longer-term foundation portfolio play.

Upside

- A solid long-term play in an otherwise uncertain economy
- Focused
- Good if you're late to the China party

Downside

- Still exposed to China boom-bust cycles
- Consumers may *never* spend—even with government prodding
- Performance underwhelming so far, may have to be patient

Just the Facts

INCEPTION DATE: **December 1, 2009**

TOTAL ASSETS: **$206.6 million**

AVERAGE DAILY VOLUME: **98,300**

TOTAL HOLDINGS: **41**

PERCENT NORTH AMERICA HOLDINGS: **0.0%**

TOP 10 HOLDINGS PERCENTAGE (CONCENTRATION): **50.41%**

PORTFOLIO TURNOVER: **6.11%**   BENCHMARK: **12.0%**

BETA COEFFICIENT: **0.39**

R-SQUARED (1 YEAR): **11.86%**

1-YEAR RETURN: **11.67%**   BENCHMARK: **30.69%**

3-YEAR RETURN: **NA**   BENCHMARK: **3.34%**

TRACKING ERROR (PRICE VS. NAV)   1 YEAR: **21.4%**   ASSET CLASS MEDIAN: **10.41%**

$10,000 Invested at inception	2006	2007	2008	2009	2010	2011
	$—	$—	$—	$10,000	$11,008	$11,073

What's Under the Hood

Symbol	Name	Percentage of fund
493:HK	Gome Electrical Appliances Holding Ltd.	6.61%
489:HK	Dongfeng Motor Group Co. Ltd.	5.72%
322:HK	Tingyi (Cayman Islands) Holding Corp.	5.66%
1044:HK	Hengan International Group Co. Ltd.	5.64%
291:HK	China Resources Enterprise Ltd.	5.23%
EDU	New Oriental Education & Technology	4.99%
151:HK	Want Want China Holdings Ltd.	4.89%
FMCN	Focus Media Holding Ltd.	4.81%
1068:HK	China Yurun Food Group Ltd.	4.74%
2238:HK	Guangzhou Automobile Group Co. Ltd.	4.71%
753:HK	Air China Ltd.	4.58%
1833:HK	Intime Department Store (Group) Co. Ltd.	4.41%
YOKU	Youkucom Inc.	4.06%
3368:HK	Parkson Retail Group Ltd.	4.01%
1066:HK	Shandong Weigao Medical Polymer Co.	3.96%
168:HK	Tsingtao Brewery Co. Ltd.	3.91%
1099:HK	Sinopharm Group Co. Ltd.	2.94%
606:HK	China Agri Industries Holdings Ltd.	2.71%
HMIN	Home Inns & Hotels Management Inc.	2.62%
2333:HK	Great Wall Motor Co. Ltd.	2.11%

Global X Management Company LLC
410 Park Avenue, 4th Floor
New York, NY 10022
(888) 493-8631
Website: *www.globalxfunds.com*

SPDR Russell/Nomura Prime Japan ETF

Ticker Symbol: JPP ❑ Issuer: State Street Global Advisors ❑ Description: Equity Country Selection ❑ Geography: Japan ❑ Morningstar Rating: 3 stars ❑ Marco Polo XTF Rating: 2.3 ❑ Yield: 2.37% ❑ Expense Ratio: 0.50% (Benchmark: 0.60%)

Stated Purpose

The investment seeks to replicate the total return performance of an equity index based upon the Japanese equity market. The fund uses a passive management strategy and sampling methodology designed to track the total return performance of the Russell/ Nomura PRIME Index. The PRIME Index is made up of the 1,000 largest stocks in terms of float-adjusted market capitalization of the index and is designed to take into account liquidity and to serve as a benchmark for passive investment strategies. The PRIME Index includes stocks from a broad universe of Japanese equities.

Our Take

Most investment professionals these days are still advising folks to stay away from Japan. No growth, debt problems, an ineffective central bank, a dysfunctional government and leadership structure—and almost twenty years of varying degrees of recession because of all of that. (If any of that sounds like today's United States, that's a pure coincidence . . . .)

But Japan has a few things that the United States doesn't have, or at least the United States doesn't have

any longer. First, it has a first-order manufacturing capability. True, some of that, especially the labor intensive, low value-add part of it, has shipped off to other Asian countries. But Japan still has a huge high-value-add industrial infrastructure mostly intact save for the short-term earthquake destruction.

Second, Japan still funds its own debt and deficits. Japanese savers still supply enough capital to fund the country's debt needs; there is no need to go to others, particularly China, to sell bonds. The economy may be slow, but it is still self-sufficient, and part of the reason it is slow is the strong yen, which results in part from this self-sufficiency.

So we think that Japan's problems aren't as severe as the markets have made them out to be, especially long term, and, at least for patient investors, we support the idea of adding some Japan to a portfolio. The SPDR Russell/Nomura Prime Japan ETF is a safe, broad, and well-diversified way to do this. About 85 percent of the fund is large-cap, with familiar names like Toyota, Honda, and Canon. The rest is made up of smaller and more aggressive plays.

Why Should I Care?
If you believe in a Japan turnaround and in the core strength of Japanese manufacturers, this is a good place to put some long-term capital.

Upside
• Good way to play Japan turnaround

• Attractive yield
• Safely diversified

Downside
• Strong yen hurts
• Turnarounds can take a long time
• Small and not very liquid

Just the Facts

INCEPTION DATE: **November 9, 2006**

TOTAL ASSETS: **$15.7 million**

AVERAGE DAILY VOLUME: **2,000**

TOTAL HOLDINGS: **379**

PERCENT NORTH AMERICA HOLDINGS: **0.80%**

TOP 10 HOLDINGS PERCENTAGE (CONCENTRATION): **18.81%**

PORTFOLIO TURNOVER: **3.0%**   BENCHMARK: **12.0%**

BETA COEFFICIENT: **0.50**

R-SQUARED (1 YEAR): **39.08%**

1-YEAR RETURN: **11.86%**   BENCHMARK: **30.69%**

3-YEAR RETURN: **-4.13**   BENCHMARK: **3.34%**

TRACKING ERROR (PRICE VS. NAV)   1 YEAR: **16.26%**   ASSET CLASS MEDIAN: **10.41%**

$10,000 Invested at inception	2006	2007	2008	2009	2010	2011
	$10,187	$9,673	$7,023	$7,324	$8,476	$8,079

What's Under the Hood

Symbol	Name	Percentage of fund
7203:JP	Toyota Motor Corp.	3.27%
8306:JP	Mitsubishi UFJ Financial Group Inc.	2.57%
7267:JP	Honda Motor Co Ltd.	2.36%
7751:JP	Canon Inc.	2.27%
9432:JP	Nippon Telegraph And Telephone Corp.	1.57%
8316:JP	Sumitomo Mitsui Financial Group Inc.	1.55%

Symbol	Name	Percentage of fund
4502:JP	Takeda Pharmaceutical Co. Ltd.	1.46%
6954:JP	Fanuc Corp.	1.40%
8058:JP	Mitsubishi Corp.	1.25%
8031:JP	Mitsui & Co. Ltd.	1.16%
8411:JP	Mizuho Financial Group Inc.	1.11%
9437:JP	NTT Docomo Inc.	1.11%
9984:JP	Softbank Corp.	1.06%
6758:JP	Sony Corp.	1.06%
6301:JP	Komatsu Ltd.	1.05%
9433:JP	Kddi Corp.	1.00%
6501:JP	Hitachi Ltd.	0.99%
9020:JP	East Japan Railway Co.	0.93%
8802:JP	Mitsubishi Estate Co. Ltd.	0.88%
6752:JP	Panasonic Corp.	0.87%

State Street Global Advisors
State Street Financial Center
1 Lincoln Street
Boston, MA 02111–2900
Phone: (617) 786-3000
Website: *www.spdrs.com*

100 BEST STRATEGY: **FOUNDATION/ROTATIONAL/OPPORTUNISTIC**

100 BEST CATEGORY: **COUNTRY/REGION**

SPDR Russell/Nomura Small Cap Japan ETF

Ticker Symbol: JSC ⬛ Issuer: State Street Global Advisors ⬛ Description: Equity Country Small-Cap Selection ⬛ Geography: Japan ⬛ Morningstar Rating: 4 stars ⬛ Marco Polo XTF Rating: NR ⬛ Yield: 1.46% ⬛ Expense Ratio: 0.55% (Benchmark: 0.60%)

Stated Purpose

The investment seeks to replicate as closely as possible, before fees and expenses, the total return performance of an equity index based upon the Japanese small cap equity market. The fund uses a passive management strategy and sampling methodology designed to track the total return performance of the float-adjusted Russell/Nomura Japan Small-Cap Index. The Small-Cap

Japan Index is made up of the smallest 15 percent of stocks, in terms of float-adjusted market capitalization, of the Russell/Nomura Total Market Index.

Our Take

Do you think that Japan has what it really takes to shake off twenty years of debt problems, the unwinding of an asset bubble, and an ineffectual government policy?

If you do, we agree with you. These problems sound alarmingly similar to what we're experiencing in the United States today, but Japan differs in two ways: First, it has kept most of its high value-add engineering and manufacturing capability intact. While some low value-add work has gone elsewhere in Asia (and to the United States in the case of the auto industry), the core manufacturing infrastructure and its supply chains are still in the country. Second, the Japanese are big savers, and the country is thus able to fund its own debt without soliciting foreign borrowing.

We think these two factors will eventually allow Japan to resume its world-leading economic position. And when it does, the big companies will prosper, but the smaller names may prosper even more, since some of the bigger names like those in our other Japan pick, the SPDR Russell/Nomura Prime

Japan ETF (JPP) may be too big to really grow that much. But smaller companies may shine, especially if the yen weakens and Japanese goods become even more competitive on the world stage. We feel they're already pretty competitive because of technology and quality, so they don't need so much of a currency push as in other countries.

The fund is well diversified with 397 holdings. By sector, 24 percent are industrials, 22 percent are consumer, 13 percent are financial, 12 percent are IT, 12 percent are materials, 10 percent are consumer staples, and 5 percent are in health care.

So if you want to bet with us on this turnaround—and the recovery from the March 2011 earthquake might make this turnaround more pronounced—the SPDR Russell/Nomura Small Cap Japan ETF should work well.

Why Should I Care?

This fund would work for more aggressive international portions of a foundation portfolio. Those believing an economic turnaround is imminent, or that earthquake recovery will give these companies a boost, could use this fund in a rotational or even opportunistic portfolio.

Upside

- Good assortment of companies and sectors
- Attractive yield for this type of fund
- Well positioned for Japan recovery

Downside

- Will recovery ever happen? May require patience
- Overdiversified, not focused?
- China may eat their lunch

Just the Facts

INCEPTION DATE: **November 9, 2006**

TOTAL ASSETS: **$123.7 million**

AVERAGE DAILY VOLUME: **31,700**

TOTAL HOLDINGS: **397**

PERCENT NORTH AMERICA HOLDINGS: **0.71%**

TOP 10 HOLDINGS PERCENTAGE (CONCENTRATION): **5.84%**

PORTFOLIO TURNOVER: **8.0%**   BENCHMARK: **12.0%**

BETA COEFFICIENT: **0.38**

R-SQUARED (1 YEAR): **25.0%**

1-YEAR RETURN: **13.90%**   BENCHMARK: **30.69%**

3-YEAR RETURN: **-1.77**   BENCHMARK: **3.34%**

TRACKING ERROR (PRICE VS. NAV)   1 YEAR: **16.59%**   ASSET CLASS MEDIAN: **10.41%**

$10,000 Invested at inception	2006	2007	2008	2009	2010	2011
	$10,045	$8,855	$7,276	$7,648	$8,448	$9,239

What's Under the Hood

Symbol	Name	Percentage of fund
CASH	Cash	0.76%
4521:JP	Kaken Pharmaceutical Co Ltd.	0.62%
6474:JP	Nachi Fujikoshi Corp.	0.58%
4114:JP	Nippon Shokubai Co. Ltd.	0.58%
8388:JP	Awa Bank Ltd.	0.57%
6366:JP	Chiyoda Corp.	0.57%
6976:JP	Taiyo Yuden Co. Ltd.	0.56%
2908:JP	FujicCo Co. Ltd.	0.56%
4527	Rohto Pharmaceutical Co. Ltd.	0.53%

Symbol	Name	Percentage of fund
8153:JP	Mos Food Services Inc.	0.53%
2206:JP	Ezaki Glico Co. Ltd.	0.51%
7966:JP	Lintec Corp.	0.49%
4045:JP	Toagosei Co. Ltd.	0.49%
4912:JP	Lion Corp.	0.48%
4205:JP	Zeon Corp.	0.48%
6754:JP	Anritsu Corp.	0.48%
8088:JP	Iwatani Corp.	0.47%
7988	Nifco Inc.	0.47%
4534:JP	Mochida Pharmaceutical Co. Ltd.	0.47%
5991:JP	NHK Spring Co. Ltd.	0.47%

State Street Global Advisors
State Street Financial Center
1 Lincoln Street
Boston, MA 02111–2900
Phone: (617) 786-3000
Website: *www.spdrs.com*

100 BEST STRATEGY: **FOUNDATION**

100 BEST CATEGORY: **COUNTRY/REGION**

iShares S&P Latin America 40 Index Fund

Ticker Symbol: ILF ▢ Issuer: BlackRock/iShares ▢ Description: Equity Regional Large Cap Selection ▢ Geography: Latin America ▢ Morningstar Rating: 5 stars ▢ Marco Polo XTF Rating: 5.7 ▢ Yield: 2.19% ▢ Expense Ratio: 0.50% (Benchmark: 0.60%)

Stated Purpose

The investment seeks to replicate, net of expenses, the S&P Latin America 40 index. The fund invests at least 90 percent of its assets in securities of the index and in depositary receipts representing in the index. The index is comprised of selected equities trading on the exchanges of four Latin American countries: Mexico, Brazil, Argentina, and Chile.

Our Take

While we advocate exchange-traded funds as a prudent and reasonably safe way to invest in today's markets, we also like to remind people of the fact that tripling, quadrupling, or quintupling your money over a period of time is not likely. Not to say that it doesn't happen, but entire economies, regions, countries, sectors, industries, and most other portfolios rarely have those kinds of gains in value—especially in a ten-year period.

So here's a fund that most people wouldn't have thought of investing in ten years ago. The iShares S&P Latin America 40 Index Fund has gained almost seven times its original $10,000 investment in 2001. Latin America? Really?

Yes, really. Not only has the level and profitability of Latin American business grown internally but the region has also become a big player on the world stage. China and many other countries now look south of the border for resource supply agreements and for many manufactured products coming from the prosperous four countries mentioned above. Government intervention has diminished, inflation has largely been tamed, the work force is more educated, there are considerable infrastructure investments, people have more confidence—these are among the many reasons these largest forty companies, and many smaller ones, have worked so well.

By country, Brazil is 53 percent of the portfolio, Mexico is 22 percent, Chile is 7 percent, and others make up the rest. By sector, materials is 23 percent, financials are 22 percent, consumer products are 16 percent, energy is 12 percent, telecom is 12 percent, and utilities are 8 percent. We feel this is a healthy mix going forward and should remain fairly stable into the future.

Why Should I Care?

This fund works for those looking for a strong and less-mainstream international component for a foundation portfolio.

Upside

- Well balanced portfolio, steady performer
- Decent yield
- Large, liquid, and experienced

Downside

- Always some political risk
- Always some inflation risk
- Easy gains already made?

Just the Facts

INCEPTION DATE: **October 25, 2001**

TOTAL ASSETS: **$2.3 billion**

AVERAGE DAILY VOLUME: **1.6 million**

TOTAL HOLDINGS: **34**

PERCENT NORTH AMERICA HOLDINGS: **4.2%**

TOP 10 HOLDINGS PERCENTAGE (CONCENTRATION): **64.18%**

PORTFOLIO TURNOVER: **6.0%**   BENCHMARK: **21.0%**

BETA COEFFICIENT: **0.82**

R-SQUARED (1 YEAR): **63.69%**

1-YEAR RETURN: **26.94%**   BENCHMARK: **30.39%**

3-YEAR RETURN: **0.40%**   BENCHMARK: **-1.77%**

TRACKING ERROR (PRICE VS. NAV)   1 YEAR: **12.08%**   ASSET CLASS MEDIAN: **11.1%**

$10,000 Invested at inception	2006	2007	2008	2009	2010	2011
	$45,700	$67,996	$35,597	$68,586	$79,004	$76,868

What's Under the Hood

Symbol	Name	Percentage of fund
VALE/P	Vale SA	11.97%
AMX_L:MX	America Movil SAB de CV	9.97%
ITUB	Itau Unibanco Holding SA	8.95%
PBR	Petroleo Brasileiro SA Petrobras	7.24%
BBD	Banco Bradesco SA	5.89%
PBR/A	Petroleo Brasileiro SA Petrobras	5.08%
ABV	Companhia De Bebidas Das Americas	4.53%
WALMEX_V:MX	Wal-Mart de Mexico SAB de CV	3.68%
SAN	BANCO SANTANDER CHILE	3.67%
FEMSA_UBD:MX	Fomento Economico Mexicano SA de CV	3.55%
BRFS	BRF Brasil Foods SA	2.82%
CIG	Energy Co of Minas Gerais	2.21%
SQM	Sociedad Quimica y Minera de Chile SA	2.21%
TLEVISA_CPO:MX	Grupo Televisa SAB	2.07%
SID	National Steel Co	2.06%
EOC	Empresa Nacional de Electricidad SA	2.00%
LFL	Lan Airlines SA	1.89%
GGB	Gerdau SA	1.88%
BAP	Credicorp Ltd.	1.78%
BVN	Compania De Minas Buenaventura SAA	1.73%

BlackRock iShares
525 Washington Boulevard, Suite 1405
Jersey City, NJ 07310
(800) 474-2737
Website: *www.ishares.com*

100 BEST STRATEGY: **FOUNDATION**

100 BEST CATEGORY: **COUNTRY/REGION**

SPDR S&P Emerging Latin America ETF

Ticker Symbol: GML ▢ Issuer: State Street Global Advisors ▢ Description: Equity Regional Blend
▢ Geography: Latin America ▢ Morningstar Rating: 4 stars ▢ Marco Polo XTF Rating: 1.6 ▢ Yield:
1.8% ▢ Expense Ratio: 0.59% (Benchmark: 0.60%)

Stated Purpose

The investment seeks to replicate, net of expenses, the S&P Latin America BMI index. The fund invests at least 80 percent of its assets in the securities comprising the index. The index is a market capitalization weighted index that measures the investable universe of publicly traded companies domiciled in emerging Latin America markets.

Our Take

Latin America is a region much maligned for its past and the headlines that past generated about inflation, dictators, government regulation, government-owned companies, popular apathy with the system . . . you name it. But we think Latin America has changed a lot for the better, especially in the past ten years.

Governments, notably in Brazil and Mexico, have become much more accommodating to business, and guess what? Business and private sector prosperity have created jobs and tax revenues for these governments, while the governments themselves have worked to become a bit less of a drag on their economies. Add a more prosperous middle class and considerable foreign demand from developing nations, notably China, and you get a pretty attractive business environment.

The SPDR S&P Emerging Latin America ETF, like our other Latin America pick, the iShares S&P Latin America 40 Index Fund, is well positioned to capitalize on this opportunity. Unlike that fund, this one is more diversified, with 114 holdings. Although the fund has the phrase "Emerging Latin America" in its name, connoting lots of smaller companies in smaller countries, it is still primarily centered in Brazil (59 percent of holdings), Mexico (20 percent), and Chile (8 percent). In their view, these countries are emerging. We don't disagree.

Why Should I Care?

This portfolio makes sense mainly as a more aggressive play in a foundation portfolio.

Upside

- Broad industry coverage
- Reasonable yield
- Safety: right amount of diversification

Downside

- Vulnerable to politics and inflation
- Not strong recently
- Pretty big dip during 2008 downturn (but recovered quickly)

Just the Facts

INCEPTION DATE: **March 10, 2007**

TOTAL ASSETS: **$198.8 million**

AVERAGE DAILY VOLUME: **21,340**

TOTAL HOLDINGS: **114**

PERCENT NORTH AMERICA HOLDINGS: **1.97%**

TOP 10 HOLDINGS PERCENTAGE (CONCENTRATION): **44.54%**

PORTFOLIO TURNOVER: **7%**   BENCHMARK: **12.0%**

BETA COEFFICIENT: **0.82**

R-SQUARED (1 YEAR): **63.69%**

1-YEAR RETURN: **26.07%**   BENCHMARK: **30.39%**

3-YEAR RETURN: **1.84%**   BENCHMARK: **-1.77%**

TRACKING ERROR (PRICE VS. NAV)   1 YEAR: **12.47%**   ASSET CLASS MEDIAN: **11.1%**

$10,000 Invested at inception	2006	2007	2008	2009	2010	2011
	$—	$13,665	$6,881	$14,095	$16,322	$15,888

What's Under the Hood

Symbol	Name	Percentage of fund
VALE/P	Vale SA	6.68%
PBR/A	Petroleo Brasileiro SA Petrobras	6.38%
AMX_L:MX	America Movil SAB de CV	5.47%
PBR	Petroleo Brasileiro SA Petrobras	5.14%
ITUB	Itau Unibanco Holding SA	4.92%
VALE	Vale SA	4.87%
BBD	Banco Bradesco SA	4.01%

Symbol	Name	Percentage of fund
ABV	Companhia De Bebidas Das Americas AMBEV	3.00%
FEMSA_UBD:MX	Fomento Economico Mexicano SA de CV	2.10%
ITSA4:BR	Itausa Investimentos Itau SA	2.03%
WALMEX_V:MX	Wal-Mart de Mexico SAB de CV	2.02%
GMEXICO_B:MX	Grupo MexiCo SAB De CV	1.66%
FALAB	SA Comercial Industrial Falabella SACIF	1.27%
BVMF3:BR	BM&F Bovespa SA Bolsa de Valores Mercadorias e Futuros	1.22%
BVN	Compania De Minas Buenaventura SAA	1.15%
TLPP4:BR	Telecomunicacoes de Sao Paulo SA Telesp	1.14%
COPEC	Empresas Copec SA	1.06%
BBAS3:BR	Banco do Brasil SA	1.04%
CIG	Energy Co of Minas Gerais	1.03%
SID	National Steel Co.	1.03%

State Street Global Advisors
State Street Financial Center
1 Lincoln Street
Boston, MA 02111–2900
Phone: (617) 786-3000
Website: *www.spdrs.com*

Real Estate

The following four funds provide exposure to real estate, for those wishing to add real estate to their portfolio without worrying about specific locations and neighborhoods, fixing toilets, and so forth. These funds operate through buying REITs—real estate investment trusts—normally a safe and income-producing way to invest in the real estate market. Expenses range widely from 0.12 percent for the Vanguard REIT ETF to 0.58 percent for the more specialized and international WisdomTree Global Ex-U.S. Real Estate Fund.

100 BEST STRATEGY: **FOUNDATION/ROTATIONAL**

100 BEST CATEGORY: **REAL ESTATE**

Vanguard REIT ETF

Ticker Symbol: VNQ ❑ Issuer: Vanguard ❑ Description: U.S. Large Cap REIT Fund ❑ Geography: U.S. ❑ Morningstar Rating: 3 stars ❑ Marco Polo XTF Rating: 10.0 ❑ Yield: 3.56% ❑ Expense Ratio: 0.12% (Benchmark: 0.48%)

Stated Purpose

The investment seeks to provide a high level of income and moderate long-term capital appreciation by tracking the performance of a benchmark index that measures the performance of publicly traded equity REITs. The fund employs a "passive management"—or indexing—investment approach designed to track the performance of the MSCI U.S. REIT Index. The index is composed of stocks of publicly traded equity real estate investment trusts (REITs). It attempts to replicate the index by investing all, or substantially all, of its assets in the stocks that make up the index, holding each stock in approximately the same proportion as its weighting in the index.

Our Take

Real Estate Investment Trusts (REITs) have been a solid way to invest in real estate without the chores, risks, and asset commitment of picking out individual properties to buy and own. They offer diversification, good yields, and in today's real estate market, a good way to play a rebound in real estate prices.

ETFs are an effective way to buy into the REIT market, because effectively you get a basket of

REITs—residential, commercial, health care, hospitality, self-storage, and other REITS all under one investing roof. If you're playing for a broad turnaround in real estate prices, and want a decent yield while you wait, a generalized REIT ETF is pretty compelling.

Most of the big ETF sponsors offer a generalized REIT ETF. Most, as we discovered, hold just about the same REITs in the same proportion. We selected the Vanguard REIT ETF mainly because of its low expenses and solid, diversified portfolio. Those looking for higher yields and/or international exposure or more specific sector selections could look at the other three real estate ETFs on our *100 Best ETF* list: REZ, DRW, and KBWY.

Why Should I Care?

REIT ETFs make sense as a long-term, income-generating real estate investment for a foundation portfolio; those who feel that real estate is currently undervalued can use them in a rotational context also.

Upside

- Attractive yield
- Low expenses
- Large, liquid, and experienced

Downside

- Assumes all real estate will recover
- Overdiversified?
- Big hit in 2008 downturn—but recovered well

Just the Facts

INCEPTION DATE: **September 23, 2004**

TOTAL ASSETS: **$9.8 billion**

AVERAGE DAILY VOLUME: **2.5 million**

TOTAL HOLDINGS: **106**

PERCENT NORTH AMERICA HOLDINGS: **100%**

TOP 10 HOLDINGS PERCENTAGE (CONCENTRATION): **47.10%**

PORTFOLIO TURNOVER: **12.0%**   BENCHMARK: **11.0%**

BETA COEFFICIENT: **0.61**

R-SQUARED (1 YEAR): **55.56**

1-YEAR RETURN: **37.64%**   BENCHMARK: **30.69%**

3-YEAR RETURN: **6.60%**   BENCHMARK: **3.43%**

TRACKING ERROR (PRICE VS. NAV)   1 YEAR: **8.95%**   ASSET CLASS MEDIAN: **9.65%**

$10,000 Invested at inception	2006	2007	2008	2009	2010	2011
	$16,992	$14,206	$8,944	$11,604	$14,911	$16,701

What's Under the Hood

Symbol	Name	Percentage of fund
SPG	Simon Property Group Inc.	10.17%
EQR	Equity Residential	5.21%
PSA	Public Storage	5.19%
BXP	Boston Properties Inc.	4.35%
HCP	HCP Inc.	4.30%
VTR	Ventas Inc.	4.22%
VNO	Vornado Realty Trust	4.09%
AVB	Avalonbay Communities Inc.	3.70%
PLD	Prologis Inc.	3.48%
HCN	Health Care REIT Inc.	2.52%
HST	Host Hotels and Resorts Inc.	2.21%
KIM	Kimco Realty Corp.	2.07%
MAC	Macerich Co.	1.83%
GGP	General Growth Properties Inc.	1.70%
UDR	UDR Inc.	1.65%
FRT	Federal Realty Investment Trust	1.63%
DLR	Digital Realty Trust Inc.	1.58%
SLG	SL Green Realty Corp.	1.55%
CPT	Camden Property Trust	1.35%
ARE	Alexandria Real Estate Equities Inc.	1.52%

Vanguard
P.O. Box 1110
Valley Forge, PA 19482–1110
(877) 241-1395
Website: *www.vanguard.com*

100 BEST STRATEGY: **FOUNDATION/ROTATIONAL**

100 BEST CATEGORY: **REAL ESTATE**

iShares FTSE NAREIT Residential Plus Capped Index Fund

Ticker Symbol: REZ ◻ Issuer: BlackRock/iShares ◻ Description: U.S. REIT Selection ◻ Geography: U.S. ◻ Morningstar Rating: 5 stars ◻ Marco Polo XTF Rating: 7.0 ◻ Yield: 3.06% ◻ Expense Ratio: 0.48% (Benchmark: 0.48%)

Stated Purpose

The investment seeks to replicate, net of expenses, the FTSE NAREIT All Residential Capped Index. The fund invests at least 90 percent of its assets in securities of the underlying index and in depositary receipts representing securities of the index. The index measures the performance of the residential, health care, and self-storage real estate sectors of the U.S. equity market.

Our Take

Perhaps you're looking for a broad-based ETF to invest in real estate, or real estate investment trusts (or REITs), in particular. REITs offer investors a diverse, relatively risk-free, and relatively high yielding way to invest in real estate, particularly as compared to buying individual properties.

But you're not sure you want to play the entire real estate market (if you do, check out our general REIT ETF selection, the Vanguard REIT ETF, VNQ). If you think that residential real estate has bottomed, and want the steady and secure income of health care and self-storage REITs blended in, the iShares FTSE NAREIT Residential Plus Capped Index Fund might be for you.

Now the index, created by the National Association of Real Estate Investment Trusts (NAREIT), picks thirty-five of the biggest players in the residential, health care, and self-storage segments. We like this focus for those who want to concentrate on these segments.

Why Should I Care?

REIT ETFs make sense as a long-term, income-generating real estate investment for a foundation portfolio. If you feel that residential real estate has bottomed, this fund could also make sense for a rotational portfolio.

Upside

- Attractive yield
- Focused play on three segments
- Good recent returns

Downside
- Residential recovery could take a while
- More exposure to health care might be good (only two in top 20)
- Rising interest rates or double dip could hurt

Just the Facts
INCEPTION DATE: **May 1, 2007**

TOTAL ASSETS: **$159.6 million**

AVERAGE DAILY VOLUME: **54,000**

TOTAL HOLDINGS: **35**

PERCENT NORTH AMERICA HOLDINGS: **100%**

TOP 10 HOLDINGS PERCENTAGE (CONCENTRATION): **66.80%**

PORTFOLIO TURNOVER: **16.0%**   BENCHMARK: **11.0%**

BETA COEFFICIENT: **0.42**

R-SQUARED (1 YEAR): **34.70**

1-YEAR RETURN: **41.04%**   BENCHMARK: **30.69%**

3-YEAR RETURN: **7.76%**   BENCHMARK: **3.43%**

TRACKING ERROR (PRICE VS. NAV)   1 YEAR: **10.90%**   ASSET CLASS MEDIAN: **9.65%**

$10,000 Invested at inception	2006	2007	2008	2009	2010	2011
	$—	$7,465	$5,586	$6,772	$8,866	$10,139

What's Under the Hood

Symbol	Name	Percentage of fund
EQR	Equity Residential	10.30%
VTR	Ventas Inc.	9.40%
PSA	Public Storage	9.09%
HCP	HCP Inc.	8.60%
AVB	Avalonbay Communities Inc.	6.79%
UDR	UDR Inc.	5.23%
HCN	Health Care REIT Inc.	5.12%
ESS	Essex Property Trust Inc.	4.42%
CPT	Camden Property Trust	4.40%
BRE	BRE Properties Inc.	3.53%

Symbol	Name	Percentage of fund
SNH	Senior Housing Properties Trust	3.14%
AIV	Apartment Investment and Management Co.	2.92%
ACC	American Campus Communities Inc.	2.53%
ELS	Equity Lifestyle Properties Inc.	2.48%
HME	Home Properties Inc.	2.45%
MAA	Mid America Apartment Communities Inc.	2.45%
PPS	Post Properties Inc.	1.97%
EXR	Extra Space Storage Inc.	1.91%
OHI	Omega Healthcare Investors Inc.	1.74%
CLP	Colonial Properties Trust	1.60%

BlackRock iShares
525 Washington Boulevard, Suite 1405
Jersey City, NJ 07310
(800) 474-2737
Website: www.ishares.com

---

100 BEST STRATEGY: FOUNDATION

100 BEST CATEGORY: REAL ESTATE

WisdomTree Global Ex-U.S. Real Estate Fund

Ticker Symbol: DRW ▫ Issuer: WisdomTree ▫ Description: Ex-U.S. REIT Equity Blend ▫ Geography: ex-U.S. ▫ Morningstar Rating: 2 stars ▫ Marco Polo XTF Rating: 3.3 ▫ Yield: 12.17% ▫ Expense Ratio: 0.58% (Benchmark: 0.48%)

Stated Purpose

The investment seeks to track the price and yield performance, before fees and expenses, of the Wisdom-Tree Global Ex-U.S. Real Estate Index. The fund employs a "passive management"—or indexing—investment approach designed to track the performance of the WisdomTree Global Ex-U.S. Real Estate Index. It attempts to invest all or substantially all of its assets in

the stocks that make up the index. The fund normally invests 95 percent of total assets in the component securities of the index.

Our Take

Suppose you like real estate, and you know something about real estate investment trusts (REITs), and like their diversification and attractive yields. You may have already checked out our other broad U.S.-based

REIT ETFs on the *100 Best* list, from Vanguard, iShares, and PowerShares (VNQ, DRW, and KBWY if you haven't). You think U.S. real estate may be poised for somewhat of a bounce back, but aren't sure the macroeconomics are right now or will be for some time. Oversupply, no jobs, a flat or moribund economy. You want your real estate pick to be where the growth is.

That makes sense—where there's growth, there's sure to be demand for real estate in all forms—residential, commercial, you name it. The WisdomTree Global Ex-U.S. Real Estate Fund owns property companies (not so much REITs, that specific form doesn't exist for the most part overseas) outside the United States and most particularly in Asia. In fact, 63 percent of the companies are in Asia, 21 percent in Europe, 9 percent in Canada, and the rest are in other places.

There is undoubtedly more risk here. It is harder to follow these companies, and an economic downturn or even rising interest rates in an effort to combat inflation in China could dampen the real estate market. There could be bubbles in the image of Japan twenty years ago. But in return for taking that risk, you get a 12 percent current return (yes, it's real), a play on foreign currency, and a play on the major growth sectors of the world.

Why Should I Care?

For those wanting to add a little foreign real estate (and a strong yield generator) to a foundation portfolio, this fund would work.

Upside

- Very attractive yield
- International diversification, China growth
- Good time to buy?

Downside

- Component companies not easy to understand
- Inflation and interest rate risks
- Bubbles always a risk

Just the Facts

INCEPTION DATE: **June 5, 2007**

TOTAL ASSETS: **$132 million**

AVERAGE DAILY VOLUME: **28,100**

TOTAL HOLDINGS: **145**

PERCENT NORTH AMERICA HOLDINGS: **8.69%**

TOP 10 HOLDINGS PERCENTAGE (CONCENTRATION): **34.12%**

PORTFOLIO TURNOVER: **15.0%**   BENCHMARK: **11.0%**

BETA COEFFICIENT: **0.58**

R-SQUARED (1 YEAR): **55.06**

1-YEAR RETURN: **35.40%**   BENCHMARK: **30.69%**

3-YEAR RETURN: **1.36%**   BENCHMARK: **3.43%**

TRACKING ERROR (PRICE VS. NAV)   1 YEAR: **5.71%**   ASSET CLASS MEDIAN: **9.65%**

$10,000 Invested at inception	2006	2007	2008	2009	2010	2011
	$—	$10,173	$4,407	$6,457	$7,529	$7,744

What's Under the Hood

Symbol	Name	Percentage of fund
WDC:AU	Westfield Group	9.52%
16:HK	Sun Hung Kai Properties Ltd.	4.25%
1:HK	Cheung Kong (Holdings) Ltd.	4.24%
SGP:AU	Stockland Corp. Ltd.	3.40%
UL:FR	Unibail Rodamco SE	3.25%
CFX:AU	CFS Retail Property Trust	2.32%
GPT:AU	GPT Group	2.25%
REI_UN:CA	RioCan Real Estate Investment Trust	1.80%
MGR	Mirvac Group	1.72%
101:HK	Hang Lung Properties Ltd.	1.67%
BLND:GB	British Land Co Plc	1.63%
19:HK	Swire Pacific Ltd.	1.55%
DXS:AU	Dexus Property Group	1.54%
688:HK	China Overseas Land & Investment Ltd.	1.54%
4:HK	Wharf (Holdings) Ltd.	1.45%
GFC	Gecina SA	1.43%
CORA:NL	Corio NV	1.43%
GMG	Goodman Group	1.41%
1878:JP	Daito Trust Construction Co. Ltd.	1.38%
LI	Klepierre SA	1.37%

WisdomTree Investments
380 Madison Avenue, 21st Floor
New York, NY 10017
(866) 909- 9473
Website: *www.wisdomtree.com*

PowerShares KBW Premium Yield Equity REIT Portfolio

Ticker Symbol: KBWY ❑ Issuer: Invesco ❑ Description: U.S. Enhanced Small/Mid Cap REIT Blend ❑ Geography: U.S. ❑ Morningstar Rating: NR ❑ Marco Polo XTF Rating: 2.7 ❑ Yield: 4.23% ❑ Expense Ratio: 0.35% (Benchmark: 0.48%)

Stated Purpose

The investment seeks results that correspond (before fees and expenses) generally to the price and yield of an index called the KBW Premium Yield Equity REIT Index. The fund invests at least 80 percent of total assets in equity securities of real estate investment trusts (REITs). It normally invests at least 90 percent of total assets in the securities that comprise the underlying index. The underlying index is calculated using a dividend yield weighted methodology that seeks to reflect the performance of approximately twenty-four to forty small- and mid-cap equity REITs in the United States. The fund intends to concentrate in the real estate industry.

Our Take

Real estate investment trusts (REITs) are a broad, diversified, and typically yield-bearing way to add some real estate to your portfolio. And most REITs are big outfits that buy and manage big properties

in big cities—large office buildings, warehouses, suburban developments, apartment complexes, and the like. The other two U.S. REITs on our *100 Best ETF* list, the Vanguard REIT ETF (VNQ) and the iShares FTSE NAREIT Residential Plus Capped Index Fund (REZ) both invest in the largest and most familiar REIT names.

Just as we like the flexibility, innovation, and growth opportunity of small- and mid-cap stocks, we also believe that smaller REITs can be compelling. They operate in targeted niches by geography or type of property they invest in. Many are in the health care sector, specialized retail, government offices, and other targeted niches that we feel will be steady and attractive going forward. Partly due to its dividend weighting method, the fund pays a higher yield than our other two U.S.-based selections, and it has relatively low expense levels.

Why Should I Care?

Those wanting more of a "niche" exposure to real estate for a foundation portfolio, or who might want a more aggressive play for a rotational portfolio, might consider this ETF.

Upside

- Attractive yield
- Relatively low expenses
- Niche players

Downside

- Very small and very untested
- Does size matter?
- Understanding component companies could be difficult

Just the Facts

INCEPTION DATE: **December 2, 2010**

TOTAL ASSETS: **$7.7 million**

AVERAGE DAILY VOLUME: **3,600**

TOTAL HOLDINGS: **31**

PERCENT NORTH AMERICA HOLDINGS: **100%**

TOP 10 HOLDINGS PERCENTAGE (CONCENTRATION): **40.57%**

PORTFOLIO TURNOVER: **NA**   BENCHMARK: **11.0%**

BETA COEFFICIENT: **NA**

R-SQUARED (1 YEAR): **NA**

1-YEAR RETURN: **NA**   BENCHMARK: **30.69%**

3-YEAR RETURN: **NA**   BENCHMARK: **3.43%**

TRACKING ERROR (PRICE VS. NAV)   1 YEAR: **NA**   ASSET CLASS MEDIAN: **9.65%**

$10,000 Invested at inception	2006	2007	2008	2009	2010	2011
	$—	$—	$—	$—	$10,000	$10,331

What's Under the Hood

Symbol	Name	Percentage of fund
HPT	Hospitality Properties Trust	5.06%
ADC	Agree Realty Corp.	4.57%
NNN	National Retail Properties Inc.	4.19%
SUI	Sun Communities Inc.	4.11%
OHI	Omega Healthcare Investors Inc.	4.07%
CWH	Commonwealth REIT	3.95%
MPW	Medical Properties Trust Inc.	3.77%
GOV	Government Properties Income Trust	3.75%
IRC	Inland Real Estate Corp.	3.59%
LTC	LTC Properties Inc.	3.51%
NHI	National Health Investors Inc.	3.48%
GTY	Getty Realty Corp.	3.43%
UHT	Universal Health Realty Income Trust	3.40%
EPR	Entertainment Properties Trust	3.31%
CLI	Mack Cali Realty Corp.	3.27%
HCP	HCP Inc.	3.20%
HCN	Health Care REIT Inc.	3.18%
WRE	Washington Real Estate Investment Trust	3.18%
UBA	Urstadt Biddle Properties Inc.	3.11%
EQY	Equity One Inc.	2.99%

Invesco PowerShares Capital Management LLC
301 West Roosevelt Road
Wheaton, IL 60187
(800) 803-0903
Website: *www.invescopowershares.com*

Actively Managed

The ETF industry was built around the idea of reducing costs, increasing transparency, and increasing trading flexibility. One of the keys to accomplishing all three is the use of "passive" indexes to define the contents of a fund, instead of the services of an "active" fund manager seeking and selecting individual investments for the fund. That formula has worked, but many foresee the day when the ETF format can be applied to more actively managed funds, that is, where a fund manager may start with an index and add his or her own insight to it, or do away with the index altogether. Many foresee a day when actively managed funds replace traditional mutual funds, but with only thirty-two actively managed funds in existence today (and only eleven of those in the equity space) it's still a fairly new idea. With that in mind, we offer the following four actively managed ETFs, with expense ratios ranging from 0.50 to 0.80 percent.

The Russell Equity ETF, noted below, is a "fund of funds"—an active selection of ten other ETFs for those who like the idea of having someone else choose their ETFs for them.

---

100 BEST STRATEGY: FOUNDATION

100 BEST CATEGORY: ACTIVELY MANAGED

Russell Equity ETF

Ticker Symbol: ONEF □ Issuer: Russell Investments □ Description: Actively Managed Fund of Funds Selection □ Geography: Global □ Morningstar Rating: NR □ Marco Polo XTF Rating: 5.5 □ Yield: 1.52% □ Expense Ratio: 0.51% (Benchmark: 0.60%)

Stated Purpose

The investment seeks long-term capital appreciation. The fund is a "fund of funds" and normally invests primarily in shares of other exchange-traded funds. It will invest at least 80 percent of the value of its net assets in shares of equity ETFs. The fund normally invests in ETFs that seek to track various indices. These indices include those that track the performance of equity securities of large-, medium-, and small-capitalization companies across the globe including developed countries and emerging countries. The fund invests at least 30 percent of assets in non-U.S. securities through U.S.-listed ETFs. It generally remains fully invested in ETFs.

Our Take

Here's a small and relatively new actively managed fund that does something that few, if any, funds do (none crossed our radar during our research): It buys and actively manages a portfolio of other ETFs. Such a "fund of funds" approach has become fairly common in the hedge-fund world. As an individual investor, if you can't really decide what funds you want to own, the simply named Russell Equity ETF might be worth a look.

There are only ten funds in this portfolio, so it isn't too hard to grasp the strategy and intent of the fund. The largest holding is—not surprisingly—a fund based on Russell's own 1000 Index, and provides a broad equity blend. From there the fund holds an assortment of low-cost Vanguard international funds, four of which are on our *100 Best ETFs* list, giving a multidimensional international exposure for close to half the fund.

For this kind of fund, we think "actively managed" is a good thing, because a fund manager can make his or her own rotations according to what's hot and what's not. That said,

the fund manager hasn't gone out on a limb too far here to pick something we couldn't have found ourselves. The expense ratio of 0.50 percent, while a bit low for actively managed funds, seems a bit high here for managing a portfolio of only ten funds, but long-term results will prove this to be true or not.

Why Should I Care?

The Russell Equity ETF leaves some of the fund selection "driving" to someone else, while still providing a solid and diverse base for your foundation portfolio. Before placing other ETFs into your foundation portfolio, you should check for overlaps with this one.

Upside

- Keeps things simple
- You, too, can be a hedge fund (or at least act like one)
- Plenty of diversification

Downside

- Should active management make more focused picks?
- Expenses could be lower for a relatively simple fund
- New and largely untested

Just the Facts

INCEPTION DATE: **May 11, 2010**

TOTAL ASSETS: **$12.9 million**

AVERAGE DAILY VOLUME: **6,400**

TOTAL HOLDINGS: **10**

PERCENT NORTH AMERICA HOLDINGS: **53.65%**

TOP 10 HOLDINGS PERCENTAGE (CONCENTRATION): **100%**

PORTFOLIO TURNOVER: **0.0%**   BENCHMARK: **21.0%**

BETA COEFFICIENT: **1.81**

R-SQUARED (1 YEAR): **86.85%**

1-YEAR RETURN: **33.63%**   BENCHMARK: **32.60%**

3-YEAR RETURN: **NA**   BENCHMARK: **3.34%**

TRACKING ERROR (PRICE VS. NAV)   1 YEAR: **7.1%**   ASSET CLASS MEDIAN: **10.41%**

$10,000 Invested at inception	2006	2007	2008	2009	2010	2011
	$—	$—	$—	$—	$12,012	$12,434

What's Under the Hood

Symbol	Name	Percentage of fund
IWB	iShares Russell 1000 Index Fund	42.05%
VEA	Vanguard MSCI EAFE ETF	19.97%
VWO	Vanguard MSCI Emerging Markets Fund ETF	9.93%
VGK	Vanguard MSCI Europe ETF	7.91%
VTWO	Vanguard Russell 2000 ETF	6.68%
VPL	Vanguard MSCI Pacific ETF	5.25%
IWF	iShares Russell 1000 Growth Index Fund	3.06%
SCZ	iShares MSCI EAFE Small Cap Index Fund	3.02%
EWC	Ishares Msci Canada Index	1.93%
CASH	Cash	0.21%

Russell Investments
1301 Second Avenue, 18th Floor
Seattle, WA 98101
(206) 505-7877
Website: *www.russelletfs.com*

PowerShares Active Real Estate Fund

Ticker Symbol: PSR ▫ Issuer: Invesco ▫ Description: Actively Managed Real Estate Fund ▫ Geography: Global ▫ Morningstar Rating: NR ▫ Marco Polo XTF Rating: 4.3 ▫ Yield: 1.63% ▫ Expense Ratio: 0.80% (Benchmark: 0.48%)

Stated Purpose

The PowerShares Active U.S. Real Estate Fund structures and selects its investments primarily from a universe of securities that are included within the FTSE NAREIT All Equity REITs Index at the time of purchase. The selection methodology uses quantitative and statistical metrics to identify attractively priced securities and manage risk. The fund will invest principally in equity real estate investment trusts (REITs).

Our Take

If you think real estate is a good place to invest now, this is certainly one well-diversified and historically successful way to do it. The PowerShares Active Real Estate fund actively manages choices among REITs *within* the FTSE NAREIT (National Association of Real Estate Trusts) index, so it doesn't stray from that set of boundaries.

The resulting assortment of fifty-six REITS is well diversified

between residential, commercial, hospitality, storage, and health care REITs. The actual breakdown is as follows:

* Specialized REITs   27.86%
* Retail REITs   24.06%
* Residential REITs   20.21%
* Office REITs   15.39%
* Diversified REITs   8.26%
* Industrial REITs   4.22%

Payouts are irregular, but in 2010 the fund made income and capital gains distributions amounting to about 1.63 percent of the average fund price. With the recent market pullback, yields may be more attractive in coming years, and we're a little surprised that yields haven't been a bit better.

Why Should I Care?

We like this fund as a moderately aggressive play in a foundation portfolio or rotational portfolio anticipating a real estate recovery.

Upside

- Broad exposure to real estate
- Solid gains over last four years
- Plenty of diversification

Downside

- Yield could be better
- High expenses, is it worth it?
- Small and may not be liquid

Just the Facts

INCEPTION DATE: **November 20, 2008**

TOTAL ASSETS: **$23.4 million**

AVERAGE DAILY VOLUME: **7,400**

TOTAL HOLDINGS: **56**

PERCENT NORTH AMERICA HOLDINGS: **100%**

TOP 10 HOLDINGS PERCENTAGE (CONCENTRATION): **51.34%**

PORTFOLIO TURNOVER: **20.0%**   BENCHMARK: **11.0%**

BETA COEFFICIENT: **0.57**

R-SQUARED (1 YEAR): **53.87%**

1-YEAR RETURN: **24.90%**   BENCHMARK: **23.72%**

3-YEAR RETURN: **NA**   BENCHMARK: **4.55%**

TRACKING ERROR (PRICE VS. NAV)   1 YEAR: **NM**   ASSET CLASS MEDIAN: **NM**

$10,000 Invested at inception	2006	2007	2008	2009	2010	2011
	$—	$—	$11,555	$14,363	$18,222	$20,639

What's Under the Hood

Symbol	Name	Percentage of fund
SPG	Simon Property Group Inc.	11.50%
EQR	Equity Residential	5.80%
VNO	Vornado Realty Trust	5.34%
HCP	HCP Inc.	5.09%
BXP	Boston Properties Inc.	5.00%
VTR	Ventas Inc.	4.76%
PSA	Public Storage	4.19%
AVB	Avalonbay Communities Inc.	3.72%
HCN	Health Care REIT Inc.	3.03%
PLD	Prologis Inc.	2.96%
HST	Host Hotels and Resorts Inc.	2.65%
WY	Weyerhaeuser Co.	2.42%

Symbol	Name	Percentage of fund
KIM	Kimco Realty Corp.	2.40%
SLG	SL Green Realty Corp.	1.94%
DLR	Digital Realty Trust Inc.	1.94%
FRT	Federal Realty Investment Trust	1.92%
UDR	UDR Inc.	1.81%
GGP	General Growth Properties Inc.	1.74%
MAC	Macerich Co.	1.68%
ARE	Alexandria Real Estate Equities Inc.	1.52%

Invesco PowerShares Capital Management LLC
301 West Roosevelt Road
Wheaton, IL 60187
(800) 803-0903
Website: *www.invescopowershares.com*

100 BEST STRATEGY: **FOUNDATION**

100 BEST CATEGORY: **ACTIVELY MANAGED**

PowerShares Active AlphaQ Fund

Ticker Symbol: PQY ◻ Issuer: Invesco ◻ Description: Actively Managed NASDAQ Equity Selection ◻ Geography: Global ◻ Morningstar Rating: 4 stars ◻ Marco Polo XTF Rating: 2.6 ◻ Yield: 0.60% ◻ Expense Ratio: 0.75% (Benchmark: 0.60%)

Stated Purpose

The PowerShares Active AlphaQ Fund rates the stocks of companies with more than $400 million market cap (about 3,000 stocks) that are traded in the United States. Weekly, the fund's subadvisor generates a master stock list that ranks these stocks, segmented by market cap, based on its proprietary stock-ranking methodology. Stocks are selected based on factors such as strong earnings growth, low

valuations, and positive money flow. Fund managers then define their universe as the 100 largest NASDAQ-listed stocks from their master stock list, excluding securities traded on other exchanges. The fund then generally selects and purchases approximately fifty stocks.

Our Take

The actively managed ETF space still isn't very active itself, with currently only a total of thirty-two selections and of those, eleven selections in the equity space. So there aren't many choices, and the choices that are available are mostly large-cap funds where the fund manager has "picked" (or used an algorithm to pick) most of the same stocks you would find in a passively managed general equity index fund, or that you would pick for yourself. So why bother? Why pay 0.75 percent or more in fees for this active management?

That's why our only straight-up actively managed equity choice is the PowerShares Active AlphaQ fund. For those who don't understand Wall Street lingo, "alpha" represents return beyond the averages for an asset class; we're not sure about the "Q" but believe it refers to the use of quantitative tools to assist the selecting managers (the "proprietary stock-ranking methodology"). Anyway, whatever's in the black box and however the fund manager chooses to use it, we like the resulting portfolio, and for the most part, we like the results. The

selected stocks, such as Perrigo, O'Reilly, and Apple are among our more dynamic favorites; it appears that by letting these fund managers and their black boxes do their thing, you get a result that might be worth paying for—time will tell.

Why Should I Care?

This fund makes sense for a relatively aggressive portion of a foundation portfolio; it's a good way to get some exposure to active management from someone other than yourself.

Upside

- Slightly aggressive; active management cheaper than most traditional funds
- Attractive portfolio
- Good recent performance after sharp 2008 dip

Downside

- Yield could be better
- High expenses; is it worth it?
- Small and illiquid

Just the Facts

INCEPTION DATE: **April 11, 2008**

TOTAL ASSETS: **$10.2 million**

AVERAGE DAILY VOLUME: **1,700**

TOTAL HOLDINGS: **51**

PERCENT NORTH AMERICA HOLDINGS: **78.97%**

TOP 10 HOLDINGS PERCENTAGE (CONCENTRATION): **25.46%**

PORTFOLIO TURNOVER: **64.0%**   BENCHMARK: **20.0%**

BETA COEFFICIENT: **1.04**

R-SQUARED (1 YEAR): **64.67%**

1-YEAR RETURN: **39.06%**   BENCHMARK: **30.69%**

3-YEAR RETURN: **NA**   BENCHMARK: **4.55%**

TRACKING ERROR (PRICE VS. NAV)   1 YEAR: **NM**   ASSET CLASS MEDIAN: **NM**

$10,000 Invested at inception	2006	2007	2008	2009	2010	2011
	$—	$—	$6,079	$8,846	$10,798	$11,271

What's Under the Hood

Symbol	Name	Percentage of fund
ORLY	O'Reilly Automotive Inc.	2.93%
PRGO	Perrigo Co.	2.82%
DTV	DirecTV	2.73%
HANS	Hansen Natural Corp.	2.64%
EBAY	eBay Inc.	2.45%
ACGL	Arch Capital Group Ltd.	2.43%
AAPL	Apple Inc.	2.40%
EXPE	Expedia Inc.	2.38%
BBBY	Bed Bath & Beyond Inc.	2.37%
QCOM	Qualcomm Inc.	2.31%
CTSH	Cognizant Technology Solutions Corp.	2.30%
WYNN	Wynn Resorts Ltd.	2.26%
CELG	Celgene Corp.	2.23%
ASIA	Asiainfo Linkage Inc.	2.15%
BRCM	Broadcom Corp.	2.15%
XLNX	Xilinx Inc.	2.12%
NTAP	NetApp Inc.	2.11%
AVGO	Avago Technologies Ltd.	2.10%
ARMH	ARM Holdings Plc	2.05%
ARE	Alexandria Real Estate Equities Inc.	1.52%

Invesco PowerShares Capital Management LLC
301 West Roosevelt Road
Wheaton, IL 60187
(800) 803-0903
Website: *www.invescopowershares.com*

100 BEST STRATEGY: **FOUNDATION/ROTATIONAL**

100 BEST CATEGORY: **ACTIVELY MANAGED**

WisdomTree Dreyfus Commodity Currency Fund

Ticker Symbol: CCX ❑ Issuer: WisdomTree Investments ❑ Description: Actively Managed Currency Selection ❑ Geography: Global ❑ Morningstar Rating: NR ❑ Marco Polo XTF Rating: NR ❑ Yield: nil ❑ Expense Ratio: 0.55% (Benchmark: 0.48%)

Stated Purpose

The investment seeks to achieve total returns. The fund is designed to provide exposure to both the currencies and money market rates available to foreign investors in selected commodity-producing countries. It intends to invest in commodity-producing countries such as Australia, Brazil, Canada, Chile, Indonesia, Mexico, New Zealand, Norway, Russia, and South Africa. The fund invests primarily in short-term U.S. money market securities and forward currency contracts and currency swaps. In order to reduce interest rate risk, it generally expects to maintain an average portfolio maturity of ninety days or less.

Our Take

Okay, here we may have stepped outside of our self-imposed boundaries of "buying what we understand." But we think one or two ventures into uncharted territory are probably justified, especially when talking about actively managed funds as we are here. We also think we're justified in that most of the thirty-two

actively managed funds (eleven in equities) available to evaluate wound up with fairly bland portfolios that weren't really worth the effort or cost to actively manage.

We've stepped out of our normal bounds in more ways than one. The WisdomTree Dreyfus Commodity Currency Fund is a currency fund (it is *not* a commodity fund). Now, for the most part we think currency trading for most traders is mainly a substitute for gambling; it has an investment purpose only in the very highest echelons of international finance. That said, some exposure to a broad basket of currencies managed via a long-term strategy probably makes sense.

As stated above, the WisdomTree Dreyfus Commodity Currency Fund is not a commodity fund. Rather, it invests in the currencies in countries that are commodity producers. These countries, most of which are listed above, are prospering, and their currencies are prospering, from the global supply/demand situation for commodities. In addition—and this is important—the yields available in these countries are higher than in most domestic government securities. So this fund makes money in two ways:

1. By capitalizing on the strength of commodity-producing countries
2. By investing in the "carry" trade, the differences in interest rates between the United States and these countries

The fund manager also points out that currencies in commodity-exporting countries have less downside risk than the commodities themselves.

So that may or may not help. There isn't a lot of data to go on from our traditional sources, but we do see that a fair amount of money has already gone into this fund. We also know that it invests in many of the currencies favored by today's "weak dollar" economists

and diversification is adequate. This is an intriguing fund that still needs to prove itself, but it may be worth the ride.

Why Should I Care?

Despite some of its unknowns and relative newness, this fund should work as a hedge against a depreciating dollar and a current income generator for foundation and rotational portfolios.

Upside

- Currency holdings match what most "weak dollar" experts recommend
- Attractive double-edged strategy
- Reasonable expenses for this type of fund

Downside

- Very new and untested
- Transparency could be better
- Stronger U.S. or weaker China economy would hurt

Just the Facts

INCEPTION DATE: **September 24, 2010**

TOTAL ASSETS: **$65.1 million**

AVERAGE DAILY VOLUME: **112,900**

TOTAL HOLDINGS: **8**

PERCENT NORTH AMERICA HOLDINGS: **NA**

TOP 10 HOLDINGS PERCENTAGE (CONCENTRATION): **100%**

PORTFOLIO TURNOVER: **NA**   BENCHMARK: **20.0%**

BETA COEFFICIENT: **NA**

R-SQUARED (1 YEAR): **NA**

1-YEAR RETURN: **NA**   BENCHMARK: **30.69%**

3-YEAR RETURN: **NA**   BENCHMARK: **4.55%**

TRACKING ERROR (PRICE VS. NAV)   1 YEAR: **NM**   ASSET CLASS MEDIAN: **NM**

$10,000 Invested at inception	2006	2007	2008	2009	2010	2011
	$—	$—	$—	$—	$10,419	$11,249

What's Under the Hood

The exact percentages of holdings were not available at the time this was assembled, but according to fund documents, investments were made in short-term money market securities with maturities of ninety days or less in Australian dollars, Canadian dollars, Norwegian krone, New Zealand dollars, Brazilian reals, Chilean pesos, Russian rubles, and South African rands.

WisdomTree Investments
380 Madison Avenue, 21st Floor
New York, NY 10017
(866) 909-9473
Website: *www.wisdomtree.com*

Inverse/Leveraged

Our last group of funds may be our most esoteric, and for many, the scariest group. Like fire, they should be used only if used properly! Inverse funds bet the opposite direction of the market; that is, if the broader market drops, these funds will gain, and vice versa. Leveraged funds are "juiced" with special investment vehicles—derivatives—to magnify gains (and losses) according to market or market segment moves. Both of these subgroups can be appropriate tools to play a short-term market change or reversal in a rotational portfolio context. For intrepid investors wanting more ways to play these short-term movements, there are hundreds of inverse and leveraged funds out there. For this year's *100 Best ETFs* list, we chose just to scratch the surface with these four funds. Expenses are fairly high with this group; these funds range from 0.70 percent to 0.95 percent.

100 BEST STRATEGY: **ROTATIONAL**

100 BEST CATEGORY: **INVERSE/LEVERAGED**

ProShares Short S&P 500

Ticker Symbol: SH ❑ Issuer: ProShares ❑ Description: Inverse General Equity/Index Fund ❑ Geography: U.S. ❑ Morningstar Rating: NR ❑ Marco Polo XTF Rating: 5.1 ❑ Yield: NA ❑ Expense Ratio: 0.92% (Benchmark: 0.60%)

Stated Purpose

The investment seeks daily results, before fees and expenses, which correspond to the inverse (opposite) of the daily performance of the S&P 500. The fund invests in derivatives that ProShare advisors believe should have similar daily return characteristics as the inverse of the daily return of the index. It typically invests the rest of the assets in money market instruments.

Our Take

Suppose you think the broader markets are going to go down. Or at least you want to have a stake in the downside to hedge all the rest of your "up" investments, to take some of the sting out if the market were to take a dip.

Investment professionals typically do this by "selling short," that is, by borrowing shares from their broker, selling them into the market, collecting the proceeds, and buying back "to cover" at a lower price (hopefully) later on. This strategy has its risks, especially for an individual investor. First and simplest, the stock price could go up, meaning you'd have to cover at a higher price, losing money. And, theoretically at least, that stock price could go up indefinitely. Second, you're borrowing shares, so you have to pay interest, and you have to compensate whomever you borrowed from for any dividends paid during your possession. Third, you might just call the next market dip, but guess what? The company you short just happens to get bought out by Berkshire Hathaway or someone, so you lose big even as the market falls.

The bottom line—when you're shorting stocks, you must be very accurate and very willing to take a loss. So shorting the whole market is a more conservative, less anxious way to play—and that's where the ProShares Short S&P 500 fund comes in.

By buying this fund, you're essentially shorting the entire market. If the S&P 500 falls, you'll gain about the same as its decline. The beta of -0.95 means that this fund is almost 100 percent negatively correlated to the S&P 500, and that's what we like—if the market goes down a buck, you'll gain ninety-five

cents. But beware—the opposite is also true—if the market goes up a buck, this fund will drop ninety-five cents. These funds in general have gotten better at tracking the market (or the inverse of the market) over the past few years.

To play "short" more specific sectors of the market, see the related ProShares Short QQQ Fund (PSQ) for the NASDAQ 100 stocks and the ProShares Short Small Cap 600 Fund (SBB), also on our *100 Best* list. Of course, there are many other "short" ETFs to choose from to short more specific market sectors, but they are too specific to include on this list. We only *wish* we could tell you what sectors will go down next year.

Why Should I Care?

This fund makes sense as a hedge to capitalize on market declines; it belongs in the rotational portfolio.

Upside
- Strong inverse correlation
- Broad market coverage
- Large and liquid

Downside
- No current yield
- High expense ratio
- Derivative tactics not transparent

Just the Facts

INCEPTION DATE: **June 19, 2006**

TOTAL ASSETS: **$1.8 billion**

AVERAGE DAILY VOLUME: **5.2 million**

TOTAL HOLDINGS: **500**

PERCENT NORTH AMERICA HOLDINGS: **98.81%**

TOP 10 HOLDINGS PERCENTAGE (CONCENTRATION): **19.95%**

PORTFOLIO TURNOVER: **NA**   BENCHMARK: **17.0%**

BETA COEFFICIENT: **-0.95**

R-SQUARED (1 YEAR): **99.90%**

1-YEAR RETURN: **-18.55%**   BENCHMARK: **19.65%**

3-YEAR RETURN: **-11.03%**   BENCHMARK: **2.92%**

TRACKING ERROR (PRICE VS. NAV)   1 YEAR: **26.13%**   ASSET CLASS MEDIAN: **10.52%**

$10,000 Invested at inception	2006	2007	2008	2009	2010	2011
	$9,209	$9,393	$13,096	$9,551	$7,975	$7,570

What's Under the Hood

Symbol	Name	Percentage of fund
XOM	Exxon Mobil Corp.	3.33%
AAPL	Apple Inc.	3.30%
IBM	International Business Machines Corp.	1.91%
CVX	Chevron Corp.	1.81%
MSFT	Microsoft Corp.	1.74%
JNJ	Johnson & Johnson	1.64%
PG	Procter & Gamble Co.	1.63%
T	AT&T Inc.	1.60%
GE	General Electric Company	1.53%
KO	Coca Cola Co.	1.46%
JPM	J P Morgan Chase and Co.	1.34%
PFE	Pfizer Inc.	1.34%
GOOG	Google Inc.	1.24%
WFC	Wells Fargo & Co.	1.21%
PM	Philip Morris International Inc.	1.15%
BRK/B	Berkshire Hathaway Inc.	1.12%

Symbol	Name	Percentage of fund
INTC	Intel Corp.	0.98%
ORCL	Oracle Corp.	0.97%
SLB	Schlumberger NV	0.95%
VZ	Verizon Communications Inc.	0.94%

Note: This fund is *short* these securities (or long on equivalent inverse derivative securities)—so it doesn't actually own them outright.

ProShares
7501 Wisconsin Avenue, Suite 1000E
Bethesda, MD 20814
(866) 776-5125
Website: *www.proshares.com*

100 BEST STRATEGY: **ROTATIONAL**

100 BEST CATEGORY: **INVERSE/LEVERAGED**

ProShares Short QQQ

Ticker Symbol: PSQ ▫ Issuer: ProShares ▫ Description: Inverse General Equity/Index Fund ▫ Geography: U.S. ▫ Morningstar Rating: NR ▫ Marco Polo XTF Rating: 3.9 ▫ Yield: NA ▫ Expense Ratio: 0.95% (Benchmark: 0.60%)

Stated Purpose

The investment seeks daily results, before fees and expenses, which correspond to the inverse (opposite) of the daily performance of the NASDAQ 100 Index. The fund invests in derivatives that ProShare advisors believe should have similar daily performance characteristics as the inverse of the daily return of the index. It typically invests the rest of the assets in money market instruments.

Our Take

As an "inverse" fund, the ProShares Short QQQ is designed to be a broad-market "short" play, that is, to go in the opposite direction of the market; as represented in this case by the NASDAQ 100 Index. Note that while this fund is "inverse," it is not "leveraged"; that is, it moves in equal proportions to the market move.

To avoid repetition of the general discussion of going "short," that is, betting on a market decline through individual stocks or through ETFs, please refer to our take on this fund's big brother—the ProShares Short S&P 500 ETF (SH).

The ProShares Short QQQ does a pretty good job of matching market moves one for one in the opposite direction, as evidenced by its beta of -1.03. A careful look at the one-year and three-year performance statistics suggests that it has gotten better at this over time. One caution: The largest holding is Apple at 15 percent of the fund; investors have gotten burned for years trying to short Apple stock, which tends to go up even when the rest of the market is down.

Why Should I Care?

This fund makes sense as a hedge to capitalize on market declines; it belongs in the rotational portfolio.

Upside

- Strong inverse correlation
- Fairly focused market coverage
- Large and liquid

Downside

- No current yield
- Apple stock a danger
- High expense ratio

Just the Facts

INCEPTION DATE: **June 19, 2006**

TOTAL ASSETS: **$245.6 million**

AVERAGE DAILY VOLUME: **1.1 million**

TOTAL HOLDINGS: **101**

PERCENT NORTH AMERICA HOLDINGS: **93.54%**

TOP 10 HOLDINGS PERCENTAGE (CONCENTRATION): **54.03%**

PORTFOLIO TURNOVER: **NA**   BENCHMARK: **17.0%**

BETA COEFFICIENT: **-1.03**

R-SQUARED (1 YEAR): **85.34%**

1-YEAR RETURN: **-24.41%**   BENCHMARK: **27.78%**

3-YEAR RETURN: **-16.80%**   BENCHMARK: **9.30%**

TRACKING ERROR (PRICE VS. NAV)   1 YEAR: **27.62%**   ASSET CLASS MEDIAN: **10.52%**

$10,000 Invested at inception	2006	2007	2008	2009	2010	2011
	$9,269	$8,222	$12,074	$7,208	$5,723	$5,242

What's Under the Hood

Symbol	Name	Percentage of fund
AAPL	Apple Inc.	14.86%
MSFT	Microsoft Corp.	8.92%
ORCL	Oracle Corp.	5.65%
GOOG	Google Inc.	5.58%
INTC	Intel Corp.	4.39%
AMZN	Amazon.com Inc.	3.77%
CSCO	Cisco Systems Inc.	3.53%
QCOM	Qualcomm Inc.	3.42%
AMGN	Amgen Inc.	2.11%
CMCSA	Comcast Corp.	1.80%
EBAY	eBay Inc.	1.60%
BIDU	Baidu Inc.	1.59%
COST	Costco Wholesale Corp.	1.41%
DTV	DirecTV	1.37%
NWSA	News Corp.	1.29%
GILD	Gilead Sciences Inc.	1.28%
SBUX	Starbucks Corp.	1.17%
TEVA	Teva Pharmaceutical Industries Ltd.	1.16%
DELL	Dell Inc.	1.16%
CELG	Celgene Corp.	1.11%

Note: This fund is *short* these securities (or long on equivalent inverse derivative securities)—so it doesn't actually own them outright.

ProShares
7501 Wisconsin Avenue, Suite 1000E
Bethesda, MD 20814
(866) 776-5125
Website: *www.proshares.com*

ProShares Short Small Cap 600

Ticker Symbol: SBB ▫ Issuer: ProShares ▫ Description: Inverse Small-Cap Index Fund ▫ Geography: U.S. ▫ Morningstar Rating: NR ▫ Marco Polo XTF Rating: 1.4 ▫ Yield: NA ▫ Expense Ratio: 0.95% (Benchmark: 0.60%)

Stated Purpose

The investment seeks daily results, before fees and expenses, which correspond to the inverse (opposite) of the daily performance of the S&P Small Cap 600. The fund invests in derivatives that ProShare advisors believe should have similar daily return characteristics as the inverse of the daily return of the index. It typically invests the rest of the assets in money market instruments.

Our Take

As an "inverse" fund, the ProShares Short Small Cap 600 is set up as a "short" play for the relatively more volatile small-cap sector of the market. As a "short" fund, it moves in the opposite direction of the market; in this case, the S&P Small Cap 600 index. Note that while this fund is "inverse," it is not "leveraged"; that is, it moves in roughly equal proportions to the market move.

To avoid repetition of the general discussion of going "short," that is, betting on a market decline through individual stocks or through ETFs, please refer to our take on this fund's big brother—the ProShares Short S&P 500 ETF (SH).

The ProShares Short Small Cap not only matches, but as a small-cap fund, slightly amplifies moves in the broader market as evidenced by its beta of -1.16. A careful look at the one-year and three-year performance statistics suggests that it has gotten better at closely following market performance over time.

Why Should I Care?

This fund makes sense as a hedge to capitalize on market declines; it belongs in the rotational portfolio.

Upside

• Strong and slightly amplified inverse correlation
• Broad coverage, not vulnerable to rises in single stocks
• Small caps tend to fall farther in bear markets

Downside

• No current yield
• High expense ratio
• Derivative tactics not transparent

Just the Facts

INCEPTION DATE: **January 23, 2007**

TOTAL ASSETS: **$60.7 million**

AVERAGE DAILY VOLUME: **69,400**

TOTAL HOLDINGS: **592**

PERCENT NORTH AMERICA HOLDINGS: **99.48%**

TOP 10 HOLDINGS PERCENTAGE (CONCENTRATION): **6.08%**

PORTFOLIO TURNOVER: **NA**   BENCHMARK: **17.0%**

BETA COEFFICIENT: **-1.16**

R-SQUARED (1 YEAR): **85.78%**

1-YEAR RETURN: **-23.03%**   BENCHMARK: **24.42%**

3-YEAR RETURN: **-16.90%**   BENCHMARK: **6.26%**

TRACKING ERROR (PRICE VS. NAV)   1 YEAR: **29.52%**   ASSET CLASS MEDIAN: **10.52%**

$10,000 Invested at inception	2006	2007	2008	2009	2010	2011
	$—	$10,730	$13,378	$9,275	$6,847	$6,410

What's Under the Hood

Symbol	Name	Percentage of fund
REGN	Regeneron Pharmaceuticals Inc.	0.98%
HS	HealthSpring Inc.	0.60%
INT	World Fuel Services Corp.	0.59%
HME	Home Properties Inc.	0.59%
MAA	Mid-America Apartment Communities Inc.	0.59%
CROX	Crocs Inc.	0.57%
SBNY	Signature Bank	0.56%
BMR	Biomed Realty Trust Inc.	0.54%
SKT	Tanger Factory Outlet Centers Inc.	0.54%
NNN	National Retail Properties Inc.	0.52%
HMSY	HMS Holdings Corp.	0.51%
CLC	CLARCOR Inc.	0.51%
PNY	Piedmont Natural Gas Co Inc.	0.51%
PRA	ProAssurance Corp.	0.50%
RBN	Robbins & Myers Inc.	0.49%
PPS	Post Properties Inc.	0.47%

Symbol	Name	Percentage of fund
KRC	Kilroy Realty Corp.	0.47%
CBST	Cubist Pharmaceuticals Inc.	0.46%
TDY	Teledyne Technologies Inc.	0.45%
EXR	Extra Space Storage Inc.	0.45%

Note: This fund is *short* these securities (or long on equivalent inverse derivative securities)—so it doesn't actually own them outright.

ProShares
7501 Wisconsin Avenue, Suite 1000E
Bethesda, MD 20814
(866) 776-5125
Website: *www.proshares.com*

100 BEST STRATEGY: **ROTATIONAL/OPPORTUNISTIC**

100 BEST CATEGORY: **INVERSE/LEVERAGED**

Rydex 2X S&P 500 ETF

Ticker Symbol: RSU ◻ Issuer: Rydex Investments ◻ Description: Leveraged (2X) General Equity/Index Fund ◻ Geography: U.S. ◻ Morningstar rating: 1 star ◻ Marco Polo XTF Rating: 3.8 ◻ Yield: 1.17% ◻ Expense Ratio: 0.70% (Benchmark: 0.60%)

Stated Purpose

The investment seeks to replicate, net of expenses, 200 percent of the daily performance of the S&P 500 Index. The fund employs as its investment strategy a program of investing in equity securities contained in the underlying index, and leveraged derivative instruments, such as equity index swaps, futures contracts, and options on securities, futures contracts, and stock indices. It holds U.S. government securities or cash equivalents to collateralize its derivative positions.

Our Take

The idea behind a leveraged fund is to magnify, or "lever" the returns of the underlying market or market segment—whether good or bad. So a "2X" fund will gain—or lose—approximately twice what the underlying index is gaining or losing. These funds create this leverage through the use of *derivative* securities—specialized options, futures, or swap contract securities specifically designed to perform to a multiple of what the underlying index is doing.

The idea, again, is leverage. For investors who are pretty sure they know which way the market is going, or who want to put down a relatively small amount of investment capital to take a position, such a 2X (and there are 3X funds too) can make sense.

While the concept of leverage adds a degree of speculation to an ETF investment, we wanted to stick our toes into the water and include at least one leveraged fund—and the Rydex 2X S&P 500 ETF is the one for *The 100 Best ETFs You Can Buy 2012*. We may include a few more of these next year. The fund does pretty much what the name says—it gains, or loses, twice what the S&P 500 does over a given period.

Why Should I Care?

Leveraged funds give investors a way to put a small portion of their portfolio at a greater risk in order to achieve a greater return. This fund—and others like it—should be used to juice short-term returns a bit especially during times of market volatility. Investors should look to buy in cheap, watch closely, and be quick to take this bet off the table if things run the wrong way.

Upside

- Relatively safe and diversified for a 2X fund
- Relatively low expenses
- Tracks the index well

Downside

- Greater downside risk too
- Yield only half a conventional S&P 500 index fund
- Derivative tactics not transparent

Just the Facts

INCEPTION DATE: **November 5, 2007**

TOTAL ASSETS: **$86.8 million**

AVERAGE DAILY VOLUME: **110,100**

TOTAL HOLDINGS: **500**

PERCENT NORTH AMERICA HOLDINGS: **98.81%**

TOP 10 HOLDINGS PERCENTAGE (CONCENTRATION): **19.94%**

PORTFOLIO TURNOVER: **23.0%**   BENCHMARK: **17.0%**

BETA COEFFICIENT: **2.05**

R-SQUARED (ONE YEAR): **99.97%**

1-YEAR RETURN: **39.25%**   BENCHMARK: **19.65%**

3-YEAR RETURN: **-4.37%**   BENCHMARK: **2.92%**

TRACKING ERROR (PRICE VS. NAV)   1 YEAR: **14.49%**   ASSET CLASS MEDIAN: **10.52%**

$10,000 Invested at inception	2006	2007	2008	2009	2010	2011
	$—	$9,791	$3,168	$4,635	$5,885	$6,244

What's Under the Hood

Symbol	Name	Percentage of fund
XOM	Exxon Mobil Corp.	3.33%
AAPL	Apple Inc.	3.30%
IBM	International Business Machines Corp.	1.90%
CVX	Chevron Corp.	1.81%
MSFT	Microsoft Corp.	1.74%
JNJ	Johnson & Johnson	1.64%
PG	Procter & Gamble Co.	1.63%
T	AT&T Inc.	1.60%
GE	General Electric Company	1.53%
KO	Coca Cola Co.	1.46%
JPM	JPMorgan Chase and Co.	1.34%
PFE	Pfizer Inc.	1.34%
GOOG	Google Inc.	1.24%
WFC	Wells Fargo & Co.	1.21%
PM	Philip Morris International Inc.	1.14%
BRK/B	Berkshire Hathaway Inc.	1.13%
INTC	Intel Corp.	0.98%
ORCL	Oracle Corp.	0.97%
VZ	Verizon Communications Inc.	0.94%
WMT	Wal-Mart Stores Inc.	0.94%

Rydex SGI
P.O. Box 758567
Topeka, KS 66675–8567
(800) 820-0888
Website: *www.rydex-sgi.com*

ETF

syn AUSE 2
syn IXP 2
syn. PFF 4